PAX AMERICANA

Also by Ronald Steel

The End of Alliance:
America and the Future of Europe

Ronald Steel **PAX**

AMERICANA

A New Revised Edition

THE VIKING PRESS / *New York*

For TIB, JAMES, *and* GWEN

Preface

"What kind of peace do we seek?" President Kennedy asked in June 1963 when he urged his countrymen to re-examine the inherited attitudes of the cold war. "Not a Pax Americana enforced on the world by American weapons of war . . . not merely peace for Americans but peace for all men and women—not merely peace in our time but peace in all time." In its rejection of imperialistic ambitions, and in its almost utopian idealism about the possibilities of universal peace, this reflects the assumptions of the American people about the goal of their foreign policy.

Yet however deep and sincerely felt these assumptions of American benevolence may be, they are not often shared by the nations that feel the direct effects of American power. Nor are they always consistent with our own behavior throughout the world. As the most powerful nation on earth—the richest, the most deeply involved, and in some ways the most ideologically committed—the United States has intervened massively in the affairs of other nations. She has done so expressing the most noble motives and the most generous impulses. Her high ideals, however, have not diminished the impact of her power, nor has her generosity necessarily convinced others that her ambitions are purely philanthropic. In the eyes of much of the world, America is a nation possessed of an empire of nominally independent client states and pursuing ambitions consistent with those of a great imperial power. Although we do not consciously seek hegemony over other nations and covet no other territory, there is more than one kind of empire, more than one way of exerting control over others, and more than one justification for doing so.

The following pages are an attempt to examine how the American empire came into existence, how it is maintained, why it appears justified to many Americans, and what the price of its pursuit might be. Of necessity this book is, to some degree, an examination of the cold war: how we responded to it in terms of our national history, our political ideals, our unexpressed ambitions, our psychological insecurities. It is, beyond that, an inquiry into the world beyond the cold war—the world in which we are already living, but which we have only dimly begun to recognize through the fog of an inherited political rhetoric.

This book grew out of an earlier study, published a few years ago, on the demise of the NATO alliance and on the changing relationship between America and a resurgent Europe. Like *The End of Alliance*, it is a critique of current policies and a call for a new diplomacy that will more realistically reflect the world we live in—one which will more effectively preserve the national interest of the United States and reflect the political ideals of her people. Just as our preoccupations have, as a result of the cold war, expanded from Europe to embrace the entire world, so this book, in order to deal with the dilemma of America's global role, has expanded from *The End of Alliance* in our relations with Europe, to the global concept, and temptation, of a *Pax Americana*.

April 1967

A new printing has given me the opportunity to make some revisions in the text of the book and to add a new chapter.

RONALD STEEL

March 1970

Contents

Wherever the standard of freedom and independence has been
or shall be unfurled, there will be America's heart, her
benedictions, and her prayers. But she goes not abroad in
search of monsters to destroy. She is the well-wisher to
the freedom and independence of all. She is the champion
and vindicator only of her own. She will recommend the general
cause by the countenance of her voice, and by the benignant
sympathy of her example. She well knows that by once
enlisting under other banners than her own, were they even the
banners of foreign independence, she would involve herself
beyond the power of extrication, in all the wars of interest and
intrigue, of individual avarice, envy and ambition, which assume
the colors and usurp the standards of freedom. The fundamental
maxims of her policy would insensibly change from liberty
to force. . . . She might become the dictatress of the world.
She would no longer be the ruler of her own spirit.

—JOHN QUINCY ADAMS, address in
Washington, July 4, 1821

PAX AMERICANA

1. A Taste for Intervention

We in this country, in this generation are—by destiny rather than choice—the watchmen on the walls of world freedom.
—John F. Kennedy

The United States, delighting in her resources, feeling that she no longer had within herself sufficient scope for her energies, wishing to help those who were in misery or bondage the world over, yielded in her turn to that taste for intervention in which the instinct for domination cloaked itself.
—Charles de Gaulle

❧ ❧ ❧ "Sometimes people call me an idealist," Woodrow Wilson once said as he stumped the country trying to drum up support for the League of Nations. "Well, that's the way I know I am an American. America, my fellow citizens, . . . is the only idealistic nation in the world." Wilson, whose career is a tragic example of what happens when idealism is divorced from political realism, never spoke a truer word. America is an idealistic nation, a nation based upon the belief that the "self-evident truths" of the Declaration of Independence should be extended to unfortunate peoples wherever they may be.

For the first 170 years of our national existence, however, we were content to make this a principle rather than a program of action. America was, in John Quincy Adams' phrase, "the well-wisher to the freedom and independence of all," but "the champion and vindicator only of her own." With the exception of Mexico, the Philippines, and a few brief adventures in the Caribbean, our national idealism did not go abroad in search of new fields to conquer. The great European war of 1914-1918 entangled us more

3

against our will than by design. We entered it under the banner of idealism when neutrality became difficult, and we left Europe in disillusionment when power politics reared its ugly head at Versailles. Never again, we said. And never again we did, until the Japanese dragged us into a global war by the attack on Pearl Harbor.

From that time on, American idealism was transformed into a plan. The Word was given Flesh by the mating of American military power to a native idealism. For the first time in its history the nation had the ability to seek its idealistic goals by active intervention rather than merely by pious proclamation. The result was twin crusades, one in Europe, one in Asia: one to restore freedom to the West, one to bring it to the East. But the passing of one tyranny in Europe saw the rise of another; the defeat of Japan gave way to the resurgence of China. The triumph of the Second World War marked not the end of our labors, but only the beginning. It transformed a philosophical commitment to the principles of freedom and democracy into a political commitment to bring them about. American idealism was the foundation; American power was the instrument to achieve the ideals. From 1945 on, we were no longer simply the "well-wisher" to the world; we were its "champion and vindicator" as well. The moral purity of American isolationism gave way to the moral self-justification of American interventionism.

The change from the old isolationism to the new interventionism flowed almost inevitably from the Second World War. The unavoidable war against fascism revealed the bankruptcy of isolationism and destroyed the illusion that America could barricade herself from the immoralities of a corrupt world. It also provided the means for the dramatic growth of American military power which made the new policy of global interventionism possible. As a result of her participation in the war, America became not only a great world power but *the* world power. Her fleets roamed all the seas, her military bases extended around the earth's periphery, her soldiers stood guard from Berlin to Okinawa, and her alliances spanned the earth.

The Second World War threw the United States into the world arena, and the fear of communism prevented her from retreating. The old isolationism was buried and discredited. The crusade that was the war against fascism gave way to the new crusade that was the cold war against communism. Roused to a new sense of mission by the threat of Soviet communism, eager to bring her cherished values to the masses of mankind, a bit infatuated with the enormous power she possessed through the unleashing of the atom, America quickly accepted—and even came to cherish—her new sense of involvement in the fate of the world. The world of the early postwar era may not have been the One World of Wendell Willkie's dream, but America felt a unique sense of responsibility about its welfare.

A reaction to the old isolationism, the new globalism forced Americans to realize that they could no longer escape involvement in an imperfect world. But because the cold war, like the Second World War, was conceived as a moral crusade, it inflated an involvement that was essentially pragmatic into a moral mission. Since we were accustomed to victory in battle and were stronger than any nation had ever been in history, we believed that the world's problems could be resolved if only we willed hard enough and applied enough power. Convinced of the righteousness of our cause, we became intoxicated with our newly discovered responsibilities and saw them as a mandate to bring about the better world we so ardently desired. American military power, consecrated by the victory of the Second World War and reconfirmed by the development of the atomic bomb, joined forces with the power of American idealism to inaugurate a policy of global interventionism.

This policy of interventionism is not only military, although we have intervened massively throughout the world with our military power. Our intervention has also been economic and political. We have funneled nearly $120 billion of American money into foreign aid since the Second World War—to bring about changes in other countries that would reflect our ideals or advance our interests. We have intervened in the politics of other nations as well, trying to push some into new alignments, trying to remake the social structures of others, and helping to overthrow the governments of not a few. America, whether most of us realize it or not, has become the interventionist power par excellence. Whether we consider this to be commendable or deplorable, it is certainly undeniable.

For the past quarter-century the United States has—at a great financial, human, and even emotional cost—been pursuing a foreign policy designed to promulgate American values. This ambition inspired the policy of "containment" that followed the Second World War, and provided the rationale for a series of military involvements. Seeking universal peace and condemning war as a means for settling political grievances, America has, nonetheless, been an active belligerent in two major land wars since 1950 and the sponsor of a series of military interventions—a record unmatched by any other power. America did not enter these wars from a sense of adventure, or a quest for territorial gain, or an effort to retain distant colonies, but rather from a desire to contain communism and protect the values and boundaries of the "free world." "What America has done, and what America is doing now around the world," President Johnson declared at Catholic University a few months after he ordered the bombing of North Vietnam, "draws from deep and flowing springs of moral duty, and let none underestimate the depth of flow of those wellsprings of American purpose."

Who, indeed, would underestimate them? But to estimate them highly is not necessarily to understand them, or to find them always wise. The moral inspiration of America's involvement in foreign wars is undeniable. But it has also posed a terrible dilemma for American diplomacy, one which is rarely acknowledged openly and is often not even clearly recognized. It is the dilemma of how American ideals can be reconciled with American military actions —and, perhaps even more grave, of how American values can be made relevant to a world that seems not to want or even respect them. However deep the wellsprings of moral duty to which President Johnson refers, the means chosen to transfer these values to a recalcitrant and often unadmiring world has troubled many thoughtful Americans. American presidents have spoken in the most noble rhetoric of the need to defend freedom wherever it may be threatened and of the indivisibility of our responsibility to protect other nations from external (and even internal) aggression. Yet the pursuit of this aspiration has frequently led others to believe that our motives may be self-justifying and tinged with hypocrisy.

The United States has become an interventionist power, indeed the world's major interventionist power, without most Americans quite realizing how it happened or its full implications. Intervention has been the dominant motif of American postwar foreign policy, but the purpose, and even the methods, of this intervention have been concealed in a miasma of rhetoric and confusion. In the belief that we were containing or repelling communism, we have involved ourselves in situations that have been morally compromising, militarily frustrating, and politically indecisive.

The commitment to interventionism as a guiding principle has made it exceedingly difficult to distinguish between necessary and spurious motives for intervention—to determine which actions have a direct relation to the nation's security, and which merely represent wish-fulfillment on an international scale. In this respect it reflects a traditional weakness in American policy—a penchant for grandiose principles at the expense of a cool assessment of national interests, which has led the nation into painful involvements as a result of bold gestures carelessly made. The warning of John Quincy Adams has lately been forgotten in the intoxication of heady moral obligations, obligations which no one asked us to assume, and whose purpose we do not often understand. This is not the fault of the public but of its leaders, who are often tempted to use slogans to justify their actions, and then become prisoners of them. "American statesmen," as the historian Dexter Perkins has written,

> have believed that the best way to rally American opinion behind their purposes is to assert a moral principle. In doing so, they have

often gone far beyond the boundaries of expediency. And perhaps it is fair to say that in underemphasizing security, they have helped to form a national habit which unduly subordinates the necessities of national defense to the assertion of lofty moral principles.[1]

The rhetoric of our cold-war diplomacy rests upon the indivisibility of freedom, the belief in self-determination, the necessity for collective security, and the sanctity of peaceful reform as opposed to violent change. These are not bad ambitions, but nowhere does this noble rhetoric seem to be in touch with the crass reality of the world as it is. Freedom, we have learned, is not only divisible between nations but subject to a hundred different interpretations. One man's freedom, all too often, is another man's exploitation. Self-determination can be a formula for political instability, and one which it may not always be in our interests to further. Collective security, as applied to our postwar military pacts, has never been much more than a polite word for a unilateral guarantee by the United States to protect her clients. Even this is now being shattered by the break-up of the cold-war alliances. The commitment to peaceful social change by constitutional processes has now collided with the reality of revolution and disorder throughout much of the world.

With every expansion of our commitments, there has been a corresponding expansion of our official rhetoric. Statesmen, unable to adjust our limited means to our unlimited ends, have committed us to goals beyond the capacity of the nation to carry out. They have done this not because they are knaves intent on foreign adventurism, but because they have been carried away by the force of their own rhetoric. Infused by the belief that nothing is unattainable so long as the cause is just, and fortified by reliance on America's awesome military power, they frequently confuse the desirable with the attainable. In doing so, they commit the nation to ends that cannot be achieved, and thereby breed a national frustration that nags at the roots of American democracy. "To some extent," in the words of a Senate committee dealing with problems of national security, "every postwar administration has indulged our national taste for the grand and even the grandiose." Because the source of this comment is not one which is normally unreceptive to the application of American military power, its conclusions deserve quotation at greater length:

> The idea of manifest destiny still survives. Officials make sweeping declarations of our world mission, and often verbally commit the Nation to policies and programs far beyond our capabilities. In this way expectations may be created at home and abroad that are certain to be disappointed and that may result in a squandering of our power and influence on marginal undertakings. We may also find ourselves entangled in projects that are incompatible with the real needs of other peoples, or are, in some cases, actually repugnant to them. To some extent every postwar administration has indulged our national taste for the grand and even the grandiose.
>
> Our ability to think up desirable goals is almost limitless; our capabilities are limited. We still have much to learn about the need to balance what we would like to do with what we can do— and to establish intelligent priorities.
>
> The "can do" philosophy accords with American folklore, but even the United States cannot do everything. In policymaking, also, the assumption tends to be made that "we can find a way." We can do a lot, but our power is limited and the first claimant on it is the American people. Accordingly, it must be rationed in accordance with a responsible ordering of national interests.[2]

The alignment of national goals with national interests—of our desires with our needs—is the most pressing task facing American diplomacy. It is a task that has become increasingly urgent with each expansion of our commitments. These commitments are to be found in a tangle of regional alliances, military pacts, verbal agreements, and even unilateral decisions. They can all, to one degree or another, be traced back to the Truman Doctrine of March 1947, when the United States made the ambiguous offer to defend threatened nations from aggression, whether direct or indirect. This led, through the back door of the European Recovery Program, to NATO, under which the United States is pledged to the defense of most of Europe and even parts of the Near East—from Spitzbergen to the Berlin Wall and beyond to the Asian borders of Turkey. From there the commitments become more vague, the situations more ambiguous, the countries themselves less crucial to American security.

From the seeds of the Truman Doctrine and the precedent of NATO came the Middle East Resolution, under which Congress gave President Eisenhower permission to protect the Arabs against communism; the CENTO and SEATO treaties that John Foster Dulles constructed to fill in the alliance gap from Iran to the Philippines; the ANZUS treaty with Australia and New Zealand; special defense arrangements with Japan and Korea; an unwritten obligation to protect India; the pledge for the defense of the entire western hemisphere under the Rio Pact; various peace-keeping functions under the United Nations; and, most recently, the Tonkin Gulf Resolution, a blank check given by Congress, allowing President Johnson to intervene as he saw fit in Southeast Asia. Early in 1970 the United States had more than 1,000,000 soldiers in 30 countries, was a member of 4 regional defense alliances and an active participant in a fifth, had mutual defense treaties with 42 nations, was a member of 53 international organizations, and was furnishing military or economic aid to nearly 100 nations across the face of the globe. Put all this together and it leaves us, in James Reston's words, with "commitments the like of which no sovereign nation ever took on in the history of the world."

These entanglements were justified as a response to events. The United States became involved in the defense of Western Europe because the defeat of Nazi Germany brought Stalin's armies into Central Europe. In Asia the disintegration of the Japanese Empire brought Russia into Manchuria and the United States into Japan, Okinawa, South Korea, and Taiwan. Later we advanced into Indochina when the French, despite our financial and military support, were unable to retain their Asian territories. We had no intention of virtually annexing Okinawa, of occupying South Korea, of preventing the return of Taiwan to China, of fighting in Indochina, or of remaining in Western Europe. If one had said in 1945 that twenty-five years later there would be 225,000 American soldiers in Germany, 50,000 in Korea, and a half million Americans fighting in Vietnam, he would have been considered mad. Yet so accustomed are we to our global commitments that we take this remarkable situation for granted.

Although the postwar vacuums are receding—with the resurgence of China, the recovery of Japan, and the revival of Europe —our commitment remains unchanged. We are still playing the same role of guardian that we played twenty years ago, when America and Russia were the only important powers in the world. Our diplomacy has not kept pace with the changes in the world power structure, and we are engaged far beyond our ability to control events. The result has been a dangerous gap in our foreign policy between our involvements and our means—between what we would like to accomplish and what we can reasonably hope to accomplish.

In a way it could be said that our foreign policy has been a victim of its own success. In the decision to rebuild and defend Western Europe, the United States acted with wisdom, humanity, and an enlightened conception of her own interests. The military alliance with Western Europe worked successfully because there was a clear community of interests between America and her allies. When we built our bases in Europe and sent our own soldiers to man the front lines, it was in the knowledge that we agreed with our allies on the dangers they faced and on the means by which they should be met. We came not as an army of occupation or as foreign mercenaries, but as friends joined in a common cause. We turned our back on the isolationism of the 1930s, put the American frontier right up to the Brandenburg Gate in Berlin, pledged our atomic weapons to the defense of our allies, added our own soldiers as guarantors of this pledge, and accepted the risk of nuclear devastation. We took this terrible risk because we had to: because neither strategically nor culturally could we accept the loss of Western Europe to our adversaries. The goal we sought in Western Europe in the early postwar period had three qualities essential for military intervention: it was vital to our interests, it was within our means to achieve, and it had the support of those we were trying to protect.

The difficulty, however, arose when the principles underlying NATO and the Marshall Plan were applied indiscriminately throughout the world—when it was assumed that the success of the Atlantic alliance could be duplicated in countries which shared neither our traditions, nor our interests, nor even our assessment of the dangers facing them. Too often American diplomacy has been engaged in the effort to create miniature NATOs and Marshall Plans with countries that have only recently shaken off the yoke of Western rule, that are at a greatly inferior stage of economic and political development, that are as suspicious of us as they are of our adversaries, that are endemically poor and unstable, and that usually greet us as unwanted manipulators rather than as welcome friends.

If our policies were judged by a cold calculation of national interest, a good many of them might have been scrapped long ago. If the struggle with Russia were merely over geographical spheres of influence, if the cold war were nothing more than old-fashioned power politics on a global scale, our commitments could have been cut and our involvements drastically limited. But the cold war has not been simply a struggle of giants for supremacy; it has also been an ideological contest for the allegiance of mankind. Or so it has seemed to its leading participants. It is because we feel ourselves embroiled in a much greater struggle that we are involved in the sustenance and security of some hundred countries, that we have replaced the old isolationism with a sweeping policy of interventionism and are today fighting yet another land war in Asia.

We are there because we feel ourselves to be pledged to a worldwide struggle against communism, because we see ourselves as the defenders of freedom and democracy in the contest against tyranny, because we are, in President Kennedy's words, "by destiny rather than choice, the watchmen on the walls of world freedom." But this role of watchman is not, for all President Kennedy's noble rhetoric, imposed by destiny. It is imposed by ourselves and subject to whatever limitations we choose to put upon it. It can provide the excuse for our playing the role of global gendarme, or serve as a guideline for a measured calculation of the national interest. No task of global omniscience is imposed upon us that we do not choose for ourselves.

As we face the obligations of our global commitments, we are becoming aware of our inability to impose our will upon events or to structure the world into the form we believe it should take. We have the power to destroy most human life on the planet within a matter of minutes, yet we cannot win a guerrilla war against peasants in black pajamas. We are so rich that we can retain an army in Europe, fight a war in Asia, dispense billions in foreign aid, and increase our national wealth by $30 billion a year. Yet we cannot adequately deal with the decay of our cities, the pollution of our atmosphere, the disintegration of public services, the growing hostility between whites and blacks, and the inadequacy of our educational system. Nor, despite the fact that we have dispensed nearly $120 billion abroad during the past twenty years, have we been able seriously to alleviate the poverty and hopelessness in which most of the world's population lives. We have assumed the responsibility for creating Great Societies at home and abroad, but we have not been able to bring this goal into line with our interests or capacities.

As a nation we have what General de Gaulle uncharitably labeled "a taste for intervention." Applied intelligently and with restraint, as in Western Europe after the war, this taste has done credit to our nation and served its interests. But expanded indiscriminately and without measure, it has involved us in struggles we do not understand, in areas where we are unwanted, and in ambitions which are doomed to frustration. Intervention is neither a sin nor a panacea. It is a method, and like all methods it must be directly related to the end in view. Otherwise it is likely to become an end in itself, dragging the nation down a path it never intended to follow, toward a goal it may find repugnant.

Too often our interventions have seemed to be imposed upon us by abstract theory rather than by a cold assessment of political realities. We have found ourselves involved in areas—the Congo the day before yesterday, Santo Domingo yesterday, Vietnam today, perhaps Thailand tomorrow—where our presence has sometimes exacerbated rather than alleviated the problem, and where it was not within our power to achieve a solution. Interventionism, as a principle of foreign policy, has not served us noticeably well in recent years. But it is a principle to which we are deeply committed: in NATO and its sister pacts, CENTO and SEATO; in the Alliance for Progress; in the Rio Pact and the OAS; in foreign aid; in Southeast Asia; and in any nation which may be taken over by communists, whether from the inside or the outside. It has fostered a staggering program of involvements and it could easily lead us, as it already has in Vietnam, into conflicts whose extent we cannot possibly foresee.

We are in very deep in Europe, in Korea and Japan, in Thailand and Vietnam, in Latin America, and in the entire nexus of underdeveloped countries which are tottering between various forms of authoritarianism. This is an American dilemma: the dilemma of how to use power—sometimes economic power in the form of tractors and dollars, sometimes raw military power in the form of soldiers and napalm—for the achievement of ends which American leaders declare to be morally desirable.

The answer to that dilemma has eluded us ever since we plunged wholeheartedly into the world arena a generation ago and acquired, in a bout of moral fervor, a string of dependencies stretching around the globe—an empire, in short. It is an empire the scope of which the world has never seen, and which we, to this day, have scarcely begun to recognize ourselves.

2. The American Empire

A great empire and little minds go ill together.
—EDMUND BURKE

❧ ❧ ❧ IF the British Empire, as Macaulay once said, was acquired in a fit of absent-mindedness, the American empire came into being without the intention or the knowledge of the American people. We are a people on whom the mantle of empire fits uneasily, who are not particularly adept at running colonies. Yet, by any conventional standards for judging such things, we are indeed an imperial power, possessed of an empire on which the sun truly never sets, an empire that embraces the entire western hemisphere, the world's two great oceans, and virtually all of the Eurasian land mass that is not in communist hands.

We are the strongest and most politically active nation in the world. Our impact reaches everywhere and affects everything it touches. We have the means to destroy whole societies and rebuild them, to topple governments and create others, to impede social change or to stimulate it, to protect our friends and devastate those who oppose us. We have a capacity for action, and a restless, driving compulsion to exercise it, such as the world has never seen. We have a technology that is the wonder of the world, an energy that compels us to challenge the obdurate forces of man and nature, and an affluence that could support whole nations with its waste. We also have a taunting sense of insecurity that makes it difficult for us to accept the limitations of our own remarkable power.

Although our adventure in empire-building may have begun without regard to its consequences, it could not have occurred at all had it not appealed to a deep-rooted instinct in our national character—an instinct to help those less fortunate and permit them to emulate and perhaps one day achieve the virtues of our own society. There was nothing arrogant in this attitude; indeed, it was heavily tinged with altruism. But it did rest upon the belief that it was America's role to make the world a happier, more orderly place, one more nearly reflecting our own image. We saw this as a special responsibility fate had thrust upon us. Standing alone as the defender of Europe, the guardian of Latin America, the protector of weak and dependent nations released from the bondage of colonialism, possessing the mightiest military force in history, an economy productive beyond any man had ever known, and a standard of living the envy of the world—we naturally became persuaded of the universal validity of our institutions, and of our obligation to help those threatened by disorder, aggression, and poverty.

We acquired our empire belatedly and have maintained, and even expanded, it because we found ourselves engaged in a global struggle with an ideology. When we picked up the ruins of the German and Japanese Empires in 1945, we discovered that we could not let them go without seeing them fall under the influence of our ideological adversaries. Struggling against communism, we created a counter-empire of anti-communism. This counter-empire was built upon the idealism enshrined in the charter of the United Nations, the altruism exemplified by the Marshall Plan, the cautious improvisation of the Truman Doctrine, and the military arithmetic of the NATO pact. It spread to Korea and the Congo, to Pakistan and Vietnam, and to a hundred troubled spots where inequality bred grievances, disorder, and instability. We came to see the world as a great stage on which we choreographed an inspiring design for peace, progress, and prosperity. Through American interventionism—benignly where possible, in the form of foreign aid; surgically where necessary, in the form of American soldiers—we hoped to contain the evil forces from the East and provide a measure of hope and security for the rest of mankind. We engaged in a kind of welfare imperialism, empire-building for noble ends rather than for such base motives as profit and influence. We saw ourselves engaged, as Under Secretary of State George Ball declared shortly after we began bombing North Vietnam, in "something new and unique in world history—a role of world responsibility divorced from territorial or narrow national interests." [1]

But there are good economic reasons for our interest in the political stability of the underdeveloped countries, for American prosperity in part depends upon access to their raw materials. With only 6 per cent of the world's population, the United States consumes one-third of the world's production of bauxite, 40 per cent of its nickel, 36 per cent of its chrome, 25 percent of its tungsten and copper.

While we did not acquire our empire for profit, "history," as Arnold Toynbee has observed,

> tells us that conquest and annexation are not the only means, or indeed the most frequent and most effective means, by which empires have been built up in the past. The history of the Roman Empire's growth, for instance, is instructive when one is considering the present-day American Empire's structure and prospects. The principal method by which Rome established her political supremacy in her world was by taking her weaker neighbors under her wing and protecting them against her and their stronger neighbors; Rome's relation with these protégées of hers was a treaty relation. Juridically they retained their previous status of sovereign independence. The most that Rome asked of them in terms of territory was the cession, here and there, of a patch of ground for the plantation of a Roman fortress to provide for the common security of Rome's allies and Rome herself. [2]

Although the desire to defend other nations against communism is not an imperial ambition, it has led this country to use imperial methods: establishment of military garrisons around the globe, granting of subsidies to client governments and politicians, application of economic sanctions and even military force against recalcitrant states, and employment of a veritable army of colonial administrators working through such organizations as the State Department, the Agency for International Development, the

United States Information Agency, and the Central Intelligence Agency. Having grown accustomed to our empire and having found it pleasing, we have come to take its institutions and its assumptions for granted. Indeed, this is the mark of a convinced imperial power: its advocates never question the virtues of empire, although they may dispute the way in which it is administered, and they do not for a moment doubt that it is in the best interests of those over whom it rules. A basically anti-colonial people, we tolerate, and even cherish, our empire because it seems so benevolent, so designed to serve those embraced by it.

But, many will ask, have we not been generous with our clients and allies, sending them vast amounts of money, and even sacrificing the lives of our own soldiers on their behalf? Of course we have. But this is the role of an imperial power. If it is to enjoy influence and command obedience, it must be prepared to distribute some of its riches throughout its empire and, when necessary, to fight rival powers for the loyalty of vulnerable client states. Empires may be acquired by accident, but they can be held together only by cash, power, and even blood. We learned this in Korea, in Berlin, and in Cuba; and we are learning it again in Vietnam. Whatever the resolution of that tragic conflict, it has once again shattered the recurrent illusion that empires can be maintained on the cheap.

Our empire has not been cheap to maintain, but we have never conceived of it as an empire. Rather, we saw it as a means of containing communism, and thereby permitting other nations to enjoy the benefits of freedom, democracy, and self-determination. This was particularly true in the vast perimeter of colonial and ex-colonial states which offered an enticing field for communist exploitation—and also for our own benevolent intervention. With the European colonial powers weakened and discredited, we were in a position to implement our long-standing sentiments of anti-colonialism. Opposed to the efforts of France, Britain, and Holland to regain control of their Asian colonies, we actively encouraged the efforts of such nationalists as Nehru, Sukarno, and Ho Chi Minh to win the independence of their countries.

However, once the war-weakened European powers finally did leave their colonies, we discovered that most of the newly independent nations had neither the resources nor the ability to stand on their own. With a very few exceptions, they were untrained for independence and unable, or unwilling, to exercise it in ways we approved of. Having proclaimed self-determination as a moral principle valid on every continent and in every country, we found ourselves saddled with the responsibility for some of its consequences. As a result, we stepped into the role left vacant by the departed European powers. In many of the new states we performed the tasks of an imperial power without enjoying the economic or territorial advantages of empire. We chose politicians, paid their salaries, subsidized national budgets, equipped and trained armies, built soccer stadiums and airports, and where possible instructed the new nations in the proper principles of foreign policy. We did this with good intentions, because we really did believe in self-determination for everybody as a guiding moral principle, and because we thought it was our obligation to help the less fortunate "modernize" their societies by making them more like ours. This was our welfare imperialism, and it found its roots in our most basic and generous national instincts.

But we also plunged into the economic primitiveness and political immaturity of the new nations because we saw them as a testing-ground in the struggle between freedom and communism, the cataclysmic duel that was to determine the fate of the world. Carried away by the vocabulary of the cold war, we sought to combat communism and preserve "freedom" in whatever area, however unpromising or unlikely, the battle seemed to be joined. Confusing communism as a social doctrine with communism as a form of Soviet imperialism, we assumed that any advance of communist doctrine anywhere was an automatic gain for the Soviet Union. Thus we believed it essential to combat communism in any part of the globe, as though it were a direct threat to our security, even in cases where it was not allied to Soviet power. Our methods were foreign aid, military assistance, and, where all else failed, our own soldiers.

But while this policy was valid in Europe, where there seemed to be a real threat of a Soviet take-over and where our allies shared our feelings about the danger facing them, it was less reasonable throughout most of the ex-colonial world. There the ruling elites were worried not so much by communism as by the real or imagined "imperialism" of the Western powers. They were not particularly committed to our advocacy of free speech and democracy, having never experienced it themselves, and they were totally mystified by our praises of capitalism, which in their experience was associated with exploitation, bondage, and misery. Insofar as they thought about communism at all, they could not help being drawn to a doctrine to which the Western powers were opposed. Western antipathy in itself was a major recommendation.

Most of these new nations have genuinely tried to keep out of the struggles among the great powers. They are anti-colonial and suspicious of the West by training and instinct. But they also have not wanted to compromise their neutrality by too close an association with the communists. Insofar as communist doctrine has seemed to offer a solution for their problems of political authority and economic development, they have been receptive to it— as a doctrine. But where it has been allied with Soviet power, they have uniformly resisted it, because it represents a threat to their independence. Most of the new nations, therefore, have tried to tread a path between the conflicting demands of East and West.

Some of them, of course, have been led by clever men who learned to take advantage of our phobias. They found that a threat to "go communist" would usually win large infusions of American foreign-aid funds, just as a threat to "join the imperialists" would inspire Russian counter-bribes. They learned, with the agility of Ben Franklin at the court of Louis XVI, how to manipulate our obsessions, seek out sympathetic ears in Congress and the Pentagon, and conjure up terrible happenings that were about to befall them. The twin doctrines of communism and anti-communism became tools by which they could secure outside help to build up their feeble economies and gain a larger voice in world affairs.

These nations cannot really be blamed for any of this. Being poor, they naturally wanted to secure as much outside assistance as they could, and played upon the anxieties of the great powers to do so. They thus served their own interests and pursued legitimate objectives of their foreign policy. What was less natural, however, was that we permitted ourselves to be manipulated by those who had so little to offer us. We allowed this because we feared that the new nations would fall under the influence of communism. Just as they were inspired by sentiments of anti-colonialism, so we were inspired by an equally powerful anti-communism. It provided the stimulus which led the United States to a massive postwar interventionism and to the creation of an empire that rests upon the pledge to use American military power to combat communism not only as a form of imperialism, but even as a social doctrine in the underdeveloped states. The foundation of this American empire can be traced back to the threat to Europe as it existed more than twenty years ago.

The American empire came into being as a result of the Second World War, when the struggle against Nazi Germany and imperial Japan brought us to the center of Europe and the offshore islands of Asia. With Russian troops on the Elbe and with the governments of Western Europe tottering under the strain of reconstruction, it seemed that only American power could halt the spread of communism. Consequently, the United States intervened to meet this new European danger, first with economic aid under the Marshall Plan, and then with direct military support under NATO. This was a necessary and proper response to a potential threat, although the emphasis on military over economic support has been sharply debated by historians. However, even before the Marshall Plan was announced, and two years before the NATO pact was signed, the United States laid down the guidelines for its intervention in Europe—and ultimately throughout the world—in the Truman Doctrine of March 12, 1947. Urging Congress to grant $400 million to help the Greek royalists fight the communist rebels, and to enable the Turks to defend themselves against Russia, President Truman declared: "It must be the policy of the United States to support free peoples who are resisting attempted subjugation by armed minorities or by outside pressure."

While such military aid may have been necessary to prevent Greece and Turkey from falling into the communist camp, the language in which the Truman Doctrine was cast implied a commitment far beyond the communist threat to those nations. Had it been confined to the containment of Soviet power, the Truman Doctrine would have expressed a legitimate American security interest. But by a vocabulary which pledged the United States to oppose armed minorities and outside pressure, it involved us in the containment of an ideology. In so doing, it provided the rationale for a policy of global intervention against communism, even in areas where American security was not involved. What was, as Kenneth Thompson has written, "a national and expedient act designed to replace British with American power in Central Europe, was presented as the defense of free democratic nations everywhere in the world against 'direct or indirect aggression.' It translated a concrete American interest for a limited area of the world into a general principle of worldwide validity, to be applied regardless of the limits of American interests and power." [3]

President Truman probably did not envisage the extreme ends toward which this policy would eventually be applied. While he argued that the United States could not permit communism to overturn the status quo by aggression or armed subversion, he put the emphasis on economic assistance and self-help. And he assumed that our efforts would be made in conjunction with our allies. What he did not intend, at least at the time, was unilateral American military intervention in support of client states threatened from within by communist-inspired insurgents. He did not suggest that the Greek civil war should be fought by American troops, nor did he seriously contemplate the bombardment of

Yugoslavia, from whose territory the Greek communist rebels were being supplied. The language of the Truman Doctrine was sweeping, but its application was limited. It grew into a policy of global interventionism only with the later acknowledgment of America's imperial responsibilities.

Historically speaking, the Truman Doctrine was essentially an extension of the Monroe Doctrine across the Atlantic to non-communist Europe. Just as the Monroe Doctrine was designed to maintain the nineteenth-century balance of power between the New World and the Old, so its twentieth-century counterpart was meant to prevent communism from upsetting the political balance between East and West. Where the former used British sea-power to serve the security interests of the United States, the latter used American economic and military power to protect non-communist Europe and thereby defend American interests. The implied limitations of the Truman Doctrine were, however, swept aside by the communist attack on South Korea and the resulting assumption that the Russians were prepared to resort to a policy of open aggression. The extension of the Truman Doctrine to cover the Korean war set the stage for its expansion into a general commitment to resist communism everywhere, not only by economic and military support, but by direct American military intervention where necessary. The alliances forged by Dulles were based upon this premise, and even the war in Vietnam is a logical corollary of the Truman Doctrine.

The old limitations of spheres of influence, treaty obligations, and Congressional consent are no longer relevant in cases where the President should deem it necessary to launch a military intervention. As Dean Rusk told a Senate committee: "No would-be aggressor should suppose that the absence of a defense treaty, Congressional declaration, or United States military presence grants immunity to aggression." [4] As a hands-off warning by an imperial power, this statement is eminently logical. It does, however, take us into waters a good deal deeper than those chartered by the Truman Doctrine. By indicating that the United States would not feel itself restricted even to the military treaties it has

with more than forty nations, the Secretary of State implicitly removed all inhibitions upon a Presidential decision to intervene
against communism wherever, whenever, and however it is
deemed necessary.

Behind the warning of Secretary Rusk lies the belief that American military power is so great that the old considerations of national interest—which confined a nation's military interventions
to areas deemed vital to its security—are no longer necessary. The
growth of American military power—the enormous array of weapons, the awesome nuclear deterrent, the largest peacetime standing army in our history, and an economy that dominates the world
—has apparently convinced many in Washington that "the
illusion of American omnipotence," in D. W. Brogan's famous
phrase, may not be an illusion. The old feeling of being locked in
a closet with Russia appears to have vanished and to have been
replaced by the conviction that America alone has world responsibilities, that these are "unique in world history" and justify a
policy of global interventionism. If this is not an illusion of omnipotence, it might at least be described as intoxication with power.

Although we consciously seek no empire, we are experiencing
all the frustrations and insecurities of an imperial power. Having assumed a position of world leadership because of the abstinence of others, America has not been able to evolve a coherent
concept of what she wants and what she may reasonably expect to
attain in the world. She has not been able to relate her vision of a
universal order on the American model to the more limited imperatives of her own national interests. She is a territorially sa-
tiated power, yet plagued by terrible insecurities over her global
responsibilities and even over her own identity. America has rejected the old tradition of abstinence and isolationism without
having been able to find a new tradition that can bring her interests into line with her ideals.

One of the expressions of this insecurity has been the
emergence of anti-communism *as an ideology,* rather than as a reaction to the imperial policies followed by the Soviet Union and
other communist powers. This counter-ideology of anti-commu-

nism has been both internal and external, reflecting our anxieties about ourselves and about our position in the world at large. As an external anxiety, anti-communism arose from the frustrations of the early postwar period and the disappointments of a terrible war which brought a terrible peace. To possess a military power unequaled in human history, to have marshaled an atomic arsenal capable of eradicating an enemy in a matter of hours, to have no conscious political ambitions other than to spread the virtues of American democracy to less fortunate peoples—to experience all this and still not be able to achieve more than stalemate in the cold war has been difficult for many Americans to accept. The transformation of adversaries into demons followed almost inevitably.

Anti-communism as an ideology was a response not only to stalemate abroad, but also to the insecurities of life at home, where traditional values had been uprooted. To those whose sense of security had been destroyed by the extreme mobility of American life, who felt threatened by the demands of racial minorities for equality, and who were humiliated by the impersonality of an increasingly bureaucratized society, ideological anti-communism served as a focal point of discontent. It could not allay these anxieties, but it could explain them in a form that was acceptable to those who saw as many enemies within the gates as they did outside. The McCarthyism and the witch-hunts of the 1950s, which so debased American intellectual life and spread a blanket of conformity over the government, were a reaction to this insecurity, acts of self-exorcism by a people tormented by demons.

Plagued by domestic anxieties and faced with external dangers that defy the traditional virtues of the American character—an ability to organize, to solve problems, to get things done by sustained energy and determination—the American people have been deeply shaken throughout the whole postwar period. They have had to accept the frustrations of stalemate with Soviet Russia and learn to live in the shadow of atomic annihilation, where the very survival of America is threatened for the first time in her history. This is a situation which, after the traumas of the 1950s, we have now learned to accept with resignation, and even with a certain equanimity. But it is one which breeds deep-rooted anxieties of the kind expressed on the radical right. These frustrations conflict with the most basic elements of Americanism as a secular faith. To challenge this faith is to commit a kind of heresy, and it is as a heretical doctrine that communism has been treated in this country. This is comprehensible only if we accept the fact that Americanism is a creed, that, as a British commentator has observed,

> America is not just a place but an idea, producing a particular kind of society. When immigrants choose to become Americans they are expected to accept the political values of this society, associated with the egalitarian and democratic traditions of the American revolution. An an immigrant country, perhaps only Israel is comparable in the demands it makes for the acceptance of an ideology as well as a territorial nationality. Consequently American patriotism is more readily identified with loyalty to traditional political values; . . . the reverence paid to the American Constitution and the basic political principles of the American revolution encourages the tendency to believe that all failures of the political system must be blamed on corruption, conspiracy or some external enemy. Communism has uniquely provided both an internal and external threat.[5]

Pampered by a continent of extraordinary riches, insulated from political responsibility in the world for longer than was healthy, her soil untouched by war for more than a century, spoiled by an economy which produces a seemingly inexhaustible wealth, flattered by an unnatural dominion over temporarily indigent allies, American has found it difficult to bring her political desires into line with her real needs. We think of solving problems rather than of living with them, and we find compromise an unnatural alternative to "victory." These attitudes are a reflection of our frontier mentality, of the cult of individualism, and of a national experience where success is usually the ultimate result of a major effort.

We have fought every war on the assumption that it was the final war that would usher in universal peace. We believed that every adversary was the architect of a global conspiracy, and that

break-up of the cold-war military blocs—these are the central realities of our time. Yet our diplomacy remains frozen in the posture
of two decades ago and mesmerized by a ritual anti-communism
that has become peripheral to the real conflict of power in today's world. We are in an age of nationalism, in which both communism and capitalism are ceasing to be ideologically significant,
and in which the preoccupations of our diplomacy are often irrelevant. We are the last of the ideologues, clinging to political
assumptions that have been buried by changing time and circum-
stance, a nation possessed of an empire it did not want, does not
know how to administer, and fears to relinquish. We live in a time
of dying ideologies and obsolete slogans, where much of what
we have taken for granted is now outdated, and where even
the political condition that has dominated our lives—the cold
war—may now be over.

3. After the Cold War

The difficulty lies not in the new ideas, but in escaping from the old ones.
—JOHN MAYNARD KEYNES

❧ ❧ ❧ FOR the past two decades we have viewed the world and our place in it through the lenses of the cold war. A whole generation of Americans has come to maturity knowing incessant crisis and the threat of instant obliteration as the normal condition of everyday life. For those born in the cold war, and for those ushered into it by an implacable history, it has been the central political reality of our time. Inescapable, and seemingly inexhaustible, the cold war has become a permanent fixture of our mental vocabulary, limiting our horizons to questions of survival, security, and prestige.

The cold war has been both a stultifying and an exhilarating period in American life. It gave birth to the self-destructive hysteria of McCarthyism, but it also inspired the creation of an American empire and the euphoria of power that has gone with it. The cold war made us fear for our safety, but it also excited us with the knowledge that we were one of the arbiters of the world. With the passing of time we even, in a peculiar way, grew fond of the cold war. It became familiar, predictable, and almost comfortable, providing a rationale for actions that flattered our pride and augmented our influence over others.

The cold war has been a struggle for power, but more than that, it has also been a struggle over ideology: one, so the antagonists believed, for the soul of mankind. The Russians, while behaving in ways that augment their status as a great power, have nonetheless believed in the mythology of communism and their duty to spread it to nations oppressed by the "imperialists." The fact that they have rarely let their belief in the promulgation of the communist faith interfere with the security of Mother Russia does not diminish the fact that they conceive of themselves as a basically messianic power. They believe in communist dogma (although they persistently twist it to suit their national needs), and they have managed to convince others that they are serious.

No nation needed persuading less than the United States, whose fear of Russian power was fortified by a deep-seated hostility to communist ideology. While America initially responded to the Soviet menace in terms of national interest—pouring her troops back into Europe after the Second World War in order to prevent the Russians from marching across the Elbe—she gradually came to look upon the Russian challenge as basically an ideological one. Thus the achievement of a military balance in Central Europe did not diminish the cold war. It simply changed it from a classical power rivalry to a primarily ideological struggle. This was because the United States matched the ideology of communism with a counter-ideology of its own: anti-communism. Around these twin poles of communism and anti-communism the cold war has raged for more than twenty years.

For a long time there was good reason to fear that the cold war might erupt into a hot one. The Berlin blockade, the Korean war, the fighting in Iran and Greece, the Hungarian revolt, the Berlin crisis of 1961, and the confrontation over Cuba all brought the world near the brink of war. Yet the nuclear giants, awed by the enormity of their own powers of destruction, have always pulled back before confrontation led to open conflict. They managed to keep the peace because they knew that total war in the nuclear age was intolerable. Provocations which in an earlier period would probably have led to a declaration of war were smoothed over and disguised. The great powers have shown a healthy concern for their own survival. The atomic bomb, by positing the threat of total obliteration, has helped to keep an uneasy peace. "By a process of sublime irony," as Churchill said in 1955, we "have reached a stage in this story where safety will be the sturdy child of terror and survival the twin brother of annihilation."

The longer the equilibrium between the two nuclear giants has lasted, the more it has been possible for the smaller powers to pursue their own separate paths and for the natural process of disintegration to develop within the great rival alliances. While America and Russia have been consumed by the struggle to restrain each other from attack and to spread their rival ideologies, the once-intimidated spectators have been straying off into the wings and setting up their own sideshows. In the process, the contest between the giants has lost much of its former virulence, as even the gladiators themselves have begun to realize. The cold war between Russia and the West is no longer a struggle for global supremacy so much as it is a kind of military gymnastics. Neither side has any intention of attacking the other, and each is content to let its rival reign supreme within its own sphere of influence. A relatively stable power balance has been achieved between Russia and the West, and the centers of danger have now shifted to Asia and the underdeveloped nations. What remain are lingering commitments to ideology and a political vocabulary formed during a postwar period that is now virtually over.

Thus, though the postwar world is passing into history, its mythology stays on in the form of conventional labels—the "communist bloc," the "free world"—which conceal the remarkable changes that have occurred since the mid-1950s: the convulsions in the Soviet empire, the defection of China, the shock of decolonialization, the revival of Europe, and the development of common interests between America and Russia. The cold-war labels conceal these because they are rooted in a view of the world that has not changed to any real degree since 1948, when we assumed that the Red Army was about to sweep Western Europe into its maw. From this assumption, which seemed valid at the time, but which virtually everyone agrees is now exceedingly unlikely, sprang the NATO alliance, the rearmament of Germany, the semi-permanent garrisoning of an American army on the Continent, and the vision of an Atlantic community knitting

Europe and America together in "equal partnership." But with Europe no longer on her knees, with Russia no longer so menacing, and America no longer invulnerable, the conditions which originally inspired the Atlantic alliance, and America's presence in Europe, have largely disappeared. In their place are ambiguous and shifting relations between three changing powers: an interventionist America, a competitive Russia, and an evolving Europe. Today the whole focus of instability is switching away from Europe, where the containment of communism has been achieved, to a revolution-prone Third World. There the problems of development and the sudden transition from colonialism to independence have been accompanied by virulent nationalism and civil disorders into which the super-powers have been drawn.

Accustomed to think in the rhetoric of the cold war, we have seen these disorders as part of the global struggle between "freedom" and "communism." And because that struggle had begun in Europe, where the problem was one of defending weakened nations from the legions of the Red Army, we applied the same remedies elsewhere. Trying to reproduce NATO in contexts where virtually none of its elements applied, we created miniature alliances such as CENTO and SEATO, composed of nations which shared few of our assumptions about the dangers they faced and which had special uses of their own for the military aid we furnished.

The cold-war pacts have, for the most part, been largely forgotten by all but that handful of diplomats and generals whose job it is to attend their yearly conferences in such agreeable places as Teheran and Bangkok. But the dogma that inspired them lives on. The obsession with communism as an ideology, which burdened us for so long in Europe, has now switched its roost to Asia, and the specter of a global conspiracy directed from Moscow has been replaced by the specter of one directed from Peking. The focal point has changed: the obsession remains the same. It is one which is held with great tenacity even in the highest councils of our government.

The dogma has lingered on because it alone can justify a good many of our current involvements. Without the belief that popularly inspired revolutions are likely to fall into the hands of communists, how justify the intervention in Santo Domingo? Without the assumption that any communist government in Asia must automatically be subservient to Peking and manipulated by her, how justify the war in Vietnam? Without the dogma, how could there be public support for the policies of military intervention being pursued by the administration? Such policies are reasonable only if we assume that there is still a universal communist conspiracy and that all revolutions are master-minded by the same malevolent source—formerly Moscow, and now Peking. This assumption is the basis for current American diplomacy, and it rests upon the unexamined dogma of the cold war.

The irony of our present foreign policy, however, is that a workable power balance has been achieved between the nuclear giants, and it is now possible to speak openly of a real community of interests between Washington and Moscow. Ideological differences remain between America and Russia, but they have been reduced to secondary importance. In Asia, on the other hand, the ideological conflict between America and China is paramount, while the threat to national interest is very much secondary. Thus our relations with Russia are exactly the opposite of our relations with China, even though they are both communist powers and both theoretically dedicated to the triumph of their ideology. Paradoxically, China is considered to be a greater threat to the peace, although she is far weaker than Russia, because her ideological motivation appears so much stronger. Listening to what China says, rather than coldly judging what she has done and what she is capable of doing with her limited resources, we are terrified. Observing what Russia has done under her policy of "peaceful coexistence," rather than paying attention to her messianic vocabulary, we are reassured and believe an arrangement can be worked out with our leading adversary.

If the cold war means simply an ideological struggle between communism and anti-communism, that struggle goes on and will continue to go on so long as the major powers believe that these counter-ideologies are important. But if the cold war can be described as a power struggle between America and Russia for the allegiance of the world—one which began over the territory of Europe but which later embraced ideology—that struggle has been greatly diminished. It is highly unlikely to be resurrected in anything resembling its old form. There are at least four major reasons why this is so.

First, there is the recovery and growing independence of Western Europe. When the Second World War ended, Europe was not only in physical ruins, but in moral ruins as well. There was no talk of Europe as an independent power center because there was no conviction that the European states could ever again marshal sufficient power to stand by themselves on the world stage.

Yet as the work of economic recovery—made possible by generous American assistance through the Marshall Plan—proceeded, there was a corresponding growth of self-confidence in Western Europe. The defeat of the Italian Communist Party in the general election of 1948 brought an end to the fear that communism would come to Western Europe from within. The guarantee of American protection under the NATO alliance, signed in the spring of 1949, convinced most Europeans that communism was blocked from without as well. From that time on, the tide turned in Western Europe. The line of political demarcation was fixed and, except for the independence of Austria, it has remained untouched ever since. The invasion of Czechoslovakia in August 1968 was precisely to maintain this line.

The division of Europe was cruel and arbitrary, but it also provided stability on both sides of the Iron Curtain. It showed where communism was going to remain, and where it was unable to expand. With the eastern part of the continent under Soviet domination for an indeterminate time, something radically new was undertaken in compensation: the construction of a *Western* European community. Inspired by visions of political unification that would submerge old national rivalries, the leaders of postwar Europe launched a series of remarkable experiments: the European Coal and Steel Community, the European Defense Community, Euratom, and the Common Market. Today the economies of the six nations of the Common Market are so intertwined and interdependent that they could not be severed without causing severe damage to all the nations involved. Integration has worked, and the member nations of the EEC have a vested interest in its survival.

The resurgence of European self-confidence has been one of the most unexpected phenomena of the postwar era. The nightmare of the Nazi period has been largely forgotten, the social and economic stagnation of prewar times has been relegated to the history books, and the sense of political impotence that followed Europe's collapse is also passing. The narrow chauvinism of the past is being replaced by a growing spirit of intra-European cooperation, and the old despair has given way to a belief that Europeans must be masters within their own house. This is not so much a new chauvinism as it is the expression of a European personality. Europe has been divided and occupied by two foreign giants for nearly a quarter-century. The American occupation, while it has been a benevolent one, is now considered anachronistic. The Europeans are demanding a much greater voice not only within the Atlantic alliance but over all the decisions that affect their future.

The second factor marking the passing of the postwar world has been the disintegration of the communist bloc and the rise of a second Rome in Peking. The Soviet empire in Eastern Europe, imposed by the Red Army at the end of the Second World War and maintained by regimes subservient to Moscow, has been splintered, probably irrevocably. It is no longer accurate to speak of "satellites" when referring to such nations as Hungary, Rumania, and Poland. Solidly within the Soviet orbit, they are nonetheless free to pursue their own internal policies, often over the objections of the Kremlin. "Communism," as George Kennan has written, "has come to embrace so wide a spectrum of requirements and compulsions on the part of the respective parties and regimes that any determined attempt to reimpose unity on the movement would merely cause it to break violently apart at one point or another." [1]

Neither as a political-economic system nor as an ideology has communism been able to overcome the power of nationalism. This failure has been endemic in communism ever since the creation of the Soviet state, when Lenin waited for the workers of the West to join the Russian example, and instead faced a wall of iron hostility. If there has been any single lesson in Eastern Europe during the past twenty years, it has been that communism has failed while nationalism has triumphed. A sense of national identity which transcends ideology is as strong today in Eastern Europe as it ever was, and far stronger than it is in the West. When one considers the excesses of East European nationalism in the past, this revival is not necessarily a welcome phenomenon. But it is a fact, and a fact that communism has done nothing to alleviate.

Even the old territorial grievances are beginning to be heard again as the Rumanians aspire for the return of Bessarabia from the Soviet Union, and as the Albanians file their claim on the parts of Macedonia held by Yugoslavia. Today there is no Soviet bloc. There is simply an association of states proclaiming formal allegiance to the same ideology and dependent upon Russian power for protection against external enemies. "Polycentrism" is the word used to describe this loosening of Moscow's hold upon the other communist nations. What it means precisely is the creation of rival centers of power within the communist orbit. The heresy of the Yugoslavs and of the Italian Communist Party has now become the hallmark of the communist movement. Instead of a single communist church with the Pope sitting in Moscow, the Marxist-Leninist churches are now autocephalous. It is no longer possible to know what is the line of communist orthodoxy, because there no longer is a single orthodoxy. The Communist Party of East Germany is equal in authority to the Communist Party of the Soviet Union over questions of Marxist-Leninist dogma and, in practice, over all questions which do not involve the security of the Soviet state.

As a result of this fission within the communist bloc, communist groups throughout the world are behaving in terms of local conditions rather than along lines laid down by Moscow. The Poles seek Western trade outlets, the Yugoslavs are experimenting with mixed enterprise, the Rumanians are inviting capitalist investment, the Italian communists ponder dissolving themselves in a Popular Front movement, the Albanians daily proclaim the perfidy of Moscow, and the Chinese accuse the Russians of betraying the proletarian revolution. Heresy is now everywhere, which means that there is no longer any orthodoxy.

The break-up of communist orthodoxy has, of course, been stimulated by the rupture between China and Russia. Whatever hopes Moscow had for dominating the world communist movement were shattered by the establishment of an independent communist government in Peking. The Russians could not have foreseen the precise form the Chinese revolt against their authority would take, but they had a clear premonition of its coming. The Chinese revolution was basically an indigenous affair, and the Chinese leaders have never concealed their demand for full equality with the Russians within the world communist movement.

Caught in the flush of their revolution, and eager to reassert their national pride, the Chinese are challenging the Russians not only over the interpretation of communist scripture, but also over the disputed territories along their common frontier. The roots of this conflict extend deep into the past. If the West had not been so blinded by its own ideological blinkers it would long ago have realized that Sino-Soviet solidarity was nothing but a myth which could not long survive the test of time and clashing national interests.

Two giant nations sharing a common frontier—one committed to "peaceful coexistence" and the pursuit of affluence, the other mired in poverty and demanding world revolution—China and Russia are natural adversaries, regardless of what ideology they may share. A common dedication to Marxism-Leninism, such as they separately interpret it, has, if anything, only intensified their conflict. The open break between China and Russia has been of vital importance to the West, for it has eliminated the danger that the world communist movement could be placed at the service of the Soviet state. In this dramatic triumph of nationalism over communist unity, ideology has been relegated to the back seat. As a result of the Chinese challenge to Moscow, the smaller communist nations throughout the world now have an unprecedented freedom to pursue their own separate paths. Orthodoxy cannot be reimposed without shattering the bloc completely. The cold-war trauma of a communist monolith has been broken. In its place is a hydra with as many heads as there are communist parties.

In the world of independent states, every government—communist or non-communist—must look after its own interests. In doing so it may find, as several communist governments have found already, that its major adversary shares its ideology. Although alliances of various communist nations in the future cannot be precluded, they are unlikely to be permanent. An indigenous communist revolution in any new country can no longer be assumed to augment the power or influence of any other communist state. A communist Yugoslavia did not augment Russian power. On the contrary, it decreased it by defying Russia's sole right to speak for the communist world. By the same token, a communist North Vietnam or North Korea has not increased China's power. Here a common ideology has been allowed to mask the conflict of national interests. By refusing to recognize this, we have been the victims of a mythology that the communists themselves no longer believe in.

The third factor which has signaled the end of the postwar world has been the spectacular appearance of Africa, Asia, and Latin America in the center of the world arena. Twenty years ago the movement from colonialism to independence had barely begun. Today it has been virtually completed. Except for a few enclaves which are unlikely to hold out much longer against the tide, European colonialism is now a thing of the past. With a speed that has dazzled even the most enthusiastic spokesmen of independence, the European powers have pulled out of Asia and Africa—sometimes, indeed, too soon. In the vast underdeveloped areas that were once their colonies, some threescore newly independent states have demanded their rights to equality, prosperity, and seats in the United Nations.

This is, by any standard, one of the great revolutions of modern times, even more important than the Russian revolution of 1917. By their assertion of equality with the older nations of the West, the underdeveloped states of the Third World have transformed the world power structure. They have reduced the Russo-American cold war to a parochial power conflict and rephrased the problems of world politics in a new vocabulary. To these nations the question of communism versus anti-communism is peripheral or even irrelevant. Their concern is with economic development, political influence, and racial equality. They envy the West (in which they include Russia) its material prosperity, its economic techniques, its social discipline. They are interested in political ideology only insofar as it can be used to achieve the goals they value. They all proclaim their allegiance to "socialism," but the word itself covers such a variety of experiences and abuses that it can no longer even be defined in Western terms.

The rise to independence of the submerged peoples has undermined most of our assumptions about the world power struggle. It has demonstrated that the real struggle is not between communists and anti-communists but between haves and have-nots; not between Russians and Americans, but between economically developed societies and economically primitive ones. By rephrasing diplomacy in terms of economic development (and thus economic power) the underdeveloped nations of the Third World have taken the ideological sting out of the cold war. As their demands upon the rich nations increase, they have forced America and Russia to realize that they share a real community of interests. Prosperous, technologically advanced, politically stable societies, they have more in common with each other than with the clamorous poor in the southern hemisphere who demand their attention and their help. Compared to the new nations of Asia and Africa, the Soviet Union emerges as a status-quo power, affluent, conservative, and more interested in increasing its wealth than in spreading the world revolution.

Insofar as the new nations can find a major power that shares their problems, that power is China, the underdeveloped nation par excellence. A country that has only recently shaken off the domination of technologically advanced foreign powers, facing all the problems of a galloping rise in population, insufficient natural resources, an inadequate industrial base, and the hostility of both Russia and America, China would seem to be the ally of all the impoverished nations of the world. Hoping to win allies where they can find them, the Chinese have zealously—but with astonishing ineptitude—tried to rally the Africans, Asians, and Latin Americans into a holy alliance of the poor against the rich. Indeed, they have so twisted Marxist doctrine from its original intentions that they are using it as an instrument of class warfare between rich and poor nations, rather than between economic classes *within* nations. They have tried to make it a tool by which the poor nations may demonstrate their superiority over the rich nations and the "historical inevitability" of their triumph.

While the Chinese have proclaimed themselves the leaders of the new world revolution, they have had little success in winning anyone's allegiance. This is because the new nations are as suspicious of the Chinese as they are of the super-powers. They are basically uninterested in the ideological pretensions of communism particularly when, as in China's case, these are not even combined with large doses of foreign aid. These nations are determined to stay out of the quarrels of the great powers and are much too absorbed in their own problems of nationalism and economic development to play an active role in the cold war.

The fourth factor to diminish the cold war has been the declining importance of nuclear weapons in the world power balance. Although it may seem anomalous, experience has shown that atomic weapons have been of virtually no value in settling political disputes. Among nuclear powers, atomic weapons serve as a deterrent which inhibits direct combat. Had it not been for the atom bomb, it is likely that Russia and America would have been at war long ago over one of their many areas of dispute. The Bomb has helped them keep the peace, but it has not allowed them to settle their grievances. The grievances, in fact, remain virtually the same as they have been since the rivalry began: the partition of Germany and the division of Europe. The Bomb, in other words, has frozen the political status quo.

Similarly, between a nuclear and a non-nuclear power, atomic weapons seem to have been of little use. They have not allowed their possessors to intimidate those without such weapons, nor even to win a battle once it was engaged. What they have done, surprisingly, is to force the great to descend to the level of the small, to compel the atomic powers to fight with conventional weapons. This has been the experience of the French in Algeria, and of the British in Cyprus, Kenya, and Aden. The United States too has discovered that her atomic weapons are not really relevant in areas of limited war such as Korea and Vietnam. Despite her vast technological superiority, she has been obliged to fight guerrilla warfare on the terrain chosen by the guerrillas, not because she wants to, but because there is no alternative. Although she possesses greater power than any nation in history, the United States cannot impose her will even on a technologically backward society of a few million people. Nor can the Russians, for that matter, enforce their will on nations outside their acknowledged sphere of influence in Eastern Europe. They invaded Czechoslovakia, with whom they had a common border, because they feared she would pull loose from the Soviet bloc. But little Albania remains defiant.

Atomic bombs, it has now become apparent, exist only to deter other atomic bombs. They cannot be used even in limited combat, lest they trigger off an unlimited war. They cannot be brandished as a bluff against another atomic power, because nobody would believe a bluff that involved the threat of national suicide. They cannot be disposed of—unless both nuclear powers could reach an agreement to dispose of them at once. And even if they did, neither could be sure that the other didn't have some weapons hidden which it would use for atomic blackmail, or that a third power might not arise to threaten them both. Paradoxically, then, the atomic bomb has kept the peace between the two great powers, while providing the cover behind which lesser powers—and indeed even they themselves—carry on low-key rivalries. It has, in one sense, made the world a safer place for the nuclear powers and their allies. But it has also reduced the necessity for them to resolve their major outstanding grievances.

The irony of the Bomb is that it is really the enemy of the super-powers. So long as it remains in their hands alone, a balance can be maintained. But if it is dispersed to a host of minor powers, it will deprive the giants of the great advantages they have over their rivals: their physical size and their economic strength. Russia and America, spreading over entire continents and marshaling the most powerful economies the world has ever known, do not need nuclear weapons to be great. Without them, they are still the strongest and richest nations in the world. Because of their geography they are also the most secure from attack. But the atom has diminished the advantage of size, and the intercontinental missile has annihilated the protection of the oceans. Together these two weapons have upset the classic relationships between great powers and small ones. They have endowed the latter with a strength that belies their size and robbed the former of their power superiority. They have not made the small the equal of the great, but they have narrowed the gap between them. France, for example, will always remain inferior to Russia on any power scale. But the French Bomb has now become a serious consideration in any designs the Russians may have on Western Europe. Similarly, the Chinese Bomb will not, for a long time at least, pose any direct danger to the United States. But when China develops an effective delivery system she will be far safer from an American attack than if neither side had ever developed a Bomb.

Thus has the Bomb served as an equalizer between the small

and the great. It is, to be sure, a symbolic equalizer, since it would serve nobody's purpose if it were ever used. But in the strange world of atomic deterrence it has a certain psychological utility. No one is happy that it has been invented. But now that it is among us, no nation aspiring to major-power status feels fully armed without it. Even those nations such as West Germany, for whom the possession of a Bomb means political disaster, cannot refrain from expressing their inferiority feelings because they do not have one. And technologically advanced mini-powers, such as Israel and Switzerland, contemplate the eventual acquisition of nuclear arsenals.

America and Russia both have "overkill" power to destroy one another as organized societies, with enough weapons left over to obliterate the rest of mankind as well. But neither can shame the other into surrendering anything it considers vital. Khrushchev issued ultimatums for three years in Berlin, threatening the most dire happenings if the West did not retreat. Yet there was no retreat and there were no dire happenings because the Russians had no intention of launching a nuclear war over the status of Berlin. Even the Cuban missile crisis, which brought the world closer to the nuclear abyss than it has been at any other point in the cold war, was not resolved because President Kennedy threatened to use American nuclear weapons. On the contrary, the successful resolution of that crisis was due in large part to the fact that the United States used her non-nuclear superiority in the Caribbean— her sea and air power—to induce the Russians to withdraw their missiles.

The present hard-won nuclear balance has not only reduced the threat of atomic war and virtually nullified the advantages of atomic weapons, but also made both sides realize that they have a vital common interest in preserving the peace. To do so they must prevent lesser powers, whether allies or adversaries, from upsetting the balance and forcing them into a nuclear confrontation against their will. Thus the covert collusion between the super-powers to close the nuclear club to new members. The non-proliferation treaty, however desirable, is designed to stabilize the peace by preserving their nuclear duopoly. Everybody knows this, but the small powers are mostly willing to tolerate it because it is to their advantage. The only important nations to oppose it are those that aspire to major-power status: so far, France and China.

With the recognition by both sides that virtually nothing is worth a nuclear war, a good deal of air has gone out of the Russo-American confrontation. Fanatics in both camps—whether Birchites or Maoists—may still speak of victory, but responsible political leaders know better. President Eisenhower summed up the grim truth about the atomic balance when he said that there is "no alternative to peace." And Khrushchev, in his own vivid way, put the Chinese fanatics in their place when he said: "Is there a madman or a clever man who could tell what would happen after a nuclear war? It's stupid, stupid, stupid. . . . And there are people among communists who believe that war is good for revolution. Those who call for revolution now should go to see a psychiatrist." [2] The revolution, in case anyone had any doubts, clearly takes a back seat to the preservation of the Russo-American nuclear balance.

These, then, are the major factors which have served to topple the ideological superstructure of the cold war and replace it by perplexing and constantly shifting relationships among the great and not-so-great powers. The postwar world has been shattered beyond recognition, and much of what we have taken for granted during the past twenty years is no longer true. Strange combinations are in process of forming: unlikely alliances among long-standing foes, unexpected rivalries among close allies. There is a new freedom, and even a new anarchy, at large in the world, an anarchy that neither of the great powers is capable of mastering.

Traditionally anti-communist Spain has strengthened her diplomatic and economic ties with communist Cuba, has tried to blackmail the United States over the use of bases on her territory, has signed a consular pact with Rumania, and is moving toward full diplomatic ties with the Soviet Union. Pakistan, the fulcrum of both the CENTO and the SEATO pacts and the recipient of billions of dollars in American aid, has formed an unofficial alliance with China in a squeeze play against India. The Turks, historically anti-Russian, but bitter over the refusal of United States support in the crisis over Cyprus, are cementing a rapprochement with the Soviets. Britain, blocked in her bid to enter the Common Market and plagued by a stagnant economy, can neither lead nor speak for a resurgent Europe. Indonesia, after flirting with communism, has wandered back into the neutralist camp, but remains profoundly unstable. India, still incapable of coping with her own economic needs, contemplates the acquisition of an atomic arsenal to balance off China. Israel and Egypt threaten to follow suit and by their action induce a wholesale proliferation of nuclear weapons among the mini-powers. West Germany, the most powerful non-nuclear power on the Continent, is straying from her old policy of rigidity toward the East, and is pursuing radically new paths to reunification. France has now withdrawn from NATO, is critical of American "hegemony," and flirts with both Peking and Moscow. Latin America, which was once a secure haven for United States investment and a faithful supporter of United States diplomacy, is trying to loosen the grip of the Yankee colossus by overtures to Europe, thereby turning the Monroe Doctrine on its head. The uncommitted new states of Africa and Asia, rather than emulate either of the super-powers, have tried to play them off against each other for their own advantage. The United Nations, by the admission of scores of former colonial states, has been transformed from a tool by which the super-powers could police the world into an instrument by which the mini-powers can exert pressure on the giants. Even Russia, which was once the world's leading provocateur, joined the United States in playing the role of peacemaker in the dispute between India and Pakistan.

The shattering of the old alliances and the rise of new political constellations have threatened the dominance the two nuclear giants have enjoyed for the past quarter-century. Control is slipping out of their grasp, and the days of their hegemony now seem to be numbered. For a long time to come they will remain the most powerful nations in the world. But their ability to cajole, intimidate, or speak for others is diminishing steadily. A world which for more than two decades revolved around the rival poles of Moscow and Washington has now fragmented into scores of pieces. It is no longer One World, to be fought over between the communists and the anti-communists; or even two worlds to be divided between them. Rather it is a series of interlocking and constantly shifting relationships between great and small powers who use one another for their own temporary advantage.

With the diminishing of the ideological conflict that has given the cold war its particular virulence and meaning, America and Russia are no longer powers with a major source of conflict between them. The only place their vital interests ever collided was in Central Europe. But now that they have reached a *de facto* accord to leave well enough alone, Europe is not a major source of contention. Two great powers on opposite sides of the world, Russia and America are learning to carry on their competition in terms of a traditional power rivalry. Each remains committed to its ideology, but since neither can enforce it upon the other without inducing a nuclear war, dialogue, compromise, and even agreement are possible. The contest for the soul of the world can be carried on in a muted key.

Already a tacit cooperation between the super-powers has begun. It cannot be openly admitted, for the extremists on both sides would point out that the emperors had been shorn of their ideological clothes. But it is going on nonetheless. The nuclear-test-ban treaty of 1963, the non-proliferation treaty to close the nuclear club, and the Strategic Arms Limitation talks are simply the most obvious examples of this cooperation. Self-restraint where rival spheres of influence are concerned has been the hallmark of the Russo-American competition. This has been enforced upon them by the fear that a direct clash might ignite a nuclear war. The United States refrained from supporting the 1953 revolt in East Berlin, let the Hungarians be crushed in 1956 and the Czechs in 1968, and accepted the construction of the Berlin Wall. The Soviet Union has respected the security of West Berlin and tolerated our devastation of communist North Vietnam. In Suez

and Iraq, the Congo and Laos, Cyprus and Kashmir, the super-
powers have collaborated to limit conflicts into which they might
be drawn as participants.

This was true even in such a chronic trouble spot as the Middle
East, where America and Russia have been engaged in the dangerous game of arming rival protégés. When hostility between Israel
and her Arab neighbors again erupted into war in June 1967, the
two super-powers showed a common desire to prevent the conflict
from spreading. The Russians, while courting the Egyptians with
advanced military hardware, had no desire to unleash a general war
in the Middle East. Nor did the United States, already overextended in Vietnam, want to get involved in such a war. Indeed,
the Israeli blitzkrieg spared Washington the agonizing choice of
either abandoning the Jewish state to possible extinction, or sending in the Sixth Fleet and risking a confrontation with Russia.
Since the six-day war, the Russian decision to extend Soviet
influence by rearming Egypt has fed the flames of Arab nationalism
and inhibited a negotiated settlement. Washington and Moscow
cannot control their protégés, who have become instruments of
their rivalry and threats to their détente.

In other areas their cooperation has been more successful.
After the mutually dissatisfying experience of the Congo, they
have tried to keep the cold war out of Africa. As Russia has been
notably restrained in Latin America since the Cuban debacle, so
the United States has refrained from exploiting the explosive nationalism in Eastern Europe. Both have agreed to demilitarize the
Antarctic, ban nuclear weapons from outer space, try to stabilize
the arms race, share the burden of building up India as a potential
rival to China, and keep Fidel Castro on a short leash. Two great
powers with a vested interest in the status quo and the perpetuation of their nuclear duopoly, they have discovered that collaboration may be exceedingly beneficial to both of them.

The fear that America and Russia may be drawn into a nuclear
war by some precipitous action of their allies, such as China or
Germany, has led both sides to reconsider the value of their alliances. They are beginning to realize that the alliances may be

important less as a means of confronting each other than as a means of keeping some of the smaller powers in line. This desire of Russia and America to seek rapprochement through their rival power blocs is a clear repudiation of the theory on which the cold-war alliances have been based. These alliances are no longer directed against each other, but are, in effect, instruments by which the super-powers seek to maintain a balance. Whether they will be able to sustain their alliances once their purpose becomes apparent is exceedingly problematical. But in this interim period there is a growing belief in both rival capitals that Russian-American dominance should be maintained as long as possible in order to prevent other countries from intruding on the scene.

Faced with the growing insubordination of their allies and the obduracy of the neutrals, America and Russia are in the declining days of their condominium. Like generals of two mutinous armies, they are becoming aware of the fact that, although they are on opposite sides, the problems they face are strikingly similar, and that what is to the advantage of one is not necessarily to the disadvantage of the other. Indeed, their interests in many cases are surprisingly parallel. Trying to maintain a nuclear balance, keeping restless allies in check, paying blackmail to the underdeveloped nations, and seeking to prevent Third World revolutions from spilling over into conflagrations that might involve them, the super-powers are being drawn together into an unacknowledged, and still rather embarrassing, cooperation.

For the first time since 1945 Franklin Roosevelt's idea of a great-power directorship over the world has become theoretically possible. America and Russia now realize that it is to their interests. But is it not already too late? The time has passed when Washington could decree a German settlement without the accord of Bonn, or when Moscow could impose a solution upon Pankow. Washington cannot speak for Paris, or even for Saigon, any more than Russia can speak for Peking, or even for Bucharest.

The break-up of the old alliances and the entry upon the world scene of other powers—a resurgent Europe, an ambitious China —have destroyed the ability of the nuclear giants to impose their own conceptions of order. The agreements they can reach are limited not only by the fear and suspicion induced by the cold war, but also by their declining power over their allies.

With pretensions to world leadership they cannot easily shed, with global responsibilities that flatter their national egos, with ideological beliefs that confirm their sense of mission, and with restless allies who could throw the hard-earned détente into doubt, the super-powers remain victims of their obsessions, their fears, and their fantasies. They cannot turn their covert collaboration into an open entente because they remain committed to inherited postures and nagging ideologies. For some time to come they will remain publicly committed to the ideological goals of the cold war, even though they may privately recognize that these are unattainable (as in the case of world communism) or perhaps even undesirable (as in the case of German reunification). Thus it may be that America and Russia will try to solidify their détente, even while protesting that no collaboration is taking place. This protest is necessary not only to soothe their allies, but also to lessen the shock of such a reversal of attitudes. It also, paradoxically, may give them a certain freedom of maneuver. This is particularly true of an ideologically oriented government like that of the Soviet Union. "The continued use of the symbols 'world communism' and 'revolution'," as one historian has observed,

satisfies . . . those who desire whatever they think these symbols represent. . . . It may fill their needs as adequately as, or more so than, an actual realization of world communism and the revolution could. . . . One may expect that the more the Soviet government changes its policies from those that were once associated with the goal of world communism, the less can it afford to stop insisting that it continues to stand for this goal. It is therefore unreasonable to expect a Soviet policy change to be initiated or accompanied by an open renunciation of the Soviet goals of burying capitalism and establishing world communism. Such a renunciation can only be one of the last, rather than one of the first, concomitants of a policy change and will for a long time be as impossible psychologically and politically as a statement by an American President (no matter what his foreign policy) that he is no longer interested in fighting communism.[3]

Symbol and myth still play a predominant role in the relations between the super-powers. This is clearly true for the Russians. It is equally true, though less obviously so, for ourselves. We are not only chained to the recitation of the old dogma in order to please the fundamentalists within our own camp; we are all too often convinced that the dogma is true. We have repeated it so often and lived with it for so long that we have ended up taking it at face value. There are, of course, real points of conflict between ourselves and the Russians, between ourselves and the Chinese, between ourselves and our own allies. These are unavoidable and to be expected in the relations among nations. But they are not conflicts which can be defined within the traditional vocabulary of the cold war. The insistence on doing so has hobbled our diplomacy and made much of it irrelevant to the world in which we now live.

The cold-war world is passing, but its myths linger on, in Asia, in Latin America, in Africa, and throughout the Third World, and nowhere more than in our relations with an evolving Europe.

4. The Atlantic Mirage

There is an eternal dispute between those who imagine the world to suit their policy, and those who correct their policy to suit the realities of the world. —ALBERT SOREL

❧ ❧ ❧ NATO WAS the first of our entangling alliances, and it is still the most important. Around NATO we built our postwar diplomacy of containment and intervention. By pledging our lives, our honor, and our wealth to the war-weakened nations of Western Europe, we rejected the isolationism that two world wars had rendered impossible, and sought a new community with our friends across the Atlantic. Based upon the foundation of a common civilization and a common danger, NATO set the precedent for a series of global alliances. Although some of its offspring are often forgotten or ignored, NATO still remains close to our hearts. To many Americans it symbolizes our acceptance of world responsibility as the protector and defender of Europe.

Yet now, some twenty years after its founding, that dream has begun to go sour. The allies who once beseeched our help are now chafing under what they term our "hegemony." They claim that America dominates the alliance to such a degree that Europe is in danger of losing its identity. Some fear, or profess to fear, that the American nuclear guarantee is less credible now that the United States herself is vulnerable to retaliation. Others complain that Washington's attention is straying from Europe to the new nations of the Third World. This change in focus, some believe, might lead the United States to involve its allies in a war over an issue in which they have no interest. And among the cynical there is a suspicion that Russia and America might try to keep the

Continent divided by rival military pacts in order to retain their own dominance.

Everywhere there are complaints, suspicions, and, in France, an outright rejection of NATO itself. America's postwar role as protector of Europe is in danger now that Europeans no longer feel so threatened. The Kennedy administration's dream of a Grand Design embracing America and a united Western Europe in "equal partnership" is beginning to seem unduly optimistic and even outdated. It is not even certain that NATO itself can much longer survive in anything like its present form. The North Atlantic Treaty Organization, which found its inspiration in a moment of common peril, is giving way to the détente.

Today, some twenty years after its creation, NATO seems to have fulfilled its purpose. But in the unsettled conditions of the late 1940s it was a vital demonstration of America's intention to resist Russian expansion. It was not, as some of its more obstreperous European critics seem to imagine, an American plot foisted upon helpless allies. Nor was it an instrument of aggression designed to force the Soviets out of Eastern Europe. Rather, it was a defensive response to the chaotic conditions of postwar Europe; part of the Continent lay under Russian domination and the other part was so weak that it threatened to fall to communist-inspired coups from within.

Postwar America would have been quite happy to withdraw from Europe once the Nazi armies were defeated. But we could not leave the Continent to the mercy of the Russians, who had installed communist dictatorships in Eastern Europe to replace the mainly right-wing, and occasionally fascist, ones of the prewar era, and who menaced the war-weakened nations of Western Europe with various forms of blackmail and subversion. With the electorally powerful communist parties of France and Italy threatening to come to power via the ballot box, with communist rebels fighting the royalist government of Greece, with the Russians making threatening moves in Iran and around Berlin, and with Czechoslovakia dragged behind the Iron Curtain by a *coup d'état*, it became obvious that the United States could not insulate her-

self from the dangers that faced postwar Europe. The victory over
Hitler was not meant to be succeeded by the creation of a communist empire ruled from Moscow.

With the Truman Doctrine of March 1947 the United States
intervened directly against communism in Europe with military
support for the Greek government. Two years later this intervention in the defense of non-communist Europe was consecrated by
the signing of the North Atlantic Treaty Organization pact. The
logical corollary of the Truman Doctrine, NATO was designed
"to restore and maintain the security of the North Atlantic area"
by making American military protection available to those nations which were too weak to defend themselves. It was a wise,
and indeed an essential, measure to re-establish a military balance
in Europe against the powerful Soviet forces in the East. The
West Europeans needed American protection, and they welcomed
NATO as the codification of our assistance.

Considering the inspirational sentiments the alliance evokes today, its original intentions seem exceedingly modest. It was not
intended to be the foundation for a political union between
America and Western Europe—or for any other kind of union,
for that matter. Rather, it was conceived as a simple guarantee of
American protection, meant to tide the Europeans over until
they were able to provide for their own defense. The purpose of
NATO, according to the report of the Senate Foreign Relations
Committee, which approved the treaty, was to "facilitate long-
term economic recovery through replacing the sense of insecurity
by one of confidence in the future." NATO, in other words, was
to be the military component of a formula in which the Marshall
Plan was the basic ingredient: a temporary wall behind which the
Europeans would use American economic aid to patch up their
wartime wounds and rebuild their defenses. This effort, it was
hoped, would be accomplished within twenty years. For this reason, the member nations were given the option to drop out after
1969, a provision particularly important to the United States
Congress, which had no intention of committing the nation's
fortunes to Western Europe indefinitely.

If the original aims of the alliance were modest, they did not remain so for long. The treaty was scarcely a year old when the communist North Korean army moved across the 38th parallel. With the decision to intervene with American troops in the defense of South Korea, the Truman Doctrine was extended from a war-weary Europe to a revolution-torn Asia. The impact of the Korean war was immediately felt in Europe, where the United States, fearful that a Soviet assault was in the offing, demanded a massive military build-up to achieve parity with the Russians on the western front. This, however, could be done only by enlisting the support of the Germans, who at that point were still under Allied military occupation. Consequently, in September 1950, three months after the outbreak of the Korean war, Secretary of State Dean Acheson called for the rearmament of the three western zones of Germany and the incorporation of twelve German divisions into NATO. The creation of a new German army was to be made tolerable by the establishment of an "integrated" NATO command to which the German units would be pledged. NATO, it was argued, would serve as the safety latch on German military independence.

Whatever limitations NATO offered, most Europeans were deeply disturbed by the prospect of a new German army. The scars were too deep and the memories too fresh to welcome the reappearance of German soldiers, even if they were now dedicated to the defense of the West and formally "integrated" into a multination NATO command. Nor were the Germans themselves eager to rearm after the debacle of their last effort. Chancellor Konrad Adenauer, despite his desire to please the Americans, continually dragged his feet, with the result that the *Bundeswehr*, which Dean Acheson declared to be so urgently needed in 1950, did not achieve its full twelve-division strength until a decade and a half later, by which time the threatening situation it was designed to meet had diminished considerably.

In addition to their understandable apprehension about the rearmament of Germany, the allies were unconvinced that any crash military program was really necessary. While they formally ap-

proved at NATO Council meetings the various strategic goals
urged by the United States—including in 1952 a demand for a
ninety-division NATO army—they never assumed that Western
Europe was to be defended on the ground with foot soldiers. For
the Europeans the real deterrent to Russian aggression was not
the land armies they grudgingly assembled under American prodding, nor the GIs guarding the frontier between the two Germanys, but the awesome nuclear arsenal the United States threatened to unleash in case the Russians crossed the Elbe. All the
rest was window-dressing. The Europeans, as Henry Kissinger has
explained,

> saw in the military contribution a form of fee paid for United States
> nuclear protection. The Europeans agreed to our requests. But they
> tried to see to it that their actual contributions would be large
> enough to induce us to keep a substantial military establishment in
> Europe, yet not so high as to provide a real alternative to nuclear
> retaliation.[1]

Nor, from their point of view, did the Europeans have to provide an alternative to nuclear retaliation. So long as American soldiers remained on the Continent, the United States would be
obliged to come to Europe's defense. These GIs insure, in a way
that no promise or treaty commitment ever could, that America
will be involved in any European war from the first shot. They
are the human trip-wire which, if broken by a Russian attack,
would trigger the American nuclear deterrent. Thus the presence
of these soldiers on the Continent has seemed essential to the
Europeans, for they make the American nuclear guarantee fully
credible. The troops are, in this sense, hostages.

By making modest efforts to fulfill their own NATO goals, the
Europeans have been able to retain the American hostages. But
they have not been able to prevent a technological revolution in
weaponry which has changed the whole nature of the nuclear
guarantee. When the United States pledged itself to Europe's
defense in the late 1940s, it was virtually invulnerable to Russian
retaliation. Because of the intercontinental missile, however, the
United States now faces the same danger of instant obliteration

that the Europeans have faced from the start. Without doubting America's good faith, some of the allies have begun to wonder whether the President of the United States would now unleash nuclear missiles on Russia in retaliation for an attack on Europe, since he knows that this would almost certainly mean the destruction of the United States itself. Some profess to see the Pentagon's new strategy of "flexible response"—with its call for larger European armies to prevent a war from immediately "escalating" to the nuclear level, and for American control of all NATO nuclear weapons—as a partial retraction of the old nuclear guarantee. They fear that the United States and Russia, in order to spare themselves atomic devastation, may prefer to conduct a "limited" war on European soil. But what would be "limited" for the super-powers would most likely be total for their allies. For this reason the British maintain their mini-deterrent, the French develop their *force de frappe*, and the Germans suffer from a nuclear inferiority complex. As former Canadian Prime Minister Lester Pearson said several years ago,

> An alliance for defense only is an anachronism in the world of 1966, especially when nuclear power is not shared, by possession or by control, among its members. . . . A guarantee of nuclear support against aggression simply does not now have the credibility that would make it a fully effective deterrent and therefore a guarantee of security.[2]

Such criticisms as these reflect a deep anxiety among the allies that the interests of Europe and America, however similar they may be, are not identical where questions of national survival are concerned. Thus the allies prefer the old strategy of "massive retaliation," which threatens the Russians with instant obliteration should they move across the Elbe. Faced with such a threat, Europeans believe, the Russians would never dare risk even a conventional probe. As a result, the allies have refrained from building the thirty-division army the Pentagon has urged upon them. Indeed, even the United States does not appear to take its own strategy seriously, since it has pulled troops out of Europe to send to Vietnam and would like to cut the 225,000-man American army in Germany if it could assuage German anxieties. With the with-drawal of French forces from NATO and the cutback in both the British and the American armies in West Germany, any Russian attack would almost certainly have to be met with atomic weap-ons. "Flexible response" still remains the official policy, but "mas-sive retaliation" more realistically describes the situation.

Because of these rather dizzying changes in strategy, NATO has come to mean something different from, and perhaps a good deal less than, what it did in the past. It is no longer, if indeed it ever was, a united body in which the defense of one is the defense of all. Militarily, the Europeans were never able to offer the United States much more than advance bases from which to strike at Soviet power. Now intercontinental missiles and Polaris-firing atomic submarines, long-range F-111 fighter-bombers and giant military transport planes, have drastically reduced the need for such strategic bases. Today whole divisions can be flown across the Atlantic in hours. Ten of these transport planes could have handled the Berlin airlift; 42 of them could complete in half a day the transfer of 15,000 troops to Europe that required 234 air-planes in 1963 and took nearly 3 days. Advanced technology has rendered the NATO bases, with their elaborate military pipelines and their brass-heavy bureaucracies, far less necessary to the de-fense of Europe. Thus there have been persistent calls in the United States Senate and even in the recesses of the Pentagon for sharp reductions in American troop strength in Europe. Technolog-ical innovation, the demands of the Vietnamese war, and the steady drain on United States gold reserves have served to intensify these appeals.

The declining need for overseas bases has stimulated not only a strategic revolution, but perhaps a political one as well. Once the United States and the Soviet Union developed the means to obliterate each other with weapons fired from their own territo-ries, the importance of their European allies inevitably diminished on the strategic scale of priorities. For both sides the most vital concern has switched from the defense of ideological allies to the prevention of nuclear war. Fearful of being dragged into an atomic conflict against their will, America and Russia have developed a common interest in keeping their allies out of the nuclear business. The Russians have not the slightest intention of giving atomic weapons to their East European comrades, and the United States has discouraged France's efforts at nuclear independence. President Johnson ultimately put into the deep freeze his predecessor's plan for a multilateral nuclear force (MLF) under mixed NATO ownership and control, and firmly told the Germans that their desire for nuclear sharing must take a back seat to the Russo-American détente and the wider interests of European peace.

Today, as in the past, the Europeans have no real control over American strategy, nor over United States diplomacy outside the Atlantic area. The American deterrent, which comprises about 95 per cent of NATO's nuclear power, rests entirely in United States hands. The allies cannot insure that it be used for a cause they may consider vital, nor prevent it from being used for a cause they may disapprove of. The Cuban missile crisis and Vietnam clearly revealed the limits of collective decision-making within the alliance. From an American point of view, these limits are eminently reasonable and desirable. As the nation which bears the major responsibility, and the major cost, of defending the Atlantic area, we clearly cannot tolerate having vital decisions over our security made anywhere but in Washington.

However reasonable this may seem to most Americans, it is an attitude not shared by some of our European allies—and particularly not by General de Gaulle. Shortly after returning to power in 1958 he tried to establish a three-power directorate with America and Britain to coordinate NATO policy on a global level. When this met with a cold reception in Washington, he sought to increase Europe's leverage within the alliance by striking a special entente with Bonn. This effort, however, collapsed with the departure of Adenauer from office. De Gaulle then fell back on the assertion of French autonomy within the Atlantic alliance, an autonomy backed up by the *force de frappe* and by a diplomatic line open to Moscow. Having announced in February 1965 that France would soon end "the subordination known as 'integration' which is provided for by NATO and which hands our fate over to foreign authority," he carried out his threat scarcely a year later by withdrawing from the military structure of the alliance.

De Gaulle, of course, could not have done this had he believed that it involved any real danger for France. But behind his action was the assumption that the alliance will continue without the system of military integration under NATO, and that such integration is, in any case, no longer essential to the defense of Europe. Deterrence, he believed, rests in the American atomic arsenal, not in the NATO command structure. And the deterrent, he declared, will continue to cover France just as it covers the other members of the alliance, and even such neutrals as Switzerland and Sweden. This has nothing to do with the structure of NATO, but with vital considerations of national interest. The United States cannot allow Europe to fall into Russian hands. This would be true whether NATO existed or not. And this is why, for purposes of nuclear deterrence, NATO is largely irrelevant.

Seizing upon a widespread discontent with the subordinate role to which Europe is still confined, de Gaulle tried to establish France as the leading challenger to American "hegemony" in Western Europe. By detaching France from NATO and throwing out her diplomatic lines to the emerging countries of the Third World, he gained for France a freedom of maneuver that was denied the other members of the alliance. In so doing he tried to show that Europe must be something more than a pawn in the struggle between the super-powers. More important, he expressed, and even helped to create, a sense of European resistance to the United States that is complex in its origins but quite widespread in its effects. It is compounded of pride in what Europe has accomplished during the past two decades, embarrassment at being totally dependent upon the United States for protection, apprehension at the growing role that American industry plays in the European economy, and fear of becoming involved in America's revolution-squelching interventions in the southern hemisphere. As Washington has become increasingly preoccupied with "wars of national liberation," the Europeans have given vent to a detachment that is not yet neutralism but determinedly resists any involvement.

In challenging America's domination of the alliance, de Gaulle brought to the surface tensions and disagreements that had long been concealed by the patina of NATO unity. He revealed and even intensified these tensions, but he did not create them. The disputes within the alliance over politics and strategy began long before de Gaulle returned to power, and are continuing even though he has left the scene, for they rest upon the realities of power, not upon the provocations of an irritating personality. "You can eliminate de Gaulle completely from the picture," the former supreme commander of NATO, General Lauris Norstad has said,

> and you would not eliminate the problem. You could eliminate France from the picture but you would not eliminate the problem. The problem has been fundamental all the way through. It is always convenient to have a whipping boy. It excuses us from our action or inaction.[8]

The reality de Gaulle revealed is that the conditions that originally inspired the alliance—a menacing Russia, an invulnerable America, a helpless Europe—have been overtaken by events. The Russians have become outspoken practitioners of "peaceful coexistence" and have been more interested in holding their own shaky political bloc together than in threatening Western Europe. The United States is still the world's greatest military power, but her defense policy for Europe is based upon a threat to commit national suicide. The Europeans have recovered from their war-time wounds to such a degree that they can now ponder the possibility of a reunited Continent from which both Russian and American troops will have disappeared. The sense of common danger and common weakness that inspired the Atlantic pact has given way to a new sense of security that is the undoer of alliances. Having achieved so much of what it initially set out to do, NATO is in danger of foundering now that its virtues no longer seem so necessary. In this sense it has become the victim of its own success.

This decline of NATO could be considered a source of satisfaction, for it means we may be approaching the point where the Europeans can take over the major burden of their own defense, and where it will no longer be necessary for us to assume such extraordinary dangers and costs on behalf of once-indigent allies. But our satisfaction with the stability and security of today's Europe has been muted by our disappointment over the failure of NATO to stimulate the united European community we desired. For most Americans, NATO was always more than merely a defense alliance: it was to be the means by which the old European enmities would be healed, by which Germany could make her peace with her neighbors, by which corrosive European nationalism would be buried, and by which the states of Eastern Europe could eventually be pried loose from the Soviet Union. Having twice been drawn into Europe's civil wars, we believed that Europe had to be made into something better than it had been. Applying the virtues of our own federal system to the chronic troubles of the Continent, we believed that the Europeans could end their endemic rivalries by forming a more perfect union: a United States of Europe.

This ambition was not selfish, for it was shared by many Europeans, and particularly by those who saw it as a means of ending the self-destructive rivalries of modern European history. Inspired by visions of a post-nationalist Europe, statesmen on both sides of the Atlantic drew up blueprints for a united Continent with a single army, a single parliament, and a single diplomacy. The communist capture of Eastern Europe limited the scope of this vision, but it also offered the opportunity of achieving the experiment on a smaller and more manageable scale in the countries west of the Iron Curtain. In this "little Europe" some of the great experiments in postwar cooperation were introduced: the Marshall Plan, NATO, the Coal and Steel Community, Euratom, the West European Union, and, perhaps most important of all, the Common Market.

From a fragmented, fratricidal Europe there would arise a great new power in the world, one which would be an "equal partner" to America in the Atlantic alliance, and which would exert such a powerful attraction on the communist states of Eastern Europe that the Russians would be forced to relinquish their empire peacefully. This was what came in time to be known as the Grand Design, a blueprint for a transatlantic partnership between the United States and the western half of Europe. Within the restricted scope of the Atlantic pact it promised the hope of One World that had been frustrated by Soviet ambitions and the collapse of great-power unity. To the former isolationists whom the cold war had transformed into fervent interventionists, the Grand Design affirmed the wisdom of American institutions by transposing them to a corrupted Europe. To the liberals committed to a benevolent imperialism, it affirmed America's readiness to assume the burdens of world leadership. Through the fusion of their economies and the federation of their governments, the nations of Western Europe would help the United States combat the communist menace, aid the underdeveloped states, lower tariff barriers, and even, in the words of President Kennedy in his "declaration of interdependence" at Philadelphia on July 4, 1962, offer the means by which "we can help to achieve a world of law and free choice, banishing the world of war and coercion."

It was an inspiring vision, noble in sentiment, honorable in aspiration, and deeply felt in its idealism. It was also a bit specious, more impressive in the effusion of its rhetoric than in the depth of its analysis. In positing a permanent "equal partnership" between America and a united Western Europe, it held out the hope of a world that might have been, rather than of one that was in process of becoming—as Kennedy himself grew to suspect before his death. From the start it should have been clear that the allies did not have the same conception of the partnership as did Washington. At best it could only be a substitute for the kind of Europe that the Iron Curtain and the cold war had made impossible. This was particularly true when it became obvious to Europeans that the United States did not intend to participate

in the equal partnership on an equal basis: that it had no intention of tearing down its tariff walls, sharing its deterrent, or sub-
ordinating the United States Congress to a European parliament.
Nor did Washington ever seem to realize that a Europe that would
be an equal partner would also want to be equal in the implements of power—that it would expect to have its own economic
policy, its own diplomacy, and perhaps even its own Bomb.
Equality, if it is to be anything more than rhetoric, means the
ability to follow independent policies. Even those Europeans most
desirous of some form of Atlantic partnership see a united Europe as something more than America's alter ego and spear-carrier.
"Partnership," in the words of Walter Hallstein, ex-president of the
Common Market Commission and thus Europe's highest-ranking
bureaucrat,

> means the opposite of a monolithic Atlantic community in which
> the European states would play the part of a bridgehead towards
> the East, as were the Hellenic settlements in Asia Minor. . . . Free
> Europe must develop its own personality in order to become a part-
> ner for America and to serve as a magnet for the countries of
> Eastern Europe.[4]

American diplomacy has run parallel to European interests because it has been based upon the military containment of Russia.
But now that the fear of Soviet attack has subsided in Western
Europe and American attention has focused on the unstable
states of the Third World, there is no longer the same clear con-
vergence of interests between the United States and her NATO
allies. Washington's attempts to solidify the détente with Moscow have raised apprehension among some of the allies, particularly the Germans, who fear that Russia and America may choose
to keep Germany partitioned in the interests of European stability. Outside the Atlantic area, the United States has found that
the Europeans have maintained a distance from our diplomacy
that borders on open detachment. Only France has so far openly
criticized American interventionism in such places as Vietnam

and Santo Domingo, but none of the NATO allies seems to share our concern about the expansion of communism in Southeast Asia, or our estimate of the aggressive intentions of China. In fact, they rather admire China for her accomplishments, see her as a potential market for European manufactured products, and recognize the usefulness of Peking as a counterbalance to Russia in the East.

Even in such mundane affairs as economics, European and American interests are not identical and sometimes not even complementary. The long and painful negotiations during the "Kennedy Round" for mutual tariff reductions have dramatized just how determined the Europeans are to protect their economic interests, and how much leverage they have gained by joining together in the Common Market. Tariff reductions have been achieved where they were to the advantage of both parties, but the hyperbole of Atlantic partnership has not secured American products a privileged entry into the Common Market, or induced the Europeans to take on a greater share of foreign aid for the underdeveloped countries.

As they try to build large-scale industries for their expanding consumer markets, the Europeans have become alarmed by the level of American private investment on the Continent, and particularly by its concentration in such vital fields as computers, automobiles, chemicals, and photographic equipment. The avalanche of American corporations jumping the Common Market tariff wall by setting up European subsidiaries has stimulated charges of "economic colonialism" and an insidious "American challenge." Many fear that the enormous American lead in growth industries such as electronics, plus the vastly greater amounts of funds available in the United States for basic research, will ultimately reduce Europe to the role of an economic satellite fated to produce American-designed products in American-owned factories on American licenses. "Europe," declared the French Socialist leader Gaston Deferre, "will be colonized by the United States unless we decide to pool our resources in order to create industrial concerns comparable in size to the American ones and able to compete with them on an equal footing."

These fears are not as imaginary as they may seem to skeptical Americans. Within recent years there has been a mounting invasion of Europe by American dollars, today in excess of $5 billion in the United Kingdom, and $6 billion on the Continent—or six times what it was in 1954. More than $2 billion is invested in West Germany alone, with another $1.5 billion in France and nearly $1 billion in Italy. The Common Market has become not only America's single most important customer and supplier, but also a magnet for United States capital in search of investment opportunities. In many respects this infusion of American funds has helped stimulate and expand European industry, providing the technical know-how and the competitive spirit that have been lacking in many areas of the European economy. But by its concentration in certain key industries, it has given rise to apprehension over foreign control. The computer industry, which holds the key to technological innovation, is controlled almost entirely by two American corporations. A similar situation applies in agricultural equipment, synthetic rubber, and chemicals. American ownership means that key areas of the European economy lie outside the effective control of European governments. "However much we welcome new American investment here as in other parts of Europe," Prime Minister Harold Wilson declared, "there is no one on either side of the Channel who wants to see capital investment in Europe involve domination or, in the last resort, subjugation." [5]

The European problem is not how to keep American firms away, for Europe needs American capital and technological skill, but how to make sure that the control of the European economy remains in European hands. This is not easy at a time when the French and Italian computer industries have been swallowed by IBM and General Electric, when the British government-owned airlines are buying American-built jets while Britain's own aircraft industries hover on the verge of bankruptcy, and when fledgling

European nuclear-power programs are being threatened by the American electrical giants. How can the Europeans compete so long as they do not have the continental-scale markets and the enormous federal research funds enjoyed by American corporations? How can they hope to challenge the United States in the basic growth industries when a single American firm such as General Motors has annual sales greater than the gross national product of the Netherlands or than that of a hundred other countries? The answer is that Europe cannot compete unless there is a domestic market comparable to that in the United States, unless European industries are able to merge into cartels as large as American corporations, unless there are massive infusions of government funds into basic research, and unless American companies can be prevented from controlling key areas of the European economy through subsidiaries. These goals cannot be achieved through an Atlantic community, since this would only institutionalize Europe's technological weakness. They can be realized only through unification—through expansion of the Common Market across the Channel and eventually across the Elbe. Whether this will happen remains to be seen. But unless there is some kind of wider economic integration, Europe cannot hope to compete with America as an equal.

European apprehension about American competition has not been confined to industry, but spreads to agriculture as well. For the past twenty years the United States has found an eager market in Western Europe for its farm products. European purchases helped cover the deficit in our balance of payments caused by overseas military expenses and foreign aid. But the same mechanization that modernized Europe's factories has also modernized her farms to the degree that the Common Market now has a farm-surplus problem of its own. Whatever their friendship toward the United States, the members of the Common Market have a primary obligation to their own family. There is nothing anti-American in the desire of European farmers to sell the crops with which a beneficent nature has provided them, but it does mean that the United States cannot much longer expect to meet its payments deficits out of money earned from selling surplus grains to Europe.

These economic disagreements have revealed just how much undue optimism there has been in Washington's vision of a free-trade area within the Atlantic community. Although an admirable design for trade liberalization on the classical model, it is full of pitfalls the Europeans are determined to avoid. Because they did not want to have their industries crushed by mass-production American imports, they have retained an external tariff. And because they wanted something more than a simple free-trade zone—more than a European supermarket—they rejected Britain's plans for diluting the integrationist ambitions of the Common Market. The Common Market nations are, in a sense, protectionist. But in that game nobody enters the arena with clean hands, not even the United States.

From these economic disagreements—which are only shadows of more important political differences—it is apparent that there has been a good deal of unjustified optimism, and even of cant, in Washington's dream of a unified Western Europe joined to America in an Atlantic community. A united Europe of 180 million people in the richest and most industrially advanced nations of the earth would be a great power in its own right, capable of defending itself and pursuing its own foreign policy. While it might be a partner to America in areas where their interests overlapped—such as the containment of Russia—it would have interests of its own to pursue, and the strength to make those interests felt. It could not be expected to remain permanently dependent on our protection, since it would have the capacity to build a Bomb of its own. Nor would it be content to play deputy sheriff to Washington in the unruly states of the Third World. A unified Europe would want a dominant voice in working out an eventual political settlement with Moscow, and in time it might even find a tamed Russia a useful ally in balancing the overwhelming weight of American economic power. As is already apparent, it would hardly share Washington's phobia about China. The Grand Design was honorable in inspiration, but too much has happened since that Fourth of July when President Kennedy outlined his sweeping vision of an Atlantic partnership. The communist empire is breaking up, the little Europe of the NATO pact has grown too small to Europeans looking beyond the Iron Curtain, and America's new role as revolution-extinguisher has instigated a growing European desire to be counted out.

The United States has been deeply involved in European affairs for half a century. Because of Europe's vital importance to our national interest, we must remain deeply concerned by what happens on the Continent. Europe will probably always remain our first line of defense, as it has long been the anchor of our deepest cultural ties. But this does not make us a European power, any more than playing a saxophone turns a man into a musical instrument. Europe is important, but it is only one of the areas of concern vital to the United States. The Atlantic demands our attention, but so do the Pacific and the Caribbean. A community is one form of political organization, but it is not one which is natural to nations separated by 3000 miles of ocean and with great discrepancies of size, wealth, power, interests, and ambitions. Our alliance with Western Europe represents our stake in Western civilization, but the lands beyond the Iron Curtain, and even Russia herself, are also part of that civilization. Europe faces west toward the Atlantic, but it also faces east toward the Urals. A Europe which is becoming absorbed in the quest for reunification will not remain forever tied to a military alliance premised upon the indefinite division of the Continent. An Atlantic community may be desirable, but it can never be built at the expense of a European community that would bring the communist nations in the east back into the European family. Nor can we allow the parochial interests of some of our NATO allies to impede the détente with Russia.

America and Europe will probably always be joined by bonds of friendship and interest, and even by some form of alliance so long as Russia remains a threat. But although they are complementary civilizations, America and Europe are not identical, and the common mold has long since been broken by two centuries of an evolving American experience. The American impact on postwar Europe has been enormous in everything from the packaging of soap to the packaging of culture. But the so-called Americanization of Europe, reflected in supermarkets and motels, is really little more than Europe's postwar adaptation to mass consumption and mass production. Prosperity has modernized the face of Europe, rebuilding its cities and jamming its narrow streets with cars. But modernization is not the same thing as Americanization, any more than hair-tinting is psychoanalysis. Despite surface similarities shared by most industrial societies, the differences between America and Europe run deep—in culture, in society, in personal relations.

This does not mean that America and Europe must, or will, become hostile, but rather that the relentless pace of industrialization may be stimulating differences even as it creates similarities. In the long run it may make it even more desirable for the peoples of the New World as well as of the Old to guard their cultural differences as a means of preserving their identities. Joined by a common heritage, sharing common cultural values and common riches in a world of poverty, America and Europe are not necessarily political partners. These two great societies are on parallel rather than identical tracks, as Americans consolidate their own unique civilization, and as Europeans strive to maintain the cherished values of their shared history and to seek a new future in some form of unification.

We had a dream of what Europe should be: a politically unified West European federation linked to the United States. It was a dream inspired by the cold war and given flesh by the existence of the NATO alliance. But in embellishing this vision we lost sight of the reason which brought us back to Europe two decades ago: to defend our friends from the Russians until they were capable of defending themselves and of achieving a political balance with the countries of Eastern Europe. Now that our allies are beginning to turn their attention to this long-neglected problem, we treat this change as though it were somehow a defeat. We have forgotten what we wanted to accomplish in Europe, and in so doing are in danger of causing a new instability on the Continent.

The time has come to stop mourning over formulas that served so well in the past, over blueprints for the future that have been made obsolete by changing events. What was reasonable in 1949 is often unreasonable today; what was visionary in the mid-1950s is reactionary in the early 1970s. What is essential in contemplating the future of NATO is that we not allow ourselves to become prisoners of our own rhetoric: that we not pursue roads that are no longer open, proclaim goals that are no longer possible, substitute a certain conception of Atlantic unity for a reconciliation of Europe, impose an abstract solution upon an intractable problem, become so mesmerized by projects that we lose sight of ends. The true issue facing us today is not one of holding desperately to an organization that was conceived in the late 1940s, or of trying to force the Europeans into certain rigid forms of political union, but of encouraging the creation of a political climate that will allow the two Europes to reconcile their differences and achieve a wider community stretching across the Elbe.

This rebuilding of the European community is the ultimate objective which we originally envisaged when we returned to Europe twenty years ago. It would be foolish and self-defeating to allow our preoccupation with certain organizational forms of Atlantic cooperation to impede this process. It would alienate our European friends and negate much of what we have tried to accomplish during these past two decades. It could even leave Europe in a more dangerous condition than the one in which we found it. This need not happen, and it would be tragic if it did. Yet it could well result if we continue trying to impose our own conception of unity upon a reluctant Europe.

NATO as a military alliance has served us well in the past and it is a construction in which we and our allies may take a good deal of pride. But it was a specific response to a specific situation, and the situation has changed so radically that the response is no longer the proper one. A revitalized Europe, a chastened Russia, a vulnerable America—these are not the conditions to which NATO is appropriate. The NATO Organization, which was appended to the North Atlantic Treaty as a military after-thought, has now largely served its purpose. It is breaking down—with the withdrawal of France, the reluctance to meet military goals, and the arguments over money—because the members themselves no longer agree upon its necessity. It is, in Walter Lippmann's striking phrase, "no longer a genuine military invest-ment but an expensive and deteriorating ruin . . . like a mansion, once the pride of the neighborhood, from which the tenants have moved away, for which no new tenants can be found." [6]

Although NATO now seems doomed to extinction as a mili-tary organization, some form of military cooperation is likely to continue between America and Western Europe so long as our allies feel themselves threatened by the Russians. The alliance does not depend upon the organization, and the demise of the organization does not preclude the need for mutual defense ar-rangements. Even General de Gaulle underlined the need for an Atlantic alliance that would assure Europe of American nuclear protection. But just as the alliance is not the same as the or-ganization we call NATO, so the alliance is not necessarily the prelude to an Atlantic "community." An expression of the cul-tural, economic, and social bonds between America and Western Europe, the Atlantic community will always exist as a manner of speech and a frame of reference. What we must not do, how-ever, is to confuse this community of values shared by the diverse peoples who border the Atlantic with a particular form of political organization between America and Western Europe. The former is a living reality based upon three hundred years of shared his-tory; the latter is a by-product of the cold war. A politically unified Atlantic community was a noble dream: but it is no longer so desirable as it once was to a Europe now in search of reconcilia-tion, and to an America which may be tempted to achieve a private accord of its own with Russia. Perhaps one day it may be resur-rected in another form, but in the new climate of détente, the emphasis in Europe is on reconciliation with the East—and in Washington, on collaboration with the Soviet Union.

Having for so long been bemused by our role as Europe's protector, and having been in search of an Atlantic mirage, we have allowed ourselves to become oblivious to the realities of a Europe that may be nobody's partner in tomorrow's world.

5. Nobody's Europe

*. . . this monster, this robot, this Europe without soul,
without backbone, without roots.* —CHARLES DE GAULLE

❧ ❧ ❧ TODAY'S Europe oscillates fitfully between two worlds:
between the world of division and dependence it has known for
more than two decades, and the world of independence and unity
it would like to achieve. Europe hesitantly seeks a new identity in
federation, but clings to national sovereignty as the only assur-
ance of national identity. It speaks of destroying old frontiers and
creating new loyalties, but it is still, in de Gaulle's memorable
phrase, "without soul, without backbone, without roots." It listens
to Washington's appeals for transatlantic partnership, but it does
not feel itself to be an equal partner, or perhaps any kind of partner. It studies the blueprints for a federated Europe in which
national boundaries will have disappeared, but doesn't know how
to build this dream house and is not even sure that it wants to.

Everywhere there is talk of independence, unity, and common
purpose; but beneath the talk there is only the reality of dependence, division, and disagreement. There is resentment of American dominance and fear that Europe may be dragged into a war
against her will as a result of United States interventions in the
Third World. But there is no consensus on how to reduce this
dominance, or how to extricate Europe from the American world
gendarmery. De Gaulle called for "the construction of a European
Europe, that is to say, independent, strong, and influential within
the free world." [1] Yet he was unwilling to dilute French sovereignty in a politically unified European community, or to replace
the United States as Europe's protector. Caught between the

dependency to which they have become accustomed and the independence toward which they aspire, the Europeans are still too divided to forge a diplomacy, or a new identity, of their own.

Europe exists in one sense, and not in another. It is a cultural force, a geographical entity, a frame of reference. But for the time being it has lost its political significance, and with it the identity that came from the centuries during which Europe dominated world affairs. Europe today, politically speaking, is not a second-rank power, or even any power at all. Rather, it is an assemblage of states squeezed together on a western peninsula of Asia and dominated by the giants de Tocqueville believed would one day rule the world: America and Russia. Whatever power Europe exerts on the world stage is by grace of these giants. Within a narrow range there is a certain freedom of action, but Suez, Budapest, and Prague brutally established the limits of European initiative. In Eastern Europe the mold is imposed by Soviet Russia: economic rigidity, political authoritarianism, social conformity. In Western Europe the pattern is American: political democracy, the welfare state, mass consumption. The two Europes have become distorted reflections of their protectors. "Were it not for America's presence, one could hardly speak of Western Europe as an entity; to the extent to which Europe has a face, it is a borrowed one." [2]

The present condition of Europe reflects the revolution in the world power structure over the past thirty years. Until the outbreak of the Second World War in 1939, Europe dominated the world through its colonies, its economic network, its political influence—to such a degree that a conflict among European states was automatically a "world war." Today Europe is no longer the center of the world stage, but a kaleidoscopic sideshow. While its economic power is greater than it has ever been, it is not being used to affect diplomacy, and its military power is at the disposition of its rival protectors. Where vital questions of foreign policy are concerned, the real centers of decision lie elsewhere.

After tormenting themselves and the world for decades over a struggle for rank and power, Europeans today seem to be more interested in affluence and leisure. In world politics, Europeans are suffering from a perfectly understandable, and indeed eminently desirable, battle fatigue. NATO, the Warsaw Pact, the Common Market, the United Nations—these are the organizational instruments of Europe's abstention. Largely content to let the Russians and Americans struggle for world leadership, the Europeans have shown only the slightest curiosity about what kind of dictators rule in the Caribbean, which tribes rig the elections in tropical Africa, or who overthrows whom in Southeast Asia. With the exception of Britain and France, which still seek to exert political and economic influence in their former colonies, the nations of Europe have shown far more interest in prosperity at home than in glory abroad. They have retreated into a kind of isolationism, thereby providing a suitably ironic reversal of the prewar roles of Europe and America.

Throughout Europe there is a lack of interest in the old ideologies which once seemed so important, and a search for a new pragmatism better suited to the needs of technological societies. That portion of the population which is seriously concerned with political ideology, whether it be communism or anti-communism, has been steadily diminishing. De-Stalinization in the Soviet Union and de-Russification in the satellites, the encyclicals of Pope John and the reforms of the Vatican Council, the process of decolonialization and the revival of nationalism—all these have contributed to the disencnantment with ideology. It has been as difficult for the United States to enlist its allies in support of its anti-communist interventions in Asia and Latin America as it has been for the Soviet Union to win anything more than perfunctory acquiescence among the states of Eastern Europe.

Europe today is disenchanted with cold-war politics but fascinated with the fruits of the new economics. Having turned away from empire, it is now in quest of prosperity. This quest is transforming the structure of European society. Duplicating the American experience, the industrially advanced countries of Western Europe are now entering an era of abundance in which the major problem is no longer one of production but one of distribution. For the first time in European history the wealth of society is not confined to a small elite with a monopoly of political and social power: it is becoming accessible to all. Class consumption is giving way to mass consumption, and throughout Western Europe—and even in parts of Eastern Europe—blue-collar workers can look forward to television sets, private cars, and holidays in the sun.

This is the second Industrial Revolution, and its effects promise to be as far-reaching as those of the first. Among its victims are the class distinctions of nineteenth-century politics, which divided the population between the property-owning few and the wage-earning masses, between those who held the reins of political power and those who sought it. It was from such a stratified social structure that Marxism was born, and it is in the more primitive economic societies of the underdeveloped world that traditional Marxism still elicits support. In the advanced industrial societies of Europe, however, it has become irrelevant. This is true even of the countries on the other side of the Iron Curtain, which are discovering that they cannot remain true to the iron laws of Marxist economics and still be able efficiently to utilize resources in accordance with national needs and consumer demand.

While the Communist states of Eastern Europe do not tolerate any threat to their political authority, they have begun to experiment with such daring concepts as consumer choice and interest rates. Today it is no longer considered heretical in communist societies to contemplate the idea of producing what people want rather than what planners say they should have. Such earth-shaking theories are not only making life more tolerable for the people in the communist countries but are also helping to move them closer toward the economies that exist in the West. These countries still remain nominally communist in structure, but in Yugoslavia the role of private enterprise has grown to such proportions that in effect a mixed capitalist-communist society is being created.

Like their counterparts in the West, the communist states compute their gross national products to see how much they have grown, and measure their virtue by the amount of goods that roll off production lines. These nations, too, have little interest in sharing their wealth with the discontented poor of the underdeveloped world. Instead of aiding their exploited comrades in Cuba or Guinea, communist workers prefer to spend their savings on television sets and their holidays in the Miami-style resorts along the Black Sea. Abstention is a game that Europeans in the East have learned to play fully as well as those in the West.

Since the communist nations themselves are trying to break out of the strictures of Marxist economics, it is not surprising that its influence in the West has become nominal. To the industrial nations of Western Europe, old-style Marxism, with its predictions of class warfare and progressive impoverishment of the proletariat, is hopelessly outdated. Where communism has not been able to adjust to the social implications of the new economic revolution, it has become a historical curiosity. In societies such as France and Italy, where the Communist Party remains numerically strong, it has had to make radical adjustments to the realities of the mass-consumption society. Where this adjustment has been made, as in Italy and increasingly in France, the Communist Parties have ceased to preach communism in the way that Karl Marx intended. Rather than urging class warfare as a means of gaining economic justice for the poor, they have had to concern themselves with questions such as the distribution of wealth and the enlargement of the welfare state. In other words, Marxism in Western Europe either has ceased to be relevant or had to cease being Marxist. As a result, the traditional vocabulary of postwar European politics, with its division into diametrically opposed communist and anti-communist forces, is no longer important or even very interesting.

The diminution of Marxism as a serious force in postwar Europe has left the political equation different from what it was a decade or two ago. The Soviet menace has receded and the class struggle is no longer a philosophical question. It is simply a matter of tactics. Throughout most of Western Europe there is general acceptance of the existing social order. The working class does not have the slightest interest in revolution because it has been admitted to the citadels of power. Whereas in communist societies the workers are exploited in their own name by a self-perpetuating managerial elite, the West European proletariat (how dated even the name is) is the direct beneficiary of the productive power of the modern industrial state. There can be no rebellion, because the workers themselves have a vested interest in the status quo. The religion of mass consumption has won out over the "historical imperatives" of mass revolution.

Now that economics has replaced politics on top of the European scale of priorities, a good many of the old political fears have wasted from lack of substance. In Western Europe the communist parties have been barred from power since 1948. During the past two decades the socialist parties, which once caused goose-pimples up and down the flesh of the European bourgeoisie, have become the primary defenders of the bourgeois society, dedicated to middle-class values and middle-class methods. The British, French, and West German socialist parties have scrubbed themselves so free of radical ideas that they no longer even favor the further nationalization of industry.

Purged of its old quest for glory and empire, Western Europe is now busy accumulating riches and enjoying the benefits of mass consumption. A rich, attractive, and increasingly expensive bazaar whose multilingual inhabitants migrate north to find work and south to seek sunshine, today's Europe is a peaceful place. Now that Europeans have been relieved of the tedium of running colonies, or of defending themselves (which the Americans are eager to do for them), they can sit back and let others worry about such problems as communism, the population explosion, races to the moon, nuclear proliferation, and the "yellow peril."

This extraordinary prosperity has taken the edge off some of the political imperatives that seemed so pressing to Europe in the early postwar period. The general boredom with NATO is accompanied by a sharp drop in enthusiasm for creating a politically federated United States of Europe. In the dark days of the late 1940s reasonable men declared that national sovereignty was outdated and that Europe must either federate or perish. Middle-sized states, it was assumed, could not hope to survive in a world of giants. But Europe did not federate, and it did not perish. Instead, it has achieved undreamed-of levels of prosperity and feels a good deal more secure than it did two decades ago.

Even the most successful experiment in European cooperation, the Common Market, has fallen far short of the ambitious political goals envisaged by its founders. Men like Robert Schuman and Jean Monnet believed that if the nations of Western Europe fused their economies they would ultimately be driven, by force of logic and necessity, to fuse their budgets, their currencies, their armies, and finally their parliaments. Once integration had begun, they believed, it would lead to full political federation. This, of course, has not happened. Economic integration has led to a new prosperity; the Common Market has been a brilliant economic success, but the vision of a United States of Europe is receding ever further into the distance. The dream of Europe has not inspired its achievement.

Perhaps de Gaulle was partly to blame for this. Certainly his exaltation of the nation-state and his refusal to dilute French sovereignty in a wider political structure did not help the cause of federation. But the revival of European nationalism is too widespread a phenomenon to lay exclusively at his doorstep. More likely he expressed, in a typically exaggerated manner, a disenchantment with federalism that would have occurred even without his prodding. This can be seen even in the institutions of the Common Market—the nearest that Europe has yet come to integration. There the nation-state still remains the final political authority, and no nation has been willing to concede to the Common Market Commission the right to decide matters deemed vital to a member's national interests.

Not only France but all the countries of Europe are reluctant to give up the sovereignty they have cherished and in which their national identities are embodied. Where national consciousness is coterminous with the nation-state, the abnegation of sovereignty is a self-denial which would be difficult under even the most extreme circumstances. In an age when virtually every other value has been thrown into question—the society, the family, and even the human personality—a sense of nationality may serve as an essential safeguard against a breakdown of civilization. If the nuclear age has made the nation-state obsolete as a political force, it has not wiped away the importance of national identity.

Perhaps a divided Europe is an anachronism in a time of nuclear giants that bestride whole continents. But a united Europe could be created only by coming to terms with the cultural, economic, and political differences which separate the individual European societies. This requires great sacrifices: practical sacrifices over tariff levels, monetary policy, and defense; and emotional ones as well. Such sacrifices are not likely to be made unless they are inspired by something more powerful than a vague sense of community. The creation of a unified Europe requires political decision which is tantamount to a will to independence. To give up what they have, the Europeans must be convinced that they will gain something more valuable in return. As they are prosperous and secure, they can only hope to gain power: power to deal as an equal with the American protector and the Soviet colossus. A united Europe, in this sense, could be built only in opposition to America, for otherwise it would have no function and the sacrifices would never be made. Thus, as Raymond Aron has written:

> The creation of a superior political unity, embracing old nations weighed down by history like Great Britain, Germany and France, demands a real political will—unless it is to be a sort of abdication. But a political will is inseparable from a will to be independent, even if it is not equivalent to a will to power. Many of the Brussels Eurocrats are conscious of this fact and see the constitution of a European state, capable of taking a stand and thus of defending itself, as the inevitable final outcome of their efforts. Such a Europe would not consequently be a third force; it would remain tied to the United States, but as a single unit, whereas today . . . the United States can easily impose its will on the plurality of states, small or middle-sized, whose connections with each other are less close than their subservient relations with the Big Brother across the Atlantic.[3]

Seizing upon this prosperous but still torpid and partitioned Europe, de Gaulle tried to rouse it to action by playing on its pride. He prodded the old nations of the Continent to "Europeanize" themselves, to shed their timidity and complacency and build a power which would be able to speak to America as an equal. As the self-appointed voice of the new and still disorganized Europe, de Gaulle came on the scene just as the Schuman-Monnet vision of a supranational Europe was reduced to the hard core of the Brussels technocracy. In a rich yet discontented and frustrated Europe, de Gaulle's call to honor struck a deep chord of response.

While recognizing Europe's dependency on America for nuclear protection so long as the Soviet menace endures, he felt that by her dominant position within the alliance America kept Europe in a strait jacket, made her fearful of speaking in her own voice, and provided a rationale for the abstentionism that is so pronounced in postwar Europe. For de Gaulle this was intolerable. Since Europe has lost its *élan* and has borrowed an American personality, it must be forced to reassume an identity. As this identity does not yet exist, it must be created. This was the task de Gaulle set for himself. Having roused France from her torpor to a new dynamism and self-respect, he then tried to induce a similar attitude elsewhere in Europe.

His foreign policy, although often unflattering toward the United States, was meant to be not so much anti-American as pro-European. If Europe can be roused from its affluent dormancy only by instilling an apprehension over American "hegemony," then this must be done for the sake of Europe's survival. Perhaps there are better ways to arouse Europe, and certainly ways that are less offensive to Washington. But de Gaulle was primarily concerned not with American sensitivities but with the need to assert Europe's separate identity. To offset an Atlantic community with its capital in Washington, he urged the creation of an independent Europe of associated, but still sovereign, states, a kind of Common Market on a Continental scale.

While de Gaulle did not have much affection for the Common

Market involvements he inherited from the Fourth Republic, he soon learned how the organization could be used for the construction of the new Europe he hoped to build. This Europe would be based on politics and power rather than on free trade and idealism. Unlike the federalists in Brussels, he did not view integration as an end in itself, but rather as the means by which Europe could recapture the predominant place in world affairs that it lost during the two terrible civil wars of this century. Such a Europe would be nobody's partner, equal or otherwise, in any Grand Design, but a great power in its own right, standing between America and Russia and tempering their rivalry.

Although never sympathetic to communism, de Gaulle always considered Russia to be an integral part of European civilization, an errant sister in the grip of an oppressive ideology, from which she will eventually emerge to join her European siblings. In the long sweep of European history the cold war is but a moment, and the Russian menace—like the Turkish menace, the Napoleonic menace, and even the Nazi menace—but a passing phenomenon. One day, after a reversal of alliances no harder to conceive than the one that occurred after the last war, the communist states of Eastern Europe, and eventually Russia herself, will be restored to a wider European community. Until that day the West must keep its powder dry and stand together in times of crisis, but it should be careful not to mistake temporary quarrels over ideology for permanent clashes of national interest.

Although de Gaulle no longer rules France, his legacy weighs heavy on his successors and on the architects of the evolving European community. It rests on the belief that Europe can be truly independent only if it is able to defend itself; and in the nuclear age this means an atomic defense. For France, as for Britain, a Bomb of one's own exerts political influence, lessens dependency on the American colossus, and provides insurance against sudden changes in American strategy or policy. To be sure, France's *force de frappe* is purely *française*, but it does form the nucleus of an arsenal which could, now that de Gaulle has departed, become an all-European deterrent. Such a European deterrent, as distinct from a purely French national arsenal, has been favored even by such "good Europeans" as Jean Monnet, who see it as essential to an equal relationship between Europe and America.

Even if Europe can develop an independent deterrent (and strategist Herman Kahn says that Europe could produce a 200-missile atomic force for less than $1 billion a year over a 5-year period [4]), why does it *need* a Bomb of its own when the American Bomb covers it so nicely? Why can Europe not spend her money more sensibly—for example, on the larger land armies favored by current Pentagon strategy? Unfortunately, Europeans are not fully convinced of the wisdom of a policy of "flexible response" where their own territory is concerned, nor can they accept the idea that they must be permanently inferior to their transatlantic protector. "Men do not live by cold truth alone," a Dutch commentator has written of his fellow Europeans:

They demand something more: the ability to *feel*, however unreasonably, that they are not just disenfranchised citizens of Pentagonia, even though that might be a much cheaper and safer way of life; their birthright, never questioned in pre-nuclear times, to a sense of responsibility for their own fate; in short, their self-respect and what they call their honor. Now that these powerful sentiments can no longer find satisfaction in national self-defense, the modern means of which have been too costly, they are bound to set up an ever growing pressure for "self defense" in a wider framework which, pending a federal Atlantis, can only be a nuclear Europe.[5]

Beyond this assuaging of European pride, an independent deterrent also gives the Europeans an escape hatch from total dependence on American strategy, should the going get too rough in the steamy lands of the southern hemisphere to which American attention is now wandering.

Thus the elements of Gaullist policy have an appeal even to those who do not admire the General's personality or his methods.

These sentiments—which may be termed Gaullism as a kind of shorthand, although they can be found all across the political spectrum—rest on a number of factors: on the extraordinary recovery of Europe from its physical and psychological wounds; on the boredom most Europeans feel with the litany of the cold war; on the lingering nationalism that inhibits the creation of a true political federation; and on the growing resistance to America that is so much a part of Europe's present temper. It is compounded of Europe's institutionalized dependency and its growing pride and self-confidence.

In an exaggerated but inescapable way, de Gaulle's abrasive personality captured the pride that is so marked in contemporary Europe: a pride in what Europe has achieved since the end of the war, a pride in being something both separate and different from the United States. In this sense Gaullism is the psychological expression of Europe's physical recovery: it is the demand to be treated as an equal by acquiring equal power. In expressing a renascent European personality, Gaullism is something a good deal more widespread and up-to-date than mere French nationalism. By seeking a recovery of status, it hopes to recaptured a lost European dignity.

De Gaulle was an eloquent and visionary statesman. But his great failure was his inability to realize that the independent Europe he wanted to create could be forged only if France herself were willing to accept certain limitations on her national sovereignty. This de Gaulle was unwilling to do, but such an acceptance, given Britain's self-imposed isolation from direct involvement in Continental integration, is the only present hope for creating a European power base. De Gaulle tried to substitute France for the United States as the protector and organizer of Europe. He failed because France does not have the power to take over America's role by herself. Only Europe as a whole could hope to exercise that power, and such a Europe does not yet exist. Power still commands power, which is why Europeans reject from Paris what they accept from Washington. American hegemony has been tolerable because it is distant and benevolent. French hegemony is intolerable because it is close at hand and not merited by the realities of power.

Yet such is the appeal of the Gaullist argument for a Europe "independent, strong, and influential within the free world," that no European statesman has been able to ignore it. Europe's leaders resented de Gaulle's imperious demands and refusal to cooperate on any terms but his own. Yet they have rendered his European policy the honor of imitation by making it their own. They phrase their thesis differently and remove some of its anti-American barbs, yet they have been prodded into declaring their desire for a more self-reliant Europe by the very tenacity of the Gaullist argument. In this sense de Gaulle served as a catalyst for a European drive toward greater independence. This ambition—which is a kind of Gaullism without de Gaulle—has been reflected in a new generation of Europeans which is itself a product of Europe's prosperity and self-confidence. Impatient with the lingering remnants of the cold war and eager to end the partition of the Continent, they share de Gaulle's desire for a Europe from which both Russian and American soldiers will have departed.

From one end of the Continent to the other there is a growing determination to shed cold-war postures and to seek a new role for Europe between the two nuclear giants. The Catholic Church, under the liberalizing influences of Pope John and Pope Paul, has launched its own private "opening to the left," seeking closer ties with the communist countries of Eastern Europe, dissociating itself from the more conservative elements of the Christian Democratic Party in Italy, calling for widespread social reform in backward and dictatorial societies, and even receiving Soviet officials in the Vatican. This *aggiornamento* in politics has been a powerful factor in opening a dialogue between the two Europes and in stimulating reform in such Catholic countries as Spain and Italy. The entry of the Catholic Church into the liberal stream of European politics is likely to have a profound effect on the evolution of European society and on the relations between the two parts of a divided Continent.

In the traditionally anti-communist countries of Europe there has been a growing spirit of independence from America and a desire to explore new paths. In Spain the Franco dictatorship is only gradually relaxing its iron grip at home, but in foreign policy it has been increasingly flexible toward the communist world, maintaining its ties with Castro's Cuba, seeking industrial contracts in Eastern Europe, and openly contemplating the establishment of diplomatic relations with Moscow. Madrid has carried on a subtle form of political blackmail for the American air and naval bases on Spanish territory, demanding billions of dollars in rental fees, which Washington has been only too willing to pay. Now that some of these bases are becoming obsolete and the Spanish economy is considerably healthier than it was a decade ago, Madrid is being tempted by French plans for restoring the Mediterranean to Europe's—rather than America's—sphere of interest. Italy, although beset by continual government instability and social unrest, continues to experiment with an "opening to the Left" that may yet bring the powerful Communist Party into the government and result in a foreign policy oriented more toward a neutral Europe than toward the Atlantic alliance.

Germany, apparently recovered from the disease of the Nazi era, is gradually emerging from the cocoon of her postwar convalescence. Long an object of the diplomacy of others rather than an active participant herself, the Federal Republic is now evolving an independent foreign policy. While this policy rests upon close association with the West, it also assumes that Germany must establish friendly ties with the communist states to the East. The immobilism of the Adenauer-Erhard-Kiesinger period is past, and with it the era of governments that were totally dependent on Washington. Bonn's formidable economic strength has now been matched by a growing political independence. The victory of the Socialists in September 1969 marked more than merely a change in the ruling party. It represented a rising German self-confidence and a desire to open the locked doors to the East. Chancellor Willy Brandt, who has long favored a policy of reconciliation with Germany's communist neighbors, is actively pursuing a détente with Moscow. This is to Europe's interest as much as it is to Germany's. But what is important is that Germany is now doing this on her own rather than as an instrument of the United States. She is becoming the leader of Europe.

France, despite the departure of de Gaulle, is not likely to revert to the good old days of the Fourth Republic, when a string of acquiescent premiers—usually dependent on Washington's good will to back up the faltering franc—faithfully declared their allegiance to American leadership. Pompidou is certainly a pale version of de Gaulle, but he is following Gaullist policies. France's arms sales to Libya and her attitude toward the Arab-Israeli dispute are dramatic, but not the only, examples. Gaullism, as an expression of the self-confidence France has gained from modernization and the ending of colonial wars, does not depend on the physical presence of the General, and in fact is as strong without him, since it is no longer chained to his abrasive personality and uncooperative approach to European integration. As far as foreign policy is concerned, virtually everyone in France today is a Gaullist, if by Gaullism we mean nationalism, resistance to the United States, and a desire for Europe to play an independent world role. Even the General's most bitter opponents on the Left approve many of the foreign-policy initiatives he took, such as the recognition of China, the ending of the Algerian war, the reconciliation with Germany, the condemnation of the American interventions in Vietnam and Santo Domingo, and the withdrawal from NATO— although not, to be sure, his fishing in Quebec's troubled waters, his expensive *force de frappe*, and his stance toward Israel.

All during the Gaullist era Washington indulged itself in a good deal of wishful thinking, imagining that the departure of the General would mean the end of Gaullism. But Pompidou is simply de Gaulle writ small—Gaullist substance without Gaullist style. He has been, to be sure, rather less abrasive toward Washington and more cooperative within NATO. But these are not substantive differences. When the chips are down and serious French interests are concerned, Paris continues to do what it thinks best—regardless of Washington's admonitions. The sale of Mirage jets to Libya is simply one example.

Even in Britain, where the belief in a "special relationship" with Washington still remains strong despite the passing of the conditions that made it possible in the past, there are likely to be some changes. These have been exceedingly slow in coming because for a long time the British have looked across the Atlantic for their foreign policy. They have been preoccupied with liquidating the remnants of empire, and hostile to the pursuit of closer relations with Continental Europe because of a deeply felt conviction that Britain is different from the rest of Europe and that her geographical setting should in no way limit her freedom of action. Accustomed to playing the role of a great imperial power, historically trained to the task of keeping Europe divided, linked by racial and cultural ties to such distant nations as Australia and Canada, and dependent on cheap food imports from America and the Commonwealth, the British have not found it easy to jump the Channel and find their future in an integrated European community. In fact, they have persistently tried to inhibit the formation of such a community on any terms that might infringe on their freedom of action. They rejected Schuman's plea to join the Coal and Steel Community in 1950 and the European Defense Community in 1952, and spurned the offer to join the Common Market at its inception in 1957. Instead, they tried to sabotage its integrationist aims by setting up the rival European Free Trade Association. But despite EFTA, the Common Market turned out to be such a success that the British finally sought to gain membership. The attempt was politically premature, for it did not have the support of a majority in Britain, nor was London ready to make the economic sacrifices that the Six demanded. De Gaulle's veto of January 1963 brought an abrupt halt to the agonizing negotiations.

Since that time, however, a good deal has happened. A persistent economic crisis has made association with the EEC more attractive, the diminishing relevance of the Commonwealth has drawn Britain more toward Europe, and the realization that London has little real influence over Washington has made many Britons wonder whether the old role of transatlantic middleman may not be about finished. Perhaps most important of all, the Labour government, which only grudgingly and against the deepest instincts of many of its leaders, accepted the need for Britain to become a full member of the Common Market, was replaced in the June 1970 elections by the Conservatives. Tory Prime Minister Edward Heath is an ardent "European" and has made entry into the EEC a cardinal point of his program.

Antipathy to the Vietnam war and fear of isolation from the Continent have contributed to the pressures now building up in London for a change in British foreign policy, away from an imperial America and a dying Commonwealth and toward a revitalized Europe. In this direction, France is the logical Continental ally of Britain, just as Britain is the logical ally for France in her attempt to forge a European diplomacy independent of the United States. There is a real, if often unexpressed, community of interests between Paris and London—one which their very similarities tend to conceal. They are both former imperial powers reluctant to accept second-class status now that their empires are gone. They are both prosperous, democratic societies which are politically stable and which believe that they have responsibilities transcending Europe. Compared to the other nations of Western Europe, they are exceedingly nationalistic and will not accept any formula of federation which imperils their national sovereignty. Bearing the scars of numerous wars, they are historically suspicious of Germany, fear the possible consequences of her reunification, and are eager to prevent her from acquiring nuclear weapons. They have each developed an independent atomic deterrent because it enhances their prestige and permits them to feel that they are not totally dependent upon the United States for survival. Their current disputes over European policy tend to spring from the fact that on essential questions of diplomacy and national power they are basically alike, rather than from their differences.

Nowhere is this likeness more obvious than in relation to the political ambitions of the Brussels technocrats for a federated Europe. De Gaulle resisted any form of association that would compromise French sovereignty, but he was a faithful, if difficult, partner for his associates in the Common Market. The British have not yet come even that far toward integration and are just as Gaullist as the General himself where European federalism is concerned. In 1961, when Britain made its initial bid to enter the Common Market, Prime Minister Macmillan told Commons: "I fully accept that there are some forces in Europe which would like a genuine federalist system. . . . They would like Europe to turn itself into a sort of United States, but I believe this to be a completely false analogy. . . . The alternative concept . . . a *Europe des patries* . . . seems to be more in tune with the national traditions of European countries and, in particular, our own." [6] Lest it be thought that the British have become ardent federalists since then, here is Harold Wilson in the election campaign of March 1966: "We believe that, given the right conditions, it would be possible to join the EEC *as an economic community* [italics added]. But we reject any idea of supranational control over Britain's foreign and defense policies. We are in Europe, but our power and influence are not, and must never be, confined to Europe." [7] In waving the banner of political independence, Wilson could have given de Gaulle a few lessons.

The quarrel between Paris and London is not eternal. De Gaulle blocked Britain's bid to enter the Common Market in 1963 because he feared she was entering as America's Trojan horse, with her heart and her nuclear weapons pledged across the Atlantic rather than across the Channel. But conditions are changing within Britain. De Gaulle's successors recognize that they cannot hope to achieve his plan for the reunification of Europe in opposition to both Germany and Britain. Given a change in British policy, Paris might come to look on London as a more cooperative ally than Bonn. Since there is always the danger that a revitalized

Germany might threaten European stability, France values a powerful counter to German ambitions.

The British, for their part, have had time to think about the consequences of their exclusion from Europe, and about the inability of either the Commonwealth or the links with America to compensate for this isolation. Gradually, but perceptibly, the tide is turning within Britain, and now that the Labour government has given way to the far more "pro-European" Conservatives, it is quite possible that Edward Heath, as de Gaulle once predicted, will lead Britain into the Common Market. The problem is whether Britain is yet willing to make the drastic changes in her own economy and in her overseas commitments. Without these changes, French opposition to British entry will continue to elicit grudging support on the Continent, for none of the Six wants the Common Market to be hobbled by Britain's enormous overseas debt and her shaky currency. Even devaluation has not solved Britain's economic problems. Nor has London, for all its desire to enter the Common Market, yet come to terms with the Gaullists' objection to her entry: that she is still too intimately bound to the United States by military and political ties. In a truly independent Europe, there is no place for a London that remains the handmaiden of Washington. But as they cut back their commitments "east of Suez" and take more drastic measures to stabilize the wobbly pound sterling, the British may be able to reduce their economic dependence on the United States. This could, in turn, make them less politically dependent as well.

Should the British decide that they are not going to be America's spear-carrier in the Third World, or a more powerful Sweden living in political isolation, they will have little choice but to throw in their lot with their Continental neighbors and use their power to shape Europe along lines favorable to their own, and to Europe's long-run, interests. Once Britain is in the Common Market, however, she is not going to be the Voice of America, translating sermons on the sanctity of Atlantic unity. She will be, along with France and Germany, a key member of a new European triumvirate that could create through unity a new and independent power in tomorrow's world. It is a heady prospect, but not at all an impossible one, and one which Washington's policy of military intervention in Asia has made more pressing. The choice is one that Britain alone can make, but Americans would be ill advised to imagine that London's current policy of financial and diplomatic dependence on Washington is likely to be permanent. Britain is an Atlantic power, but she is even more a European power. If consideration for the former position has dominated British policy since the war, an urgent necessity to come to terms with the latter is likely to become the next great task of British diplomacy.

As Britain makes her peace with the Continent, so America is going to have to come to terms with her own illusions about Europe. She will have to take a hard look at the dream of an Atlantic community, which seemed so inspiring when the Iron Curtain looked impenetrable, and which has now come to look dated. The frontiers of Europe, which were artificially fixed by the Soviet barricade along the Elbe, have now begun to open toward the east. The Europe of the rival alliances, of NATO and the Warsaw Pact, is passing into history, and in its place is an evolving collection of nations not quite sure where the future is leading but unwilling to stand still in the grooves staked out during the cold war.

In Western Europe the allies we have nourished and protected for so long are at last beginning to feel their own way and to make their own independent decisions. They are pursuing some kind of unity, but it is not the kind of construction we imagined would fit neatly into the Atlantic community, and it may not fit into any association with America. Our blueprints may have been beautiful, but they did not fit the European house or the land on which it was built. Now it is up to the Europeans to decide what kind of house they want to live in, how many rooms it shall have, and who shall be allowed a voice in family affairs. We have been generous and protective toward Europe. We have also been tiresome and nagging. We have enjoyed playing Europe's mother-in-law, but it has not been a very flattering role or one that the Europeans will allow us to play much longer.

We shall have to adjust ourselves to the fact that Europe will not be unified as we wished it to be, and that it may not be unified at all. It is quite possible that Europe may return to something resembling the power structure of the nineteenth century, in which a number of nations engaged in a subtle game of shifting alliances and rivalries. This would not be a United States of Europe such as has been enshrined in the dogma of American postwar diplomacy. But Europe could do worse than return to a modern variant of the arrangement worked out at the Congress of Vienna in 1815. This was an accord based upon the smothering of conflict through compromise and on a continual rebalancing of power centers. Ideology played a relatively insignificant role. The nineteenth century was an era of cataclysmic change, of civil wars, of revolutions and anti-revolutionary interventions, of the rise of aggressive new powers and the decline of enfeebled old ones. Yet, except for a few minor lapses, the Congress of Vienna kept the peace in Europe for nearly a hundred years, an enviable record by any standard.

A return to a balance of power in Europe strikes most people as hopelessly anachronistic and potentially dangerous. Perhaps it is. But the alternative may be equally dangerous. What if our wishes came true and Western Europe really did unite to form a single political confederation? With its extraordinary resources and its enormous power potential, would such a Europe be content to remain under a benevolent American protectorship? Might it not try to recapture the states of Eastern Europe by force from the Soviet Union, or, conversely, make some kind of deal with Moscow to America's disadvantage? Regardless of what policy it followed, a unified Europe would be as powerful as Russia and perhaps even more dangerous. This would be true even if Europe remained partitioned along the Elbe. It might be even more true if, by some miracle, a European confederation were formed from the Atlantic to somewhere west of the Urals. Before we waste any more rhetoric on the virtues of European unification, we might well ask ourselves how American interests would benefit from such an eventuality, and whether it is really to our advantage to push the Europeans into constructing a new world power. If we thought about it seriously, we might well come to the conclusion that a Europe fragmented into relatively harmless nation-states and dominated by ourselves and the Russians might be far more manageable than a united Europe with the power to challenge us both. There are indications that this may be becoming apparent to official Washington, where the old dream of the Grand Design is gradually giving way to a vision of Europe moving toward reconciliation under the tutelage of its twin protectors. Whether the Europeans will accept a Russo-American hegemony once they have the power to do otherwise remains to be seen.

Thus, in viewing the untidiness of a fragmented Europe, we would do well to recognize the advantages of a Continent in which there are currently no great powers and where the endemic European capacity for mischief-making has been drastically reduced. Europe's old dreams of glory can be revived, but it is not to our interests to stimulate them by forcing blueprints for unification down the throats of reluctant Europeans. Europe can, and should, be left in a state of political quiescence as long as it is willing. The world has suffered more than its fair share of agony from a Europe with power to exercise and missions to accomplish. Europe's current retirement from the world scene—although it may have been forced by the unnatural conditions of the cold war—has not been harmful to the world and it has been exceedingly healthy for Europe. We would do well not to jeopardize it by well-intentioned meddling that could only revive ambitions that might threaten our own interests and might well make Europe far less safe than it is today. The real centers of danger in tomorrow's world, after all, lie not in a war-chastened, ideologically cynical Europe, but in an ambitious China, a restless Russia, and a messianic America bent on saving the world from itself.

We do not need a powerful Europe to restrain Russia. We have done that by ourselves for twenty years and, if need be, we can continue doing it. But for our own sake we need to settle the grievance over Germany's partition before it becomes a threat to the peace of Europe and thus to our own security. We must, in other words, find a way of working together with Moscow to achieve a reconciliation of the European community that will end the cold war in Europe. Even if we wanted to, we could not indefinitely keep Europe partitioned. The Iron Curtain is gradually lifting, and the two Europes are beginning to move together. The crucial questions are on what terms the partition of the Continent can be ended and how two Europes can be transformed into one.

6. One Europe, or Two?

We must turn to one of the great unfinished tasks of our generation, and that unfinished task is making Europe whole again.
—LYNDON B. JOHNSON

❦ ❦ ❦ HABIT and familiarity have endowed the partition of Europe with a certain naturalness. What would once have been unthinkable—a Continent divided along the River Elbe and guarded by American and Russian soldiers for nearly a quarter of a century—has now become part of the normal course of events. The longer the cold war has lasted, the more comfortable we have become with this divided Europe. "Our Europe" is not all of Europe, but it is by far the richest and most populous part and quite enough to defend from the uncertain ambitions of the Soviet Union. The other Europe, "their Europe," remains in the hands of communist dictatorships. But even the Iron Curtain has had its advantages, for it sealed off communism at the Elbe and helped make possible such constructions as NATO and the Common Market. A partitioned Europe was a suitable symbol of a world divided into two rival power blocs.

But the decline of ideological passions, the acceptance of "peaceful coexistence" by the two great rivals, the achievement of a nuclear balance, and the pursuit of détente between Russia and the West have served to erode the military blocs dividing the two Europes. Now that the fear of nuclear war has diminished, it is becoming possible for Europeans to turn their thoughts to the reunification of the Continent. There is increasing talk of plans for a "disengagement" of Russian and American troops, for an East-West Common Market, for a nonaggression treaty between

NATO and the Warsaw Pact, for a nuclear-free zone in Central Europe; and there is speculation on the meaning of such visions as de Gaulle's Europe "from the Atlantic to the Urals."

Gradually those two strange phenomena of the postwar world, "our Europe" and "their Europe," are changing as the severed parts of a single civilization try to restore their broken links. The efforts are hesitant, and in many places politicians are just beginning to speak of them openly. But they are taking place on all levels of European life, and they are transforming the relations between the European nations and their rival protectors. For convenience, the movement can be called one toward European "reunification," although its object is not necessarily political fusion. Rather, it is an attempt to turn the present détente into a wider entente that will re-engage the European community. For the first time since the cold war began, Europeans are not merely praising the virtues of a reunited Continent but actually pondering the tactics of achieving one. Something is budging in Europe, something unfamiliar and a bit amorphous, something that is not quite yet a program but is more than an idle dream.

It is no longer a dream because it is no longer impossible. Hesitantly but surely, the two Europes are approaching each other. There is a quarter-century of division, hostility, and suspicion to overcome, and grievances to settle. But as the détente grows more solid, contacts are increasing at every level: economic, political, and cultural. Trade between Eastern and Western Europe, long held at a low level by the cold-war strategic-control restrictions, has begun to pick up sharply. While still far below its prewar level, it is gradually becoming an important element in trade calculations. Almost without exception the West Europeans have ignored the strategic-control restrictions imposed on East-West trade at American insistence, and are extending most-favored-nation treatment and long-term credit financing to the communist countries. East Europeans are increasingly looking west for high-quality capital goods and even for partners in industrial development, while West European manufacturers are exploring the potentially lucrative markets of the East. At this point the major restriction to greater East-West trade is not a lack of will on either side, nor even political impediments, but a shortage of hard currency in the communist countries, and a shortage of products for which they can find Western buyers. Even the West Germans, who long refused to extend full diplomatic recognition to the countries of Eastern Europe because they recognize the "illegal" regime in Pankow, scrapped the Hallstein Doctrine and set up trade missions in Eastern Europe. They are now going a good deal farther by seeking to normalize their relations with the communist countries and working out a modus vivendi with East Germany based on common political and economic interests.

Now that the United States is beginning to loosen its old restrictions on trade with Eastern Europe, the NATO allies are trying to stake out new markets before these are captured by their American competitors. Trade which began as a relatively low-key exchange of Hungarian jam for British light machinery, and Soviet timber for French die-tools, has now branched out to include such basic industries as oil, automobiles, and communications. Today the Italians get a quarter of their oil imports from the Soviet Union, the French have licensed their color-television system to communist countries, the Russians have permitted the Fiat company to set up an auto plant in the Soviet Union, the Warsaw government has carried on negotiations with the Krupp combine to build a factory in Poland, and the Rumanians have tried to get the Americans to build a synthetic-rubber plant in their country. The Europeans are pushing hard to expand East-West trade, and now the United States is following suit as a result of recent executive decisions to reduce export controls on non-strategic items, guarantee commercial credits, and seek Congressional approval for most-favored-nation tariff treatment to Eastern Europe.

Parallel with these moves toward greater economic cooperation has been a cultural and social rapprochement between Eastern Europe and the West. This can be felt in every area, from tourism to jazz, from film-making to athletics. The Iron Curtain has been punctured by a stream of businessmen and commissars seeking new markets, by cultural exchanges of everything from soccer teams to symphony orchestras, and even by small-scale tourist invasions. Many Americans are discovering, or revisiting, the lands of their ancestors, while West Europeans are exploring the once-forbidden lands of the East. The bus tour, the charter flight, and the private automobile full of campers are breaking down the barriers that have kept Europe divided. The Bulgarians have set up Miami-style resorts on the Black Sea, the Poles take out advertisements in the glossy color magazines of the West, and Yugoslavs are giving away land to Western film stars so that they will build villas that attract tourists. It is, of course, dangerous to draw too many political inferences from such tourism. Travel does not spread democracy or reform unfriendly governments. But it does break down the curtain of ignorance that has grown up alongside the curtain of fear. As Western travelers wander through the baroque churches of Prague, travel along the Danube from Vienna to Budapest, sun themselves on the golden sands of Varna, and ski in the Carpathian Alps, they are rediscovering that Europe is a single civilization, of which the communist countries are an integral part.

Europeans everywhere are beginning to explore new paths toward reconciliation, and the negative goal of containment is giving way to the positive search for re-engagement. This is particularly true among the younger generation, which played no part in the Second World War and no longer even recalls the worst days of the cold war. Among these young Europeans, who are probably the least chauvinistic people to be found anywhere, there is the beginning of something which could be described as a pan-European nationalism. It expresses itself in a pride in European civilization and a desire for Europe to be something more than a protectorate of America and Russia. The usual gulf between the generations that exists everywhere is particularly pronounced in Europe today. Those Europeans who have come to maturity since the war are now becoming leaders of their societies in government, commerce, and the arts. They do not, indeed they cannot, think in the cold-war clichés of their elders. They grew up in a world of atomic terror and political stalemate, of cold-war blocs and military pacts; a world where instability was the rule of life and where whole civilizations could be destroyed in a single instant, where the established values of society were daily ignored by its rulers and where traditional morality seemed little more than organized hypocrisy. It is not surprising that they could not accept the slogans that came so naturally to their parents. Nor is it surprising that they have rejected the pretensions of ideology, both communist and anti-communist. They are intellectually adventurous but emotionally detached, indifferent to ideology yet romantic about the ideal of a united Europe. They are absorbed in the quest for affluence, suspicious of all governments, and unresponsive to the vocabulary of the cold war. This is true in the West, where the young are experiencing a revulsion from party politics; it is equally true in the East, where they take "peaceful coexistence" for granted and have little interest in the rhetoric of communism.

No one is more aware than the Europeans themselves that the path to a reunified Continent is long and paved with difficulties. Reconciliation cannot come about until the Russians pull their troops out of Eastern Europe, and until the communist states gain more independence from Moscow and grant their own citizens a greater personal liberty. It is dangerous to confuse anti-Soviet actions with true liberalization, to imagine that, because Bucharest challenges Moscow's right to give orders, a brutal police state is being transformed into a democracy. Many of the East European states have never experienced a sustained period of liberal, parliamentary government. That they are authoritarian now is nothing new in their history. They all seek closer ties with the West, but the two Europes are not inspired by the same political ideals and they are not going to achieve fusion overnight. Yet such is the desire to end the cold war and bridge the partition of the Continent that Europeans are emerging from the old feelings of hopelessness and are seeking new, and often unorthodox, ways of reconciling a divided community. Reconciliation is becoming the most pressing item on the European polit-ical agenda. It is also the most difficult, for at its heart lies the dispute over Germany.

The cold war between Russia and the West began with this dispute. Today, nearly a quarter-century later, the passion has gone out of the cold war, yet the dispute continues. Germany re-mains the last and most intractable remnant of the cold war in Europe, the knot that impedes reunification of the Continent and prevents the détente from evolving into a wider settlement. The Russians, apprehensive over their own security after two German invasions, want to contain German strength by keeping the former Reich divided. The French, seeking to enlist German support for an independent power bloc in Western Europe, urge Bonn to look to Paris rather than to Washington for leadership. The Americans, fearful that the Germans might seek reunifica-tion through a deal with Moscow, have tried to buy German loy-alty through NATO. Everyone seeks to anchor Germany to a wider community. For Moscow that community is the Warsaw Pact, for Washington it is the Atlantic alliance, for Paris it is an independent Europe stretching from the Atlantic to somewhere this side of the Urals.

Germany is not only the focal point of the rival alliances but the very reason for their existence. Had the wartime allies not fallen into disagreement over the control of Central Europe, had the former Reich not been divided into Russian and Western occupation zones, had German power not become a crucial fac-tor in the new cold-war balance, there would have been no NATO and no Warsaw Pact. Germany's status remains unresolved be-cause the Western powers, in accordance with the wartime ac-cords, secured a foothold in Berlin, deep within the Russian zone of occupation. Were it not for that foothold, and the decision to continue the Western allies' presence in West Berlin, the terri-torial changes resulting from the Second World War would not still legally be in doubt. The acceptance of Germany's new fron-tier with Poland along the Oder–Neisse line, the permanent loss of the "eastern provinces," and the acknowledgment of a communist-controlled buffer state in the eastern zone—all this would have flowed logically from the end of the war. The former German capital would have been absorbed into East Germany, and we would have ceased to think about Berlin just as we have ceased to think about Dresden. It is Berlin which has kept open the wound of Germany's partition, and it is the unwillingness of Germans to accept the consequences of that partition that keeps America and Russia at odds in Central Europe.

The West has solemnly pledged itself to German reunification through the absorption of communist East Germany into the Federal Republic. Yet throughout Europe there is the belief that the partition of Germany is one of the few happy results of the Second World War. Cut off from Prussia and her former eastern territories, Germany has been able to orient herself toward the West and create a responsible parliamentary democracy. The Federal Republic, which is the product of Germany's partition, has been perhaps the most successful of all the inspiring experiments that have taken place in postwar Europe. Prosperous and democratic, a West Germany of 50 million people is on a par with France, Italy, or Britain, and can therefore be integrated in a West European community. But a reunified Germany of 75 million people, stretching from Alsace to the Polish border and with its capital in Berlin, would control, if not destroy, the Common Market, and perhaps dominate all Europe. It is with Bonn, not Berlin, that Europe has been able to make its peace. It is because of her division that Germany has acquired loyal allies in the West— allies she could not otherwise have attracted and who have no vital interest in her reunification.

What is a matter of practical politics for Germany's neighbors in the West is a question of national security for those in the East. So long as the Federal Republic continues to claim legal title to lands beyond the Oder–Neisse and in the Sudetenland, the Poles, Czechs, and Russians will continue to fear that some future German government might seek to recapture such territories by force. The Russians, having suffered 20 million dead and incalculable physical damage as a direct result of the last German invasion, see security in Germany's partition. While they might have tolerated a neutral and demilitarized Germany—as Stalin hinted in a note to Adenauer in 1952—they could never permit a reunified Germany as a member of a Western alliance. When Adenauer rejected neutralization, fearful that it might destroy Germany's reconciliation with the West, there remained no other hope for German reunification other than by a Russian withdrawal. Since this was inconceivable so long as the cold war lasted, Germany had to remain divided.

Naturally Adenauer could not have admitted this, nor could the Federal Republic's allies. To have done so would have been to repudiate the myth under which West Germany had joined NATO. Instead, an elaborate fiction was compounded, which declared that Germany's allies were dedicated to her reunification at the earliest possible moment, and that through a strong NATO the Russians would be forced to release their hold on the eastern zone. Consequently, the allies accepted Bonn's declaration that it alone has the right to speak for all Germans and that there must be no legal recognition of the East German communist regime. This "hard line" helped Adenauer integrate the Federal Republic into the West and lead the Germans away from the possible temptations of a separate deal with the Russians. But it also caused the Germans to misunderstand the purpose of the NATO alliance, and it chained American diplomacy to German demands which cannot be fulfilled short of a war which neither side has any intention of fighting.

The West Germans, grown secure and prosperous under the present partition, want to be reunited with the eastern zone—but they want NATO and the *Wirtschaftswunder* too. The West Europeans, having found a satisfactory colleague in the Federal Republic, formally proclaim their allegiance to reunification while fervently hoping that it can be put off into the indefinite future. The United States, determined to keep the Federal Republic firmly within NATO, makes ritual pledges to reunification but remains attached to a conception of alliance that presupposes Europe's indefinite partition. Even the Russians pay lip-service to a reunified Germany as they stand guard over a regime whose very existence is the core of the cold-war dispute in Europe. Everyone claims to want German reunification, but, like heaven, not just yet.

Like heaven, too, the desire for reunification among the Germans has tended to serve as a substitute for a reconciliation with some harsh realities here on earth. Among those realities are:

First, reunification cannot come by "self-determination"—that is, free elections in both zones—as the Western allies solemnly proclaim. For the East German government to accept this would mean that it would allow itself to be voted into extinction by the Federal Republic, whose population is three times as great.

Second, the Russians will never allow the Germans to reunify so long as they consider the existence of an independent East Germany essential to their security. They prefer to see German power restrained by keeping Germany divided. As Marshal Zhukov said at the Geneva summit conference in 1955, "You have your Germans and we have ours. It is much better this way." The Russians are likely to continue seeing things that way for a long time to come. Indeed, it is unlikely that they would accept German reunification even under a communist government. If China has taught them anything, it is the danger of having a powerful communist rival to challenge the authority of Moscow.

Third, there can be no German reunification so long as the cold war lasts and Germany participates in the rival cold-war alliances. Both NATO and the Warsaw Pact are predicated on the partition of Germany; without such partition they would be meaningless. Unification, if it comes, can only follow, never precede, the dismantling of the military blocs. The Socialist-led German government has now dared to recognize this. As President Gustav Heinemann declared, "NATO, as I have said often enough in the past, cannot be the ultimate goal of German policy because it is impossible to achieve a reestablishment of the community of our people in NATO just as it is impossible to achieve it in the Warsaw Pact." [1]

Fourth, to reunite Germany means to imperil the integration

of the Germans into the Western community. Not only NATO, but also the Common Market is based upon German partition. Two Germanys fit nicely into two Europes. But where is the One Europe that could absorb and contain a united Germany? Could the Common Market, could the present stability in Europe, survive German reunification? Has anyone ever seriously considered what might happen if the 17 million people of East Germany— socialist in economics, totalitarian in politics, Protestant in religion, and communist by indoctrination—were suddenly thrown into union with the free-enterprise, predominantly Catholic, Western-oriented Federal Republic? Such a fusion might lead to a convulsion that would make the present situation seem idyllic by comparison.

Fifth, the partition of Germany is not so "unnatural" that it cannot endure indefinitely. Germany existed as a single nation only from 1871, when Bismarck unified it by the sword, until 1945, when it disintegrated as the result of its own mad obsessions. Even then it did not include the Germanic state of Austria or the German-speaking parts of Switzerland. The former German Reich has now been divided more than a quarter-century. During that time the two German states have developed different identities, different traditions, and even different dialects. The longer this division continues, the less gap there will be between the "artificial" present situation and the "real" old situation.

Sixth, there is the living reality of East Germany (the DDR). However unsavory its origins and its policies, the DDR has now become a real state in its own right, with a real stake in its survival. It is not merely a pawn between East and West, or one which the Russians could easily abolish even if they wanted to. Almost entirely by its own efforts, the DDR has become the ninth industrial power in the world, with the highest per-capita income in Eastern Europe and even a foreign-aid program of its own, which Walter Ulbricht used to undermine the Hallstein Doctrine on his visit to Egypt in 1965. Totalitarian, unnatural, and illegal though it may be, the DDR has engendered loyalties among its citizens and an identity of its own that can be neither disregarded nor easily combined with the habits and institutions of the Federal Republic. Even the Berlin Wall, that grotesque symbol of the bitterness that divides Germans, has helped to make the DDR a more stable country, plugging the hemorrhage of its labor force and consolidating its economy.

Despite a Western diplomacy that has served to reinforce Pankow's dependence on Moscow, a rising generation of technicians and managers has been created with a loyalty to the East German state. These German communists are not in awe of the Russians, and they do not even want to flee across the Wall into the Federal Republic. In fact they tend to be rather contemptuous of the Germans on the other side of the Elbe, whose foibles they see magnified through the lenses of Marxism. The Russians can no longer depend upon the automatic acquiescence of the East Germans, who are now demanding the same rights as the other states of Eastern Europe and who have even been infected by the same national sentiments.

Under the rules of the Hallstein Doctrine, the Federal Republic long refused to extend diplomatic recognition to the countries of Eastern Europe, on the grounds that they recognize the "illegal" Pankow regime, and it used its considerable economic power to prevent other nations from recognizing the DDR. Bonn, however, has not been able to prevent Pankow from setting up trade missions in some thirty-four countries—nine of them members of NATO—or from industrializing a basically peasant society until today East Germany possesses, after Soviet Russia, the most powerful economy in the communist bloc. As an instrument of diplomacy the Hallstein Doctrine was about as meaningful, and about as useful, as America's ability to keep Red China out of the United Nations. Unworkable and unrealistic, it has finally been scrapped by the Brandt government.

Given the realities of East Germany today, the relevant question is not whether the DDR is legitimate—for its existence does not depend on our legal recognition—but whether its continued isolation is desirable. Whose interests does that isolation serve, ours or those of the Russians? Who gains by relegating the DDR to the status of a Soviet satrapy? Certainly not the West Germans, whose policy of non-recognition and minimal communication has served only to increase the bitterness and hostility between the two German states. Certainly not the East Germans, whose isolation has probably impeded the internal liberalization that is taking place in other Eastern European countries, and whose feeling of physical insecurity has legitimatized the presence of Russian troops in the DDR. And certainly isolation of the DDR has not served the interests of the United States, which is forced to keep more than 200,000 of her own soldiers in the Federal Republic, in large measure because Bonn has refused to accept the existence of the DDR and what it implies. It may well be that the only beneficiary of Pankow's isolation is the Soviet Union, which justifies the twenty divisions it maintains there as being essential to the security of the East European states against Bonn's "revanchism." To question the usefulness of isolating the DDR does not mean that Washington should exchange ambassadors with Pankow, for this would imperil our good relations with the Federal Republic. Rather it is to say that it is to Bonn's interests to revise its policy toward the DDR from one of hostility to one of engagement. This is the policy of Chancellor Brandt, who declared that "the principal aim of our policy is to make the renunciation of force the basis for improving our relations with all Eastern European states." [2]

Reunification, it is clear, can come only as a result of a diminution of tensions in Eastern Europe and of a reconciliation of the two European communities. And the reconciliation of the two Europes depends in large degree upon the restraint and the wisdom shown by the Federal Republic and its allies. On a practical level, reconciliation means that the Federal Republic must accept in law what she has had to accept in principle: that the 1945 frontiers, including the Oder–Neisse line, are permanent. As the Germans cannot reclaim except by a war of aggression territories which since 1945 have been incorporated into Poland, Czechoslovakia, and the Soviet Union, they have no realistic choice but to renounce them. Second, the Germans must resist the temptation to put their hands on atomic weapons, no matter how disguised or where manufactured. As the furor over the MLF showed, nothing more quickly sends the East Europeans running to Moscow for protection, or reinforces Russia's determination to hold on to East Germany, than the nightmare of a Federal Republic armed with nuclear weapons. Third, Germany would have to pull out of any exclusively Western military alliance, since the Russians would never allow the absorption of the Pankow regime into NATO. If the Germans want to get the Russians out of the DDR, they will have to accept the departure of the Americans from the Federal Republic. So long as they value security above reunification, they will not make such a choice. Nor need we spur them to do so, for their reunification is a far more pressing problem for them than it is for us. Yet the pendulum may swing as conditions change, and we would be foolish not to prepare ourselves for it. As Franz Josef Strauss, one of the most important political figures in the Federal Republic, wrote a decade ago in words that take on even greater weight today:

> In all negotiations about reunification, risks and chances must be weighed against one another. The risks will diminish, the chances will improve, the more Germany herself has to throw on the scales. . . . Although there exists a preference [among the allies] . . . for a reunited Germany to belong to a military alliance with the West, the hard political requirements of the German people might cause them to make a decision according to the Austrian pattern [of neutralization]. . . . Such a decision would have to rest on very sober political and military considerations. . . . Without possessing potential power, Germany will never have a chance to be heard.[3]

That is the voice of a rising German nationalism. We might be wrong to be appalled or intimidated by it. We would be exceedingly foolish to ignore it.

The Germans have been faithful members of the Atlantic alliance and enthusiastic builders of a West European community. But as the cold-war ideologies diminish, the demands of geography resume their old importance. Germany, for all her recent attachment to the West, is a Central European country, compelled by history and geography to look East as well as West. The conditions that forced the Germans to deal exclusively with the West have been unavoidable, but they have also been basically unnatural. They cannot endure indefinitely, and no German government, however anti-communist it may be, can allow the doors to the East to remain permanently locked. Adenauer's rigidity gave way to Kiesinger's temporizing, and finally to Brandt's efforts to assuage Russian fears of German power by a more cooperative policy toward the East.

The danger is not that the Germans may eventually turn East in their quest for reunification and make another Rapallo deal with Moscow. The Germans must eventually negotiate with the Russians, who hold the key to their reunification. But this is not 1922, and the analogy of Rapallo, an accord struck between two war-weakened and politically outcast powers, is not at all valid in today's conditions. Rather, the danger is that the Germans may feel so frustrated by their present partition that they will succumb to the temptations of a new nationalism. Such a resurgence could imperil the peace of Europe and lead to a new round of coalitions to restrain German "revanchism." For this reason it is important that the Germans feel themselves to be a part of a wider community. NATO has been one such community, and it has served German interests well by ensuring the security of the Federal Republic. But NATO cannot provide a means of reconciling Germany with her neighbors, or of breaking down the barriers between the two Europes. A military alliance based upon the partition of Europe is hardly an ideal instrument of German reunification.

This is why the Germans must not allow their alliance with America to jeopardize their intimate ties with the nations of Europe, and why we must not force such a choice upon them. It is to our interests, as well as to those of the Germans, that the Federal Republic be attached to a wider European community and that she not follow a foreign policy her neighbors would consider to be hostile. Given Britain's isolation from the Continent, the nation most capable of applying a restraining hand to German policy is France. Rather than encouraging a Franco-German entente, the United States persistently tried to break it up, presumably in the fear that the Germans might be tempted to stray from NATO loyalty to Gaullist-type neutralism. This pressure put a terrible strain on the Federal Republic and stimulated the creation of rival factions: a "pro-Washington" group led by Chancellor Erhard and Foreign Minister Schroeder, and a "Gaullist" group led by Franz Josef Strauss. This strain helped contribute to the downfall of the Erhard coalition in the fall of 1966. Erhard's successor, Kurt Georg Kiesinger, tried to bridge the gap with Paris by calling for a "close and trusting" relationship. But later his successor, Willy Brandt, carried this a good deal farther by extending this relationship to the East as well as to France. This is clearly in line with Gaullist policy, although it was never de Gaulle's intention that the political leadership of Europe pass from France to Germany.

Seeking to tie the Germans to a wider European community and to break down the barriers that keep Europeans divided, de Gaulle called for an all-European settlement of the German problem. The reunification of Germany, he declared, cannot be settled by a private deal between Washington and Moscow, as was done at Yalta in 1945, nor by the perpetuation of the rival military blocs. Rather, it is up to "the peoples of Europe to examine together, then to agree in common, finally to guarantee jointly the solution of a question which is essentially that of their Continent." [4]

In place of a Europe of NATO and a Europe of the Warsaw Pact, gradually learning to live together under the ground rules of "peaceful coexistence," de Gaulle called for a European community that would cut across the rival blocs and unite the ancient nations of the Continent in a loose and unspecified form of association stretching "from the Atlantic to the Urals." Stripped of its more grandiose vocabulary, the Gaullist program was basically a variant of the old Rapacki plan: denuclearization of Germany and the disengagement of Russian and American forces from Central Europe. The Germans would be expected to renounce the acquisition of atomic weapons by any means, and to recognize the present frontiers in the east as inviolable. America and Russia would guarantee the neutrality and denuclearization of the two Germanys and would withdraw their troops. The German promise not to acquire nuclear weapons would be insured by the vital interest of all the Europeans nations, plus America and Russia, in holding Germany to that promise. German neutrality would be acceptable because there would no longer be any Soviet troops in Eastern Europe, and the Iron Curtain would have presumably been lifted. With the Red Army gone, it would not be necessary to maintain an American garrison on the Continent. Once Joe and Ivan had returned to their respective homes, the Europeans would take over the responsibility for their own conventional defense. Russia and America would continue to provide nuclear guarantees for their respective allies until a united Europe emerged which was capable of building its own atomic deterrent.

This plan is vague and full of pitfalls. Would a reunited Germany stay denuclearized and neutral? Is there a place in Europe for a single Germany of 75 million people stretching from Alsace to the Polish border? Can Russia be counted on to maintain a European balance? Would Western Europe feel safe once American troops had been withdrawn across the Atlantic? All these are serious questions. But to raise them does not mean they are unanswerable. What is important is that de Gaulle's plan for a Pax Europa would put the major responsibility for the reunification of Europe in the hands of the Europeans. By positing a Europe open to the east it offers a balance to the overwhelming power of the United States. By expanding the little Europe of NATO and the Common Market across the Continent to the borders of Russia, it offers the creation of a Europe wide enough to support the colossus of a united Germany—and thus perhaps the only context in which German reunification is possible. The idea of a Europe stretching to the Urals is less a blueprint than a dream, but in forcing the Europeans to push their heads a little bit into the clouds de Gaulle may be helping them to pull their feet out of the mud. The hard knot of Germany's partition remains to be untied, but the frontiers of Europe are moving from the Elbe, if not to the Urals, at least to the Vistula.

De Gaulle was a cynic, but he was also a visionary, and his vision of a Europe "all entire, balanced, solving its own problems," elicits a powerful response among Europeans who have watched Russia and America moving toward an increasingly overt cooperation, yet who see the Continent still split into rival power blocs. To a Europe tiring of the cold-war ideologies and eager to return to something more resembling normality, the Gaullist vision is tantalizing, and even the Gaullist vocabulary is appealing. The inability, or the unwillingness, of the super-powers to bridge the partition of the Continent has reinforced the belief that the future of Europe must lie in the hands of the Europeans. Both America and Russia find that their dominant position in Europe is declining as the Europeans ponder the prospects and the tactics of reunification.

There is evidence to indicate that the evolution in European politics may be setting the stage for a radical change in the relations between Europe and the Soviet Union. As the East European states demand the right to follow their own path toward communism, the Russians are discovering that their *cordon sanitaire* in Eastern Europe is neither so solid nor perhaps so important as it once was. The invasion of Czechoslovakia was a desperate effort to maintain the bloc. But a more enlightened Soviet leadership will be forced to recognize that reform cannot be forever stymied by bayonets. In the age of the intercontinental missile, a territorial buffer zone no longer offers the safety it did in the past. Similarly, Soviet political influence depends upon its relations with non-communist governments.

This has become apparent throughout the Third World, where the Russians have better relations with neutral India than they do with communist China, and where they have tried to woo ambitious regimes, such as Nasser's Egypt, with military aid, regardless of political orientation. The same thing is happening in Europe, where the new rapprochement with France is more important to Soviet diplomacy than the loosening hold over communist Rumania. Should this evolution continue, it could mean a radical transformation of European politics. Less dependent on the states of Eastern Europe for military security, the Russians might allow them to join a wider European community, which would be pledged to a cold-war neutrality and withdrawal from military blocs. The demise of NATO and the concurrent dismantling of the Warsaw Pact could thus lead to a new European confederation from the Channel to the Vistula, one from which both American and Russian troops would be absent. Should such a prospect seem feasible, it would become increasingly appealing to Europeans and would put an unbearable strain on the continued cohesion of the Atlantic alliance.

As they ponder the difficulty of keeping the East Europeans in line, the Russians may also be having second thoughts about the communist parties of Western Europe. Displaying a taste for independence that mirrors the movement shaking Eastern Europe, the West European communist parties can no longer be counted on as a reliable backstop for Soviet diplomacy. The movement for autonomy that began in the Italian Communist Party, and has now spread throughout Europe, has undermined Russia's claim to Marxist infallibility. Now that Moscow can no longer be sure of controlling the West European communists, it might decide, as it did at the time of the Nazi-Soviet pact, that its ideological allies are expendable where the interests of the Soviet state are concerned.

As it emphasizes economic expansion over ideological proselytizing, Moscow must put more emphasis on cooperation with its European neighbors. To build up her industries, modernize her agriculture, and realize her extraordinary potential, Russia needs the help of Western Europe. By the same token, the Europeans need the expanding markets, the raw materials, and the manpower of the Soviet Union. Only by stretching the Common Market to the Vistula, and perhaps even to the Urals, can the Europeans gain the mass markets, the industrial base, and the technological skills to deal with America as an equal. To be truly equal to America, Russia needs the help of Western Europe, just as Western Europe needs the cooperation of the communist states.

If the nations of Eastern Europe are no longer so crucial as they once were to the security of the Soviet Union, the NATO allies are of decreasing importance to the United States. They long ago ceased to be essential as advance bases for American air power, and now they are becoming a political liability as well, since they have the power to impede the détente. Nuclear powers half a world apart can destroy each other in a matter of minutes. The concept of a *cordon sanitaire*, if it has retained any meaning, has shifted from the ground to the air—from friendly border states to radar warning systems and anti-missile missiles. In a confrontation of the super-powers, allies are often irrelevant and even a positive hindrance. While they still may be useful for purposes of prestige, and for fighting non-nuclear wars, they have lost much of the significance they once held. Small and medium-sized powers need allies to defend themselves. Super-powers, however, indulge in allies largely as a luxury to nourish their egos and spread their political influence. In the lonely world of nuclear confrontation the two super-powers, for the time being at least, stand alone. Europe is a danger to America and Russia only insofar as they refuse to arbitrate their differences over its future.

This is becoming increasingly clear to both capitals and is reflected in a tendency of Moscow and Washington to negotiate directly with each other rather than through their alliances. The Cuban missile crisis, the nuclear-test-ban and non-proliferation treaties, and the SALT talks have all been part of the new dialogue between America and Russia. It is a dialogue, not a love duet, for the differences that separate the two nations are still very great. But it does rest upon the belief that they share a community of interests with each other that they do not necessarily share with their allies.

Within Europe they have shown a willingness—indeed an

eagerness—to leave well enough alone. By their policies they seem perfectly content to accept the partition of the Continent along its present lines. Gone is all talk of "rollback" and "liberation." Just as the Russians have had to give up any illusions they may have had about bringing communism to Western Europe, so the United States has had to admit that it has no intentions of "liberating" Eastern Europe. In fact, it is even questionable whether Washington would like to see Eastern Europe liberated from Soviet control, with all the dangers of "balkanization" that might ensue. As President Johnson has said, "The wound in Europe which now cuts East from West and brother from brother . . . must be healed with the consent of Eastern European countries and consent of the Soviet Union." [5] The clear implication of such a statement—and the judgment that lies behind it—is that the peace of Europe and the interests of the super-powers can best be advanced by the continued cohesion of the cold-war blocs. Washington now apparently agrees with Moscow that attempts at mini-power independence—Gaullism in the West, the Rumanian or Yugoslav heresy in the East—are dangerous and undesirable. They are agreed, as a matter of necessity and of mutual interest, that nobody is going to chase anybody else out of Europe by force. That is the condition of the nuclear balance, and that is the meaning of "peaceful coexistence."

Under the pressure of parallel interests, America and Russia have been moving toward a *de facto* accord on Germany. They have made it clear that neither one intends to disturb the status quo by force; and since neither is interested in changing it by negotiation, the present impasse could continue indefinitely. Europe remains split through the middle of Germany, each half evolving in its own way, each firmly tied to its nuclear protector. Having tested the West's mettle on Berlin and having found it firm, the Russians have not instigated a single crisis in the former German capital since the fall of 1961. Indeed, the Berlin crisis of that year was probably due to Khrushchev's judgment—drawn from the Bay of Pigs fiasco and the meeting at Vienna—that

Kennedy was not a serious rival and should be pushed as far as possible. This judgment was radically revised after the Cuban missile episode in 1962. Thus today, on both sides of the Iron Curtain, there is a desire to leave the question of Germany's partition in the deep freeze lest it imperil the hard-won and still-fragile détente. The two nuclear giants find it perfectly possible to stabilize their relations and carry on a respectable dialogue along the lines of Europe's present partition. The pursuit of reunification is not at all necessary to the continuation of the détente, and indeed Washington has prescribed a program for reconciliation with the East that does not hinge upon the reunification of Germany.

Washington and Moscow have found a new coziness in the détente. But their freedom of movement is being hampered by their allies. As the Kremlin cooperates with the White House only at the cost of alienating a jealous Peking and frightening a worried Pankow, so Washington has found that in reducing tensions with Russia it raises them with its allies. Despite their parallel interests, the super-powers are limited in their cooperation by the demands of their alliances. The Russians cannot allow East Germany to be absorbed by Bonn without imperiling their hold over the communist regimes of Eastern Europe. Nor can they tolerate the prospect of a nuclear-armed Germany that may one day drag her allies into a war with Russia for the recapture of the "lost territories." By the same token, the United States cannot ignore Bonn's desire for reunification with the eastern zone without threatening the cohesion of NATO. Having made NATO the keystone of her foreign policy, the United States is discovering that she cannot seriously negotiate with Moscow unless she is willing to bargain over issues her allies consider vital to their own interests. This is because Europe—and particularly Germany—is not only an ally but the focal point of America's rivalry with Russia. So long as the two Germanys remain integral parts of their rival alliances, America and Russia must remain at odds in Central Europe. They are, in this sense, prisoners to their alliances—prisoners who hold the keys to their cells but are reluctant to use them for fear of losing authority over their allies.

American policy now seems to be slowly evolving toward a rapprochement with Russia, even at the cost of alienating some of the European allies. This is a sharp reversal of the attitude taken during the long Dulles-Adenauer era, when American diplomacy in Europe depended to a large degree on Bonn's illusions and anxieties. Even Kennedy was never able to turn our policy away from dependence on Bonn. While he was eager to improve relations with the Soviet Union, as he eloquently stated in his American University address in June 1963, he did not succeed in liberating himself from the Atlanticist visions of his advisers. He seemed to believe that he could have an Atlantic community with Western Europe and still retain the freedom to work out a private deal with the Soviet Union. He did not realize, or at least make it apparent that he realized, the conflict between these two goals. Unwilling to subordinate the demands of his Atlantic policy to the pursuit of a settlement with Russia, he raised anxieties among the European allies without ever arriving at an agreement with Khrushchev that might have justified a detachment from the Europeans. Perhaps Kennedy did not have enough time, for there are indications that at the time of his death he was moving away from Atlanticist policies, and toward an arrangement with Russia that put America's interests above those of her European allies. It is pointless to speculate on what might have happened had he lived, but it is to the credit of his successors that they have now recognized the inherent conflict in American policy between the pledge to the reunification of Germany on Bonn's terms and the interests of the Atlantic alliance as a whole—and, more important, the conflict between the assumption of identical interests with Western Europe and the desire to reach an entente with the Soviet Union.

In a policy-making speech of October 1966, President Johnson proposed a new rapprochement between East and West based upon the acceptance of rival blocs. "Our task," he declared, "is to achieve a reconciliation with the East, a shift from the narrow concept of coexistence to the broader vision of peaceful engagement." To this end he removed many cold-war trade restrictions, shelved plans for nuclear sharing within NATO, and told the Germans that we will withdraw our troops if Bonn does not meet their expenses. Most important, he declared that German reunification, when and if it comes, can be achieved only "with the consent of Eastern European countries and consent of the Soviet Union." Gone is all talk of trying to detach the East European states from Moscow. The emphasis has now switched from a stillborn Grand Design to a cold-war Grand Reconciliation under the watchful eyes of the super-powers.

As a declaration of intent this is an important breakthrough in American policy, away from the Bonn-Washington alliance and toward a dialogue with Russia. It is still based upon the indefinite partition of the Continent into rival blocs, but it would utilize those blocs as instruments of a Russo-American entente. A long-overdue adaptation to political reality, it could help to reduce tensions in Central Europe, although it cannot by itself solve the German problem or reconcile Germany with her neighbors. But as President Nixon has said, "We recognize that the reunion of Europe will come about not from one spectacular negotiation but from an extended historical process." [6] American policy, like that of the Soviets, is to let that process take its time.

Even a policy of overt cooperation with the Soviet Union cannot keep the German problem forever in cold storage. Reunification is becoming an important objective for Germans, and powerful forces are rising within the Federal Republic which seek to take advantage of this frustrated nationalism. NATO cannot reunify Germany or reunify Europe. As the Germans become increasingly aware of this, they will be tempted to look elsewhere in their efforts to satisfy their political frustrations. The Atlantic community was not a realistic alternative, because the United States never seriously considered relinquishing any of its own sovereignty and the Germans could not be expected to confine themselves forever to a transatlantic association. Nor has the Common Market turned out to be a substitute, since its federalist ambitions have now been largely buried. De Gaulle's efforts to anchor Germany to a Paris-led European community failed—in large part because of our own counter-pressure on Bonn—and Germany could once again approach that dangerous condition where her frustrated ambitions are not contained by adhesion to a larger political community.

Had the United States not urged the Federal Republic to rearm in 1950 and pushed her into NATO in 1955, perhaps Germany would be unified today as Austria has been, her neutrality and demilitarization guaranteed by the great powers. Then Germany's unresolved place in Europe might not be an implicit threat to world peace, and there might be a Continental entente "from the Atlantic to the Urals." That chance, however, was lost, and the problem now is to find a place for a militarily powerful and territorially dissatisfied Germany in a still partitioned Europe. This cannot be done by the confrontation of two blocs, but only by reducing the military impasse in Central Europe and opening the way to a broader European reconciliation in which Germany's quest for national union can be contained and perhaps ultimately satisfied. This means not only the re-engagement of the two blocs, but the disengagement of the super-powers from their military bridgeheads in Central Europe. If we want to get the Russians out of Eastern Europe, we shall have to be prepared ourselves to leave Western Europe.

However appealing Washington may now find the idea of a Europe moving together through the rapprochement of two rival blocs, it is unlikely to satisfy Germany's quest for reunification and the desire of Europeans on both sides of the Iron Curtain to emerge from under the guardianship of their nuclear protectors. The perpetuation of NATO and the Warsaw Pact means the continued partition of Europe, for there can be no reunification as long as the European nations are split into rival alliances. Nor is it necessarily to our interests to keep the Europeans contained within rival blocs. If we can secure the withdrawal of Russian troops from Eastern Europe and the establishment of a Continental entente among the European states, then the dismantling of NATO should become an objective of our own policy. The reason we are in Europe, after all, is not to fortify NATO but to contain the Soviet Union. If this can be done without our physical presence, then we can withdraw the bulk of our troops and permit the Europeans to work out among themselves the problem that only they can resolve: the place of Germany within the European community. We can help them to work out that problem, and we can guarantee them our nuclear protection so long as they may require it, but we are not a European power and we cannot, either by ourselves or in cooperation with the Russians, reconcile Germany with her neighbors.

The path to European reconciliation is paved with difficulties, but it is one which must be traveled, if not by us in a new adjustment to changing conditions, then by our allies, who are no longer content that Europe should remain divided into rival protectorates. To limit the United States to the outdated doctrines of NATO and the little world of the Atlantic community is to put an unworkable and intolerable chain upon American interests. By the same token, Europe too has a role to play that transcends its alliance with the United States: a role in the emerging states of Africa and Asia which were once European colonies and whose problems Europe may understand better than we; a role also in the efforts of Latin America to escape from total dependence on the Yankee colossus. To be "outward-looking," Europe must face not only toward the North Atlantic but to the world at large, a world in need of the European qualities of measure, tradition, and ideological cynicism. In a world where the cold war is ending, Europe's task is not to vanquish Russia, for there can be no peace on the Continent until the communist states are peacefully restored to a wider European community. Nor must we try to force the Europeans to turn their backs to the east. Between America and Russia, between a valued friend and an errant sister, Europe cannot, and must not, choose. The task Europeans face in the decade ahead is to help reconcile these two powerful antagonists and to find a place for Europe somewhere between them. A chastened Europe can play this role only once it learns to believe in itself, in its own vitality, in its powers of creation, in its identity as something more than a pampered protectorate.

The unnatural American protectorship over Western Europe has lasted longer than has been healthy for us or for our allies. It has inspired in us the belief that we have a global mission, and it has fed a sense of defeatism and dependency among our allies. Our position in postwar Europe has been a powerful and even a dominant one. But the conditions that made America the leader and protector of Western Europe were temporary ones, and they are now passing. What we face today is a reawakened Europe that is no longer content to be an American protectorate and is finding our policy an impediment to its quest for reunification.

This assertion of resistance on the part of our allies is a source of disappointment, and even of anger, to many Americans who saw Europe's future circumscribed to an American pattern. In our infatuation with Atlantic blueprints we must not allow ourselves to forget that the crucial consideration is not whether half of Europe will be oriented across the Atlantic, but on what terms the two Europes will be reconciled with each other. The United States has the power to achieve a viable European settlement with the Russians. She can exercise that power, or she can dissipate it and thereby leave the Europeans—and particularly the Germans—with no choice but to work out their own arrangements with the Soviet Union as best they can. The choice can be ignored; it cannot be avoided. President Johnson described the problem in declaring that "we must improve the East-West environment in order to achieve the unification of Germany in the context of a larger, peaceful, and prosperous Europe." But the implementation is all, and it has yet to be begun.

Europe is now reaching the point where it no longer needs or wants America as it once did; while America, turning from a secure and prosperous Europe where the Soviet menace has diminished and our benevolent protectorship is being challenged, has found a new mission in confronting the Chinese peril Washington believes is about to engulf all Asia.

7. Yellow Peril Revisited

Once Japan is destroyed as an aggressive force, we know of
no other challenging power that can appear in the Pacific.
. . . Japan is the one enemy and the only enemy of the
peaceful peoples whose shores overlook the Pacific Ocean.
> —AMBASSADOR JOSEPH GREW, 1942

The long-range objective of the Chinese communists is to
become dominant in the Asian, African, and Latin American
countries, and to frustrate the process of peaceful
development and free choice in the developing nations.
> —ROBERT S. MCNAMARA, 1966

❧ ❧ ❧ FOR two decades following the end of the Second World
War, American foreign policy was dominated by the effort to contain the Soviet Union. The struggle with Russia consumed our
energies and became the focal point around which so much of
American life revolved. The Marshall Plan, NATO, the Korean
war, foreign aid, the Cuban crisis, the Alliance for Progress—all
these were conceived and executed in terms of the contest with
Russia for the leadership of the world. The postwar power structure became synonymous with the cold war.

But the postwar world has passed, the struggle with Russia has
sharply diminished, and the cold war is virtually over. Yet there
is no peace. Having finally been able to establish ground rules
of peaceful coexistence with the Russians, we find ourselves on a
collision course with China. The struggle for the world has been
transferred from the Atlantic to the Pacific. Whereas the protection of Europe and the ambitions of Russia once dominated our

thoughts, now the security of Asia and the intentions of China have become an American preoccupation. The struggle continues, but in the process of time we have changed both continents and enemies.

China today stands where Russia did twenty years ago—resentful, ambitious, menacing. A revolutionary power dedicated to the demolition of the status quo and to the construction of a new order in which she will play a more predominant role, China unsurprisingly sees America as her main challenger in the Pacific. The United States has taken up that challenge. In an effort to contain Chinese power, American diplomacy has tried to apply many of the same methods in Asia today that it applied in Europe during the late 1940s. The policy of containment, which for the most part worked so well in Europe, has now become the foundation of American policy in Asia. The official policy of our government is that the ambitions of China, whatever they may be, can be contained by a combination of military, economic, and political force. Vietnam today is compared to Greece in 1947, and the effort to halt a communist insurrection there as one which will determine, as President Johnson has said, "whether might makes right."

Today we are trying to contain China not only militarily but economically, politically, and even ideologically. This effort, in its present form, is a relatively new one. It did not begin in earnest until after we had achieved the current détente with the Soviet Union. Until that time our involvements in Asia were considered in terms of blocking Soviet power as expressed through the multitudinous arms of "international communism." But that monolith is no more, and, as the Russians have preoccupied us less, the Chinese have taken their place. It is almost as though we were unable to view the world without demons—as soon as one was put to rest, another immediately appeared. Perhaps this is unfair. But there is something vaguely unsettling about the sequence of our current obsession with China and the way in which it began in deadly earnest with the expansion of the war in

Vietnam, almost at the same time that the curtain was rung down on the cold war in Europe.

Rightly or wrongly, we are now engaged in a contest with China over the future of Asia. It is a contest whose ultimate end no man can foresee but which is likely to dominate American foreign policy, and perhaps even American life, for at least a generation to come. Yet it is a contest that has not elicited the same approval among the American people that the earlier policy of containing Russia did. Perhaps the people have not had the issues adequately explained to them. Or perhaps the stakes are not so important as those we have faced in Europe.

What are those stakes? Are American interests threatened if China absorbs some of the smaller countries of Asia? Can China be contained the way we contained the Soviet Union in Europe? And even if she can be contained, does it matter whether other Asian nations turn to communism? Would this serve China's interests? Would it threaten ours? These are exceedingly difficult questions, but basic ones that must be answered if we are to emerge from the tragedy of Vietnam and avoid an even greater tragedy that looms on the horizon.

Our involvement in Asia is in large measure the result of our own wishes. We wanted to crush aggressive Japan during the Second World War, and we did, thereby making China the dominant nation in Asia. We wanted China to be a great power, even insisted that she be made a permanent member of the Security Council of the United Nations. And today China is a great power, but she is not the China we envisioned and is not in the United Nations because we will not permit her. We wanted China to be restored to her old possessions, and so we told her that at the end of the war she could have Formosa, which had been in Japanese hands for fifty years. But now we are dedicated to the defense of Formosa (Taiwan) against the government of mainland China. We wanted to eject Britain, France, and Holland from their colonies and extend Woodrow Wilson's policy of self-determination from Eastern Europe to Eastern Asia. And we did, thereby insuring the same balkanization, the same instability, and eventually the same breakdown as the new states struggle among themselves and the outside powers use them as pawns.

We got what we wanted in Asia, only to discover that we do not want it any more. China is no longer our friend, the departure of the European colonialists was no panacea, and Asia is even more unstable today than it was when we moved in more than two decades ago. Now that the Europeans are gone, and happy to have left, their problems are ours. Their attempts to assure stability, provide security, and seek cooperation must now be ours. Without ever consciously willing it, without ever quite knowing how it happened, we find ourselves responsible for the fate of Asia. Our soldiers have been dying there for seventy years, first in the Pacific islands, then in Korea, and now in Vietnam.

American involvement in Asia on a major scale began in the Spanish-American war of 1898. This was ostensibly fought for the independence of Cuba, but it was also stimulated by the spirit of Manifest Destiny and the drive for overseas economic expansion. Cuba became independent and, for all practical purposes, a colony of the United States. Yet the most important legacy of the war was the American acquisition of Spain's possessions in the Pacific, the Philippine Islands. With Admiral Dewey's victory in Manila harbor and the collapse of Spanish authority in the islands, the United States became the occupying power of the Philippines. Immediately a guerrilla insurrection (a war of "national liberation," so to speak) broke out that took thousands of Philippine lives, required 70,000 American troops to quell, and lasted from 1889 to 1902. It was our baptism by fire as an Asian power.

We thus acquired our first Pacific colony and became engaged in the imperial task of providing for its welfare and defense. The islands became a base for the economic struggle in China with the European powers. By the acquisition of the Philippines, American political and economic influence was extended across the Pacific. The traditional colonialism of the Europeans was replaced by an American non-colonial imperial expansion. To defend our Pacific possessions we had to have a powerful navy. To refuel naval vessels we had to have bases at strategic points such as Hawaii and Guam.

And to protect that navy it was important that no other navy in the Pacific become more powerful. Thus by acquiring the Philippines we became committed to the territorial integrity of China and embarked on a rivalry with Japan for economic dominance in Asia.

Whereas we had formerly allowed the Europeans to carve up China at their pleasure, we now stepped in to declare our determination to keep China open to all comers. Such a declaration, however, was contrary to our principles, and in open terms would have shocked many Americans. It was therefore cloaked in phrases of morality. Abjuring any acquisitive desires ourselves, we became the champion of China's territorial integrity. No closed enclaves in China, we told the Europeans. Let the door of trade be open to all comers, including latecomers. Free trade and *laisser passer* were the new bywords as American diplomacy found, in the Open Door doctrine at the turn of the century, a unique combination of economic self-interest and political morality. Rather than a naïve gesture, this policy was, in Professor William Appleman Williams' words, "a brilliant strategic stroke which led to the gradual extension of American economic and political power throughout the world." [1]

Time and distance have embellished the Open Door policy with a mantle of disinterested generosity, and most Americans today probably view it as evidence of our concern for the welfare of China. But the history of our relations with China is not so simple, and our record is not so unblemished by acts of self-service. For all the air of sanctimony that surrounded them, the Open Door notes of 1899 and 1900 represented another episode in the long pillage of China at the hands of the Western powers —a pillage whose fruits we enjoyed, but responsibility for which we sought to avoid. We saw ourselves as China's friend and protector, above the tawdry avarice of the European powers. But, as Professor John K. Fairbank has said:

> Americans were able in the nineteenth century to share all the special privileges of foreigners in China under the unequal treaties,

without fighting for them. The British and others fought the colonial wars and the Americans enjoyed the fruits of such aggression
without the moral responsibility. By 1900 the British, the French
and the Japanese had all fought wars with China; the Russians had
seized territory; and all of them, together with the Germans, had
seized special privileges in spheres of influence.

The Americans had done none of these things and came up instead with the "open door" doctrine, which soon expanded to include not only the open door for trade, but also the idea of China's
integrity as a nation. Thus we Americans prided ourselves on cham-
pioning China's modernization and self-determination. We considered ourselves above the nasty imperialism and power politics of
the Europeans. We developed a self-image of moral superiority.[2]

The Open Door doctrine not only secured us a share of the
lucrative China trade without soiling our hands, but also provided
an outlet for our national energies at a time when the idea of
Manifest Destiny was riding high. It confirmed our rising sense of
mission, which was launched so dramatically in the Spanish–
American war, and showed the Europeans that we were a power
to be reckoned with in Asia. As the war with Spain moved us to
the offshore islands of the Pacific, so the declaration of the Open
Door planted us squarely on the mainland of Asia. By giving us a
commitment to the territorial integrity of China at a time when
she was being dismembered by Japan, Russia, and the European
powers, it involved us in the disorder of Asia. Because of this gesture—reinforced by economic interests—we could no longer remain indifferent to what happened in China, even though it had
little relevance to our own security. Yet once we were involved in
the fate of China, we were launched on a collision course with
Japan that found its culmination at Pearl Harbor.

We thought we could be a part-time Asian power, sticking our
finger into the Chinese rice bowl, standing up to the European
colonial powers, asserting the right of less fortunate peoples to
democracy. We tried, in short, to indulge ourselves in a little
moral posturing on the cheap. It finally caught up with us on December 7, 1941, that "day of infamy" that was also a day of reck-
oning. Half unconsciously we had made ourselves Japan's chief

rival in Asia. Now there was nothing to do but follow through the drama that had begun forty-three years before on Admiral Dewey's momentous cruise into Manila harbor. The new defenders of Asia, we fought Japan in a war that became a crusade to extirpate evil from the Pacific, a crusade that culminated at Hiroshima. Under the policy of unconditional surrender that we considered the only proper conclusion to a crusade, we reduced Japan to rubble and stripped her of the territories she had acquired in Asia during the past half-century. We had punished the aggressor and, so we thought, restored peace to the Pacific.

Yet by destroying Japanese power and reducing Japan to the home islands, we automatically created a political vacuum in Asia. Having killed the tyrant, we discovered that there was no one left to keep order in the family. Asia was in a state of anarchy: Japan crushed, China in the grip of a civil war, the European colonies in a state of rebellion. Who could fill the vacuum? Not Japan, which had been demolished precisely because she was too adept at filling vacuums. Not China, where Mao Tse-tung's communists and Chiang Kai-shek's Kuomintang were busy fighting each other. Not Russia, which was all too eager to move into Asia. Who else was left? Nobody but the United States.

Thus we found that victory had saddled us with the responsibility for Japan's defense. We had become the protector of our former enemy. In doing so, we developed a vital interest in Korea, which in unfriendly hands could be a threat to Japan; in the Ryukyu Islands, which controlled the approaches to Japan; and in the government that ruled China. Through our victory we had inherited the responsibilities of an Asian power.

Aside from those we assumed as the conqueror of Japan, there were the responsibilities which we acquired as the patron of anti-colonialism. Even while the war was still being fought we declared our sympathy for the Asian nationalists who were trying to push the Dutch out of the East Indies, the British out of the Indian subcontinent, and the French out of Indochina. Here, too, we eventually got our wish, as the Europeans were evicted from their colonies. One by one the nations of Asia became independent under the proud eye of the American midwife. But instead of ushering in the new brotherhood of man, independence only compounded the anarchy of Asia. Poor in everything but ambition, the new nations were a breeding ground for misery, sedition, and aggression.

In 1945 independence for everybody seemed like the password to the brave new world; by 1951 it began to seem a prescription for disaster. What had happened in the interval to change our minds? The cold war with Russia and the outbreak of the hot war in Korea. If the Czech coup and the Berlin blockade of 1948 were the straws that broke the uneasy truce with Russia in Europe, then the Korean war was their Asian counterpart. "The attack upon Korea," President Truman declared on June 27, 1950, "makes it plain beyond all doubt that communism has passed beyond the use of subversion to conquer independent nations and will now use armed invasion and war." To nearly everyone in Washington it seemed clear that the invasion of South Korea was but a sneak preview of what lay in store for Western Europe.

The Korean war also confirmed the general opinion that the communist government which had recently come to power in Peking was merely a branch office of the Kremlin. Although there was considerable evidence to the contrary even then, we *knew* that the Chinese revolution was a conspiracy organized by Moscow. Its success was an automatic extension of Russian power. How could it be otherwise? Russia was communist; China was communist. Thus half of Asia lay in Moscow's grip. The enemy may have worn different disguises, but whether masquerading as a commissar or a coolie, it remained the same: the "international communist conspiracy." China, as we all knew, was simply Russia with chopsticks. Indeed, our highest diplomatic authorities told us so. China, as Assistant Secretary of State Dean Rusk said in 1951, is "a colonial Russian government—a Slavic Manchukuo on a large scale—it is not the government of China. It does not pass the first test. It is not Chinese." [3]

Those who did not believe in the solidity of the "bloc," who saw the seeds of disintegration where others saw unshakable solidarity, and who had the temerity to point out that the Chinese revolution was carried out independently of Moscow—and sometimes against its wishes—were rewarded for their pains by being hounded from the government as security risks. Nothing could shake our conviction that the Russians had master-minded the Chinese revolution and pulled the strings in Peking.

The facts, however, yielded a different story. Rather than ·directing the Chinese revolution, the Russians gave it little encouragement and more than once tried to squelch it. Unable to put an independent-minded Mao Tse-tung under his thumb and make the Chinese communists subservient to Moscow, Stalin preferred to work with Chiang Kai-shek. At one point he even tried to get Mao to disband his amy and throw in his lot with Chiang. Less concerned with world revolution than with the security of Mother Russia, Stalin saw the communists of other nations as instruments to be used for the advancement of Soviet interests. The Chinese were stubborn and independent. Since they wouldn't join him, he constantly double-crossed them and continued to back Chiang against Mao almost until the generalissimo took his one-way trip to Formosa.

All this was pointed out at the time by various people knowledgeable about China. Indeed, it should have been obvious from the record of Stalin's cynical use of Communist Parties in other countries. But Washington would have none of it. We were caught up in our own private vision of what had happened in China. China was lost, *our* China rudely snatched from us by the communists. Clearly the Chinese would never have done such a thing of their own accord—not the Chinese for whom we had declared the Open Door, and fought the Japanese, and whom we had educated in the American way of life through generations of missionaries. Only some sinister conspiracy could explain such a mystifying occurrence. That our diplomacy had suffered a setback was not enough; we must have been betrayed.

Like a rejected suitor, we became the victim of our hurt pride. Instead of adapting to the new situation in Asia, we longed for a return to the old one. Our Asian policy fell into the hands of that curious band of ex-generals, embittered missionaries, disappointed businessmen, and professional anti-communists known as the China Lobby. Taking seriously the aberrations of such individuals as Senator McCarthy, we consoled ourselves with the illusion that China had been stolen from us by traitors but that Chiang Kai-shek, whose unhappy exile was described in such moving terms by his gracious wife on her American lecture tours, would soon return to Peking in triumph to the cheers of adoring multitudes.

If there was ever a possibility of reaching an accommodation with the new regime in Peking, it was lost by the outbreak of the Korean war. Until then the Truman administration had tried to keep the door ajar, and the President had declared as late as January 5, 1950, that "the United States government will not pursue a course which will lead to involvement in the civil conflict in China. Similarly, it will not provide aid or advice to the Chinese forces on Formosa." It makes wry reading now, some two decades and several billion dollars later, but at the time it was a noble try at noninterference. However, it went by the board when North Korea moved against the south in June of the same year. Convinced that this was the prelude to similar Russian-directed moves elsewhere, President Truman sent American troops to Korea and the Seventh Fleet to the Straits of Formosa. The Korean war was a turning-point for American diplomacy. It stimulated a sense of alarm in Europe that led directly to the rearmament of Germany and to a vast expansion of American military power all over the world. And it made Americans aware that China too was an enemy.

Since that time China has become a kind of nightmare for American policy-makers. Because of the strange history of our relations with China, compounded as it is of feelings of guilt and rejection, we have been unable to look upon the Chinese communist government with objectivity. The lingering effects of the China Lobby and the McCarthy era have stifled any initiative in the State Department toward dealing with it. There have been a timidity of thought amounting to paralysis, a fear of facing real issues, and a habit of taking refuge in inherited rhetoric and obsolete stances. The questions of admission to the United Nations and the extension of diplomatic recognition, of trade and of expanded contacts, have not been examined and debated as real issues, but have been treated as questions of morality. We see China through the lenses of our own inflated anxieties and our own betrayed illusions.

We seem to be just as misinformed and just as prone to dogma about China's intentions toward us as she is about ours. We are the victims of our self-imposed ignorance, and the Chinese are victims of their insularity and rigidity. When China has been cautious, we see her as aggressive; when she has been ambiguous, we see her as single-minded; when she has been opportunistic, we see her as implacable. Caught up in our own fears, we have taken Chinese propaganda at face value when a good deal of it is designed to inflate China's own sense of importance and to embarrass the Russians in the contest for leadership of the communist camp. We have learned to take Moscow with a grain of salt, but we accept every Chinese boast with solemn seriousness. We tend to believe everything we hear from China's propagandists because we are still obsessed with the fact that China is communist. And because she professes communism and speaks in a Marxist vocabulary, we don't know how to distinguish China as a revolutionary troublemaker from China as an imperialistic aggressor.

We have been fighting China in one way or another ever since 1950, yet we still do not know what China is or what she wants. There seems to be not one but half a dozen Chinas. There is China as an aggressive power: the China that has absorbed Tibet, that humiliated the Indian army in the Himalayas, that aids rebellion in Vietnam, and that threatens the peace of Asia. There is China as a demonic power: the China that presumably welcomes nuclear war as the graveyard of the white man's world, a war after which the eternal China will go on, in Mao's words, to "create on the ruins of imperialism a new civilization that will be a thousand times higher." There is China as the new Rome of communism's secular religion: the China that blasts Russian "revisionists" for various un-Marxist activities, that accuses them of being the "greatest splitters of all time," and that sees herself as the true defender of the communist faith. And, perhaps most ominously of all, there is China as the would-be leader of the world revolution, a revolution which has less to do with communism than with the eternal struggle between the rich and the poor, the dominators and the dominated.

The question of how to deal with China is the greatest foreign-policy problem facing this country today, and perhaps will remain so for a generation to come. Yet we are only just beginning to come out of the dark. To most Americans, and indeed to most Westerners, China is, as Churchill once said about Russia, "a riddle wrapped in a mystery inside an enigma." To broach the subject of China is to sink into a swamp of conjecture, rumor, and speculation. We know all about China, and yet we know so little. We know how many bushels of rice and how many tons of steel she produces, how many soldiers and submarines she has, and how many grains of rice her peasants consume. We even know where her nuclear installations are concealed, and no doubt what Marshal Lin Piao has for dinner. But we do not seem to know what China wants from the world. Is it war, or is it to be left alone? Is it hegemony in Asia, or is it the defense of her frontiers? Is it the domination of the entire earth, or is it simply the prerogatives of a great power?

The answers are as varied as the questioners. Some believe that China is yearning to plunge the world into a nuclear holocaust in the conviction that, although hundreds of millions would die, half a billion Chinese would survive to inherit the earth. This, however, is to take some of Mao's whistling in the dark at a good deal more than its face value. Others think that China has been the victim of a terrible misunderstanding, that she wants only to live at peace with her neighbors and to follow at home the Tao as reinterpreted by Comrades Marx, Lenin, and Mao. This, however, may be to deny the role that both ideology and nationalism play in Chinese policy. Still others try to follow a middle course between these two extremes, seeing China as a nation restored

to national unity and independence after a century of humiliation and determined to reassert her influence over those who live
in her shadow. Whether this influence is to be exerted by conquest, or by more subtle means of economic and political pressure,
remains to be seen. That China has been awakened there can be
no doubt.

So much is conjecture because the Western world has been cut
off from China since the communists won the civil war nearly
twenty years ago. The Chinese, with their traditional xenophobia
reinforced by American hostility, have not shown much interest
in talking, while the United States has made little effort to find
out. Like the Cuban revolutionaries who followed in their foot-
steps a decade later, they seem to consider it a positive virtue to
make an enemy of the United States. Since 1949, when they ar-
rested our consul general in Manchuria just as we were contemplating formal recognition of the Peking government, the communists have preached anti-Americanism as a way of life. Like most
dictatorships, they have found the stimulation of hatred for a foreign enemy a handy device for assuring conformity at home.

But in judging the reciprocal pathology of Sino-American relations, it is worth recalling that the world looks very different
from Peking and from Washington. From our point of view, American interventions in Asia have been noble and divorced from
national advantage. With no territorial ambitions ourselves, we
have sought through our intervention only to protect free peoples
against Chinese communist aggression. This is why we fought a
war in Korea for three years, why we guard Chiang Kai-shek's
army on Formosa, why we are furnishing military aid to most of
non-communist Asia, and why our own soldiers are fighting in
Vietnam. We are there because, in the official view, only American military power prevents the Chinese from dominating Asia.

But to China's eyes, shaded by the spectacles of Marxist orthodoxy and of historical suspicion of the West, the United States
is a threatening foe which nearly invaded Chinese territory in the
Korean war, which uses her military power to prevent Formosa
from being returned to China, which has rimmed China with

military bases from Pakistan to Japan, which has kept her out of the United Nations, which continues to participate in the Chinese civil war by supporting Chiang Kai-shek, which is fighting a war with a communist ally on China's southern frontier, and which seeks to deny China her sphere of influence in Southeast Asia. To Peking, as the Australian historian Coral Bell has pointed out, the United States role along China's periphery

> may look much as Latin America would look to Washington if the Monroe Doctrine had been shattered for a hundred years and the opportunity then seemed to be presenting itself to restore the status quo ante. Before the West impinged on Southeast Asia, Chinese ascendancy over the area was certainly as great as United States ascendancy over Latin America in the palmiest days of the Monroe Doctrine, round about the time of the Roosevelt corollary, and equally regarded as part of the natural order of history.[4]

Even to a people ruled by leaders less paranoid than those who sit in Peking, the United States might appear to be something other than simply the *gendarme* of freedom. But to the Chinese, who have historical reasons to fear and distrust Westerners, the world is full of enemies. From the beginning of their contact with other cultures, the Chinese have considered foreigners to be uncultured and barbaric, and none more so than the white peoples of Europe, who thrust their power upon a helpless China by the crude force of their technology. Considering that most of the Europeans with whom the Chinese came into contact were plunderers of the opium trade, adventurers who carved European enclaves in the nation's ports and sapped her wealth, and missionaries who were often patronizing in their attitude and who preached a religion whose concepts of sin and redemption seemed vindictive in comparison to the easy-going tolerance of Taoism and Confucianism, it is not surprising that the Chinese were less than awestruck by what they saw of the West.

The Chinese distrusted, even despised the West, for they suffered at the hands of Europe as had few other people. The constructive side of Western colonialism felt in the Indian subcontinent and in Southeast Asia—the building of schools, roads, and hospitals, instruction in the theories (if not the practice) of democracy—was barely felt in China. Nor did the Chinese benefit from the rational and liberating aspects of Western culture that revolutionized modern Japan. Rather than enjoying the mixed privileges of colonialism, they were pillaged and exploited like a conquered people. The West, with its soldiers, its missionaries, its fortune-hunters, and its bankers, managed to destroy the delicate balance of Chinese civilization without being able to replace it.

Having felt themselves to be the center of world civilization for more than 2000 years, having absorbed and civilized their conquerors with the superiority of their culture, the Chinese could not bring themselves to accept the possibility that their ancient culture might be inferior to that of their would-be conquerors, and they were shattered by the calamity that their civilization suffered at the hands of the West. They sought a devil who could explain the terrible misfortune that had befallen them, and they found it in the expansive Western civilization that was undermining their own. As Professor Fairbank has written:

> Xenophobic contempt for foreign cultures became a standard part of China's long-conditioned response to the power of the Inner Asian barbarians. Until 1860, barely a century ago, China's leaders had suffered many times under foreign rule but had never met an equal, much less a superior, foreign culture. The old political myth of China's superiority was based on solid cultural realities even when inspired also by a need to rationalize military weakness. Today, to expect Chinese patriots to acknowledge a double weakness, both cultural and material, in both basic principles and practical devices, is asking too much. They will sooner claim they have what China needs and condemn the outside world as evil, fit only for salvation through Maoist-type subversion. In short, Peking's intractable mood comes out of China's history, not just from Lenin's book.[5]

The last sentence is particularly worth pondering, for it provides an insight into what has been so baffling about China's behavior: a virulent anti-Westernism that is phrased in terms of a communist ideology that is itself Western in origin; a universal call to revolution by the most chauvinistic of nations. This feeling of resentment toward the West, toward Russia as much as toward America and Europe, which is reflected in the calls for the revolt of the underdeveloped peoples against the developed ones, is no monopoly of the communists. Fear and hatred of the West are embedded in the Chinese character and are shared even by Chiang Kai-shek, who, before he was reduced to total dependency on the United States for his survival, never ceased to denounce the West for China's misfortunes. In his attitude toward the West, in his authoritarianism, and even in his economic beliefs (when in power he advocated collective farms and state ownership of industries), Chiang is a perfect companion to his successor, Mao Tse-tung. If he were still ruling from Peking, it is likely that his foreign policy would be very much like that carried out by the communists: anti-Western, racist, and expansionist.

Chinese as well as Marxist, and thus feeling resentment toward the West as well as an ideological commitment to revolution, the communist inheritors of the Middle Kingdom have made themselves the champions of an anti-Western world insurrection. Chauvinistic by nature, they see themselves as the true apostles of Marx, chosen to take over the revolutionary struggle from the "revisionist" Russians, who have now been seduced by affluence and peaceful coexistence. As proof of their worthiness to lead the world revolution they offer not only their poverty and their militancy but the example of the Long March—their time in the wilderness, during which they demonstrated that revolutions can ultimately triumph despite the gravest hardships. Their experience, they believe, offers an inspiring example to the other underdeveloped nations of the worlds, an example of how they should forge their own revolutions, and how a dedicated leadership can achieve what Marx considered to be impossible: a peasant-based revolution in a pre-industrial society.

Using her economic backwardness and her history of exploitation at the hands of the West as credentials of worthiness, China has tried to make herself the ideological leader of the Third World of poverty-stricken and ex-colonial states. Such a role naturally places her in opposition not only to the rich nations of the West, but to the rich nations of the East as well, and particularly to Soviet Russia, which China now castigates as a betrayer of the revolutionary struggle. Western "imperialism" led by the United States is equated with the "Khrushchev revisionists in Moscow who aid the American imperialists because they fear war and revolution." Both are lumped together as enemies of the downtrodden peoples, secretly conspiring to keep the lid on the Third World by quashing rebellions that might threaten their great power duopoly. As "revisionists" within the secular religion of Marxism, the Russians are even worse than the Americans, for the latter are outright enemies, while the former are traitors to the cause and thus beyond redemption.

As part of their effort to set themselves up as the true Rome of world communism, the Chinese, like most leaders of religious sects, have reinterpreted the sacred doctrines of Marxism to suit their own purposes. As China is essentially a peasant society, only peasant societies are capable of achieving the true revolution. As the Chinese have a tradition of suspicion and hostility toward the West, the West is the great enemy of that culminating point of history known as revolution. As they feel their racial dignity has been offended by the white peoples of the West, they appeal to other peoples throughout the world who have also been treated as racial inferiors by white civilization. Put these ideas together and they yield a prescription for revolution that is anti-Western, anti-white, and anti-proletarian—a prescription, in short, which accurately reflects China's own historical conditions, cultural sensitivities, and political convenience. Whether this prescription is applicable to other underdeveloped societies, however, is a matter for dispute.

Twisting ideology to suit their own purposes, the Chinese have, in effect, proved themselves to be the most agile of revisionists. While they may be right in pointing out that the Russians have turned away from the gospel of world revolution in favor of affluence at home and peaceful coexistence abroad, they have had to stretch Marx a long way to make him the prophet of Chinese-style revolutions. In truth, what Marx said was that communist revolutions could never occur in underdeveloped countries like China, but only in advanced industrial societies where capitalism was highly developed and had thereby bred its own "internal contradictions." This, he said, would lead to the increasing impoverishment of the industrial proletariat, and ultimately to their revolt against their property-owning masters. Marx imagined that the revolution would come first to Germany, rather than to a half-peasant society like Russia. For the Russian revolution, Lenin was responsible. What the Chinese have done is to apply Leninist revisionism to pre-industrial societies and combine it with a Trotskyite call for world revolution. Turning traditional Marxist doctrine on its ear and applying Leninism to situations Lenin never conceived of, the Chinese argue that the peasants of the backward nations, and not the industrial proletariat of the advanced ones, are the natural leaders of the communist revolution.

The most complete expression of the new Chinese doctrine was issued in a pronouncement by Defense Minister Marshal Lin Piao in the fall of 1965. Taking the planet as a whole, he labels North America and Western Europe as the cities of the world, while Asia, Africa, and Latin America constitute the rural areas. Ever since the Second World War, for various reasons, the proletarian revolution has been stymied in Europe and North America, while it has developed vigorously in the Third World. "In a sense," this argument continues, "the contemporary world revolution also presents a picture of the encirclement of cities by the rural areas. In the final analysis, the whole cause of world revolution hinges on the revolutionary struggles of the Asian, African, and Latin American peoples who make up the overwhelming majority of the world's population." The West, therefore, is presumably doomed, since it cannot subdue the aroused peasantry of the rural areas and will eventually find its cities surrounded.

Tailoring their doctrine to fit their own problems, the Chinese argue that because of their vast numbers the underdeveloped nations will be able to subdue the "imperialists" and nullify their more sophisticated technology. Atomic weapons will be of no use in quashing revolutions, since "the outcome of a war will be decided by the sustained fighting of ground forces." Thus the peoples of the Third World should not be intimidated by the atomic weapons of the United States and should push bravely ahead to make their own revolutions.

For all its up-to-date references, Lin Piao's doctrine is pretty much a rehash of a half-century of Bolshevik vocabulary. From the moment they seized power in 1917, the Russian Bolsheviks denounced capitalist encirclement, and even the "revisionist" Khrushchev used the phrase when it suited his convenience. The only part of the doctrine that is particularly striking is the concept of an implacable opposition between the West as a whole and the impoverished peasantry of the Third World. This has made quite an impact on unsophisticated or biased minds, and has even induced a good many who should know better to take Maoist propaganda as an accurate picture of the future. It serves China's purposes to be considered the prime mover and ultimate beneficiary of any revolution anywhere. This doctrine increases China's prestige and provides her with a powerful ideological tool to use against the Soviet Union in the Third World. Indeed, this is probably its primary purpose: a means of attacking Soviet "revisionism" and undermining Soviet influence among the underdeveloped nations. As a prescription for world revolution, however, it is not so much frightening as it is cynical and self-flattering.

What is most remarkable about the doctrine is the way in which it has been used to justify China's policies and has been adapted to her weaknesses. China as yet has no effective nuclear arsenal; therefore nuclear weapons are discounted as unusable in a revolutionary struggle. China, for all her economic backwardness, is the most populous nation on earth; therefore those with the greatest numbers will ultimately conquer. "You rely on modern weapons," the Chinese declare with a frankness that indicates their own weakness, "and we rely on highly conscious revolutionary people; you give full play to your superiority, and we give full play to ours; you have your way of fighting, and we have ours." Above all, China needs peace to consolidate her revolution and build an industrial economy. Thus the Chinese state openly, in what is perhaps the most important and neglected part of their doctrine, that "every revolution in a country stems from the demands of its own people" and that "their role cannot be replaced or taken over by any people from outside." Revolution, apparently, begins at home. Indeed the Chinese admit this by declaring that "revolution cannot be imported," thereby giving their ideological followers fair warning that they are on their own.

While they faithfully promise to applaud all revolutionary wars, the Chinese have prudently refrained from any promise to participate. They are the well-wishers of everybody's revolution but presumably the protectors only of their own. They encourage communist parties elsewhere to use violence against the "imperialists," but in a war near their own frontiers they have stayed on the sidelines, fighting to the last Vietnamese. The Chinese have tried to keep Asia in ferment, encouraging animosity between India and Pakistan, between Indonesia and Malaysia, and so far as possible between America and Russia over Vietnam. But so far they have been remarkably cautious about involving themselves in the revolutions they preach.

This caution is not so much Marxist as it is Chinese. In ancient times, generals who thought it imprudent to attack would try to intimidate their adversaries through ferocious noises. The Chinese, like the Byzantines, believed that a recourse to arms was to be avoided if there were other honorable alternatives. Today's China has not forgotten the lesson of her ancestors and conceals military caution behind verbal extravagance. This has been particularly perplexing to the United States, where Theodore Roosevelt's dictum of speaking softly but carrying a big stick seems the ideal attribute of manliness. To make a big noise and then go into the bushes when the enemy appears strikes most Americans as shameful and deceitful. The Chinese, however, come from a different tradition. They perpetually issue ultimatums they have no intention of honoring and make threats they cannot hope to fulfill.

Extravagant in word, the Chinese have been circumspect in deed, and their policies have been marked by flexibility and caution. Trumpeting their prowess in order to impress their friends and intimidate their adversaries, they have yet to overestimate their power on the battlefield or to engage in military action where they did not feel a direct threat to their own territory. "It is opportunism if one won't fight when one can win," in the revealing words of Marshal Lin Piao. "It is adventurism if one insists on fighting when one can't win." This argument too has been directed more against the Soviets than against the United States, meant as a criticism of Russia's "opportunism" in seeking peaceful coexistence with the United States and an attack on Khrushchev's adventurism in putting Soviet missiles into Cuba. It is also a lesson for Vietnam, suggesting that it is opportunism for the Russians not to back up North Vietnam, but that it would be adventurism for the Chinese to enter a fight that might extend to their own territory.

Despite the anxieties of official Washington, the Chinese have had little luck in subverting their neighbors by the force of their ideology. For the most part, the underdeveloped nations have rejected China's missionary efforts and have even thrown their own communists in jail. The Chinese have been kicked out of countries like Kenya, which they tried to subvert by buying off disgruntled politicians, discredited throughout much of the Third World for their blatant interference in the internal affairs of other nations, and subjected to a staggering defeat in Indonesia, where the Peking-oriented Communist Party was virtually exterminated. China has cut herself off from Russia, which should have been a powerful ally, and has lost the support of the other communist nations, which should be her natural sympathizers. The only place the Chinese have had any success in spreading their doctrine has been in South Vietnam, where a corrupt and oppressive regime has pushed the opposition into the arms of the communists. Yet even there it has not been a Chinese success so much as one for the Vietnamese communists, who have always tried to stay independent of Peking, and who drove the French from Indochina mostly by their own efforts. The Chinese prescription for instant revolution via an anti-Western crusade is not being bought by the underdeveloped nations. Indeed, Lin Piao's doctrine seems to be taken at face value only in Peking and in Washington.

In Korea, China entered the war only when MacArthur pushed to the Yalu and she felt her own territory was in danger. In Tibet she regained control of a territory which had been under Chinese suzerainty from the days of the emperors. In India she consolidated her claim to Himalayan territories which have been in dispute since the frontier lines were drawn by the British, and which even the Nationalist government on Taiwan claims are Chinese. After occupying the disputed territories and humiliating the Indians, China retired to the line of her original claim, when she could have marched across the plains of Assam.

Coupled with this military caution has been a willingness to practice "peaceful coexistence" with other neighbors. The Chinese have struck up friendships with Pakistan and Indonesia, live at peace with such neutrals as Burma and Cambodia, and in the eyes of most of the world interfere rather less in the internal affairs of other states than does the United States, which has her soldiers stationed in thirty foreign countries and her CIA and AID missions everywhere. Washington's view of China as a land-grabbing monster about to gobble up all Southeast Asia may cause nightmares along the Potomac, but it does not seem to be shared by most Asians. While they may fear China's intentions, they are not frightened by her propaganda, for they know that China's military capacity is, for the time being, sharply limited and largely defensive in nature.

The Chinese, for all their blustering, currently lack the power to pose a serious military danger to their neighbors. Their nuclear arsenal is still in the testing stage, and it is far from certain whether it is primarily designed to intimidate China's neighbors or to deter Russian or American attack. China's army of two and a half million men is the largest in Asia, but has only four armored divisions equipped with weapons less modern than those of such American-supplied neighbors as Pakistan, India, and South Korea. China has only a primitive airlift ability for launching mobile operations, has virtually no capacity for making modern jet aircraft or modern heavy weapons, and has exceedingly limited oil reserves. Her navy is minuscule, consisting mostly of submarines, torpedo boats, and armed junks, and its 2500-plane air force is composed largely of obsolescent Soviet fighters. China's army is strong on the ground, but lacks strategic mobility, and is more designed for defending her own territory than for full-scale campaigns beyond her borders. The dominant military power in Asia is not China but the United States, whose forces include the Seventh Fleet, with bases in the Philippines and Taiwan; ground and air units in Japan, Okinawa, South Korea, and Guam; and a powerful army in South Vietnam. In addition to this formidable tactical force, there is American nuclear power, which is not yet matched by a Chinese deterrent.

Chinese aggressiveness, therefore, is limited by the current incapacity of China to conduct major operations much beyond her present frontiers. There is, of course, always the danger of another Korea. But the essential point about Korea is not that the Chinese entered the war despite MacArthur's assurances to the contrary, but that they entered it only when the American army pushed deep into North Korea and approached the Chinese frontiers. China can be provoked into war, but in view of her current military weakness she is in no position to take on an aggressive role. "While it is important to recognize Peking's ambitious goals," one scholar has stated,

> it is equally important to note that, on the basis of available evidence and communist China's performance to date, the Chinese communists do not appear to think primarily in terms of spreading their influence through direct military and territorial expansion; they appear to recognize the limits to their capabilities for military action outside of China's borders; they have usually been quite realistic in assessing the power balance in concrete situations; they have generally been calculating and even cautious in avoiding military "adventurism" and limiting their risks; they have tended to think in long-range terms about their most ambitious goals; and they have repeatedly been flexible and pragmatic (at least until recently) in adapting their strategy and tactics to fit changing situations in pursuit of their short-run goals.[6]

This is for the present. But what about the future? What will happen when China develops her own nuclear arsenal? Will she not then be capable of carrying out a war for hegemony in Asia, beginning with the weak states along her southern frontier? This, of course, is a real possibility and a danger that American policy must be prepared for. While the acquisition of a nuclear delivery system will hardly make China the equal of the United States, it would dramatically affect the power equation in Asia. Yet even so, it is important to keep a sense of perspective about the use to which a Chinese Bomb could be put. It could not be used aggressively without inviting a massive American—or Soviet—retaliation, a retaliation that China would not dare to risk unless her very survival was at stake. The Bomb, in other words, would greatly increase China's ability to deter an attack upon herself, but would be of little, if any, use in aggressive operations. In the words of an authority on Chinese military policy:

> The Chinese are unlikely to see their development of nuclear weapons as opening up wholly new possibilities for expanding Chinese influence in Asia; rather, it will simply reinforce Chinese conventional military power and Chinese ability to support wars of national liberation in enabling the Peking regime to make an implicit threat of military action against her neighbors while relying on political moves to bring these countries into the Chinese orbit. There would seem to be no situation in which the actual employment of nuclear weapons would be contemplated by the Chinese or would, in fact, be useful in expanding Chinese influence.[7]

The Bomb will change the power equation, but it will not rewrite it completely. With or without the Bomb, China is determined to expand her influence. Whether her power is to be used for military domination, or whether it can be constrained within a framework that will guarantee the integrity of China's neighbors is the question on which the peace of Asia hinges. For nearly two decades the United States has been embroiled in Asia in the struggle against communism. We are now faced with the problem of something considerably more serious: the containment of a resurgent China.

8. Chinese Checkers

Let China sleep. When she wakes, the world will be sorry.
—NAPOLEON

❧ ❧ ❧ THE containment of China has become the great preoccupation of American foreign policy. It has replaced the containment of Russia as the main focus of our anxieties and has involved us in the role of protector of the Pacific, just as we have been protector of Europe throughout the cold war. The policy of containing China has rested primarily upon a ring of American military bases around her periphery in a great arc from Japan to Pakistan, via Taiwan, South Vietnam, and Thailand. Military containment has been combined with a policy of political and economic isolation amounting to a virtual quarantine.

Our Asian policy rests upon the belief that China can be contained through the maintenance of anti-communist states along her frontiers. These states, with the exception of the two neutrals, Cambodia and Burma, are nourished and protected by the United States. Some, such as Thailand and Pakistan, are joined to us by formal alliance. Others, such as Taiwan, South Korea, and South Vietnam, are American dependencies. India, although formally non-aligned, receives massive doses of military and economic assistance, as well as an unofficial American nuclear guarantee of her independence. Even chronically mismanaged Indonesia is once again benefiting from American economic aid following the anti-communist military coup. The remaining major nation of Asia, Japan, is tied to the United States economically, politically, and by a formal mutual defense treaty.

These are the nations which will presumably check Chinese expansion and prevent the spread of communism throughout the rest of Asia. To American eyes the two dangers are synonymous, and thus the containment of China is indistinguishable from the containment of communism. This, of course, has not always been our attitude. A few years ago, when we worried more about Moscow than about Peking, we saw the containment of communism in Asia as part of our cold-war struggle with the Russians. Communism, we believed, was an "international conspiracy" directed from Moscow, with a branch office in Peking. To contain that conspiracy it became our policy to extend our system of military alliance from Western Europe to the unstable states of southern Asia.

The forging of regional alliances was the antidote John Foster Dulles applied to the infection of communism. With a lawyer's passion for pacts and formal contracts, he built alliances in the way that others issued declarations. For him alliances were a form of political carpentry, and from the scaffolding of his regional pacts he sought to create the impression of an invulnerable bastion against the communists. Military alliance had set the pattern in Western Europe, where NATO had effectively thwarted any aggressive designs of the Soviet Union. It seemed logical to apply the same formula in Southeast Asia, where communism had suddenly appeared in the form of a Chinese dragon. An Asian alliance seemed to be an ideal way to ward off the Russians, contain the Chinese, and provide an American-supported military bulwark in the new states of Asia only recently liberated from the bondage of European colonialism.

Seeking to create a miniature NATO in southern Asia, Dulles searched for allies in the struggle against international communism. The search, however, was not very productive. India, Burma, Ceylon, and Indonesia refused to repudiate their ostensible neutrality; the states of former French Indochina—Vietnam, Laos, and Cambodia—were forbidden by the Geneva agreement to join foreign military pacts; and Taiwan was already an American client. As a result, Dulles was left proclaiming the formation of a

Southeast Asian Treaty Organization which contained only a single Southeast Asian nation, Thailand.

With its unfortunately abbreviated membership list, SEATO
was off to a shaky start. It could hardly claim, like NATO, to be
an integrated alliance of like-minded nations organized for defense against a common foe, for it was neither integrated nor like-
minded, nor did it have a common foe. It was a very old-fashioned
kind of alliance in which the members agreed to come to one
another's defense under certain conditions, if attacked. Attacked
by whom? That question was left up in the air, and better so, for
if answered it might have revealed a startling difference of opinion. For the United States that foe could only be that many-
armed demon "international communism," manipulated from the
Kremlin and operating through one of its Asian tentacles. For the
Philippines the foe was probably Indonesia, insofar as there
seemed to be a serious danger from anybody. For Thailand the
foes were its traditional enemies, Vietnam and Cambodia—and
perhaps one day China. For Pakistan the foe was obviously India,
and SEATO a means of securing a powerful ally against its menacing Hindu neighbor.

Pakistan perhaps illustrates best the self-deception on which
our Asian alliances were built. The American infatuation with
Pakistan began in the mid-1950s, when French power collapsed
in Indochina, when India proclaimed her neutrality between East
and West, and when the Moscow–Peking axis was considered to
be an imminent threat to all the nations of Asia. In Pakistan,
which had been carved as a Moslem state from British India in
the panicked partition of 1947, Washington saw an ideal partner
in the struggle against communism. Headed by a vigorous general
who was eager to build up his army with American help and who
loudly proclaimed his anti-communism, Pakistan quickly became
one of Washington's most favored clients. Economic aid and
military hardware, totaling more than $3.5 billion, flowed in to
build up Pakistan's economy and endow her with one of the
world's most modern armies. Pakistan was the fulcrum of the
system of alliances Dulles was trying to extend from Europe to

the Middle East and Asia. One of our few solid allies between Turkey and Japan, she was a key member of both SEATO and its Middle Eastern equivalent, CENTO (or the Baghdad Pact, before Baghdad pulled out).

While Dulles may have seen Pakistan as a faithful ally in the struggle against "international communism," the Pakistanis were not particularly alarmed by that danger. They put their own communists in jail and did not feel any serious threat of attack from either Russia or China. The nation they really feared was nominally neutral India, whose population outnumbered theirs four to one, and with whom they were embroiled in a bitter dispute over the ownership of Kashmir. But Washington, absorbed in the effort to contain communism, could not be bothered to take such regional rivalries seriously. It poured billions of dollars of military equipment into both India and Pakistan—assuming, of course, that they would use our weapons only to defend themselves against the communists. This pipe-dream finally exploded in the fall of 1965 when our official ally Pakistan and our unofficial ally India went to war against each other with American-made weapons.

This outcome might have been predicted by anyone who had not been blinded by the presumption that anti-communism was a cause which could inspire the allegiance of Asians. Yet such was our own preoccupation with communism that we assumed the leaders of non-communist Asia would naturally share it. We believed that we could harness the nationalism of the newly independent countries of Asia to anti-communism, which we believed to be in their interests as well as ours. Unfortunately, however, the major nations of Asia did not seem to agree, and we were left basing our Asian policy largely upon the creation of isolated bastions under the rule of such self-proclaimed "strong men" as Syngman Rhee, Chiang Kai-shek, and Ngo Dinh Diem.

They were, for the most part, anti-communist by instinct and training. But the mere fact of their anti-communism did not make them valuable allies, any more than a common distaste for poverty is a basis for a sound business partnership. There was nothing morally wrong in trying to use them for our purposes, for they certainly tried to use us for theirs. But we were naïve in trying to use them when they had virtually nothing to offer us other than a distaste for communism and a desire to hold on to power themselves. Had these "strong men" been strong enough to command loyalty within their countries and to exercise power without dependence on our help, they might have made worth-while allies. Yet except for Ayub Khan in Pakistan, they were mostly weak despots who needed us far more than we needed them. We thought they were holding the line against communism, whereas they thought we could be used to help them stay in power by providing weapons to subdue their internal opposition. As it turned out, their assumption was nearer the truth than ours. It was not so much that they cynically deceived us as that they provided the means for us to deceive ourselves.

Our policy of military containment of communism through a system of alliances has been rejected by the only Asian nations that might have made it viable: Indonesia, Japan, and India. It has not built strong anti-communist governments in the one area where its need was supposedly the greatest: the former states of Indochina. It has not advanced the cause of democracy, if that was to be one of its ambitions. It has not convinced the Asians that communism as an ideology is a danger to their survival. It has not won us anybody's friendship, if that is important. And above all, it has not been capable of doing the one thing most Asians would agree is important: stemming the growth of Chinese power. As a means of defending American interests, the policy of peripheral military alliances has been disastrous; as a means of containing China, it has been useless. Its futility is now being demonstrated every day in the jungles of Vietnam.

Our involvement in Vietnam originated in the effort of Dulles to salvage an anti-communist state from the wreckage of the French empire in Indochina. This effort began even before the French were defeated by the armies of the Vietnamese communist leader Ho Chi Minh. The United States, which had once supported Ho in his struggles against the Japanese during the

Second World War, turned against him during the cold war and aided the French in their efforts to subdue his nationalist forces. As these efforts became increasingly costly and onerous for the French, the United States took over much of the financial burden of the Indochinese war. Yet despite American aid and encouragement, the French were unable to subdue the communist-led rebels. The war became increasingly frustrating and politically unpopular in France. During the long siege of the French garrison at Dien Bien Phu, such figures as Vice-President Nixon and Admiral Radford urged President Eisenhower to send American planes and forces to prevent a French defeat. The British, however, refused to go along with such an expansion of the war, and eventually the garrison fell. This provoked strong sentiments for withdrawal within France, where the people had been told the war was in its "last quarter-hour" ever since it began in 1946. An international conference was called at Geneva in 1954 to probe the terms of a settlement between France and the Indochinese communist-led rebels. Shortly after the conference began, a new government came to power in Paris under Pierre Mendès-France —a government pledged to seek a negotiated settlement on honorable terms. After hard bargaining at Geneva, aided by Russian willingness to see the war ended, and by the mediation of Anthony Eden for the British government, an accord was worked out which provided for the independence of Laos and Cambodia, two of the three states of old French Indochina, and for the temporary partition of Vietnam along the 17th parallel. Free elections were to be held within two years to form an all-Vietnam government. In this regard the Final Declaration at Geneva stated: "The Conference recognizes . . . that the military demarcation line is provisional and should not in any way be interpreted as constituting a political or territorial boundary." The United States, while not a signatory to the Final Agreement, agreed to respect its terms.

The end of the fighting, however, was not the end of the war. The French withdrew their forces, the communists moved north of the 17th parallel to establish the provisional state of North

Vietnam, the anti-communists set up a government of South Vietnam in Saigon, and the Americans gradually moved in to replace the French. Although the United States had agreed to respect the Geneva accords for the unification of Vietnam by free elections, she could not easily tolerate the prospect of a Vietnam unified under communist control. Yet observers generally agreed, and President Eisenhower himself admitted, that Ho Chi Minh's communists would probably win any all-Vietnamese elections.

The only way to block this was to try to build up a viable state in the South, one which would be anti-communist and linked to the United States. While this plan may have sounded good in the abstract—however contrary it was to the intention of the Geneva agreement—the odds were heavily against it. First was the problem that South Vietnam was a nation which had no independent existence and no leader. It was a face-saving device of the Geneva conference that was expected to evaporate within two years. Second, even if a leader could be found among the religious and tribal groups struggling for power, anarchy mastered, and a sense of nationhood established, there was the crucial problem of whether South Vietnam could ever survive as an anti-communist bastion. Assuming that dikes against communism were possible in Southeast Asia, was the 17th parallel a reasonable place to put the dike? Third was the question whether the United States had a serious enough interest to intervene where the French had failed. It was one thing to help a real state guard its independence against foreign invaders. It was something quite different to create a state where none had existed, find a leader where there was nothing but rival gangs, and hold the line against a communist-led army that had already won its war and was waiting to unify the country as had been promised at Geneva.

These were questions worth asking, but 1954 was not a time for answers. Despite the death of Stalin and the more cooperative line followed by Malenkov, it was a time for building barricades against the communists and demonstrating the strong purpose of the administration in Washington. Trying to do after the Geneva conference what he was unable to do before, Dulles embarked upon a search for a leader who could keep South Vietnam within the "free world." He found Ngo Dinh Diem. Plied with American aid and weapons, Diem eliminated his competitors by one means or another, restored some semblance of order, and proceeded to establish South Vietnam as an independent state. Repudiating the Geneva accords, first by accepting United States military aid, then by refusing to hold the scheduled elections in 1956, Diem thwarted the establishment of a unified communist Vietnam which Ho Chi Minh thought he had won on the battlefield.

But as Diem used increasingly repressive measures to enforce his personal rule in South Vietnam, an organized resistance movement was formed in the South from the remnants of the old Vietminh and from non-communists as well. By 1959 the southern resistance movement had joined forces with Ho Chi Minh, who furnished active support and guidance. A communist-oriented political body called the National Liberation Front was formed, and the second war for Vietnam was under way. Though the roots of the war are to be found in the South, and in the inability of the Saigon regime to win the support of the population, the support from the North was largely inspired by the refusal of Diem to permit all-Vietnamese elections. As an authoritative French commentator has observed:

> It was the categorical and apparently definitive refusal of Ngo Dinh Diem and his government to envisage general elections in which the regime in the South would confront the communists that caused the leaders in Hanoi to organize, finance, and equip subversion in the South, provoking the constant aggravation of American intervention and the progressive internationalization of the conflict which, had it been confined to Vietnamese alone, would have led to the collapse of the South.[1]

American officials encouraged Diem in his refusal to permit all-Vietnamese elections in part because pro-communist terrorist groups operating in the South would have made free elections exceedingly difficult, and in part because it was generally agreed that even if such elections could be held in the disturbed conditions at the time, the communists would probably win them and thus unify Vietnam under a government headed by Ho Chi Minh. It was precisely to prevent such a prospect that Dulles had chosen Diem, backed him against a host of rivals, and provided the military and economic support that allowed his government to survive. It was because Dulles believed that the survival of South Vietnam as an independent, non-communist state was essential to American interests that he committed the prestige of the United States to the Diem regime. South Vietnam was to be the barrier beyond which communism would not be allowed to pass. First with foreign aid, then with military assistance, and now with our own soldiers, we have been trying to assure the permanent partition of Vietnam so that the portion south of the 17th parallel will remain anti-communist.

We are fighting in Vietnam not for freedom and democracy, because they do not exist in that unhappy country, but because we are convinced that if one nation "falls" to communism, all the others will follow suit; that if the United States fails to protect one of her client regimes with her military power, her allies everywhere will lose faith in America's word and immediately succumb to the seductions of communism. Carried away by our obsession with communism as an ideology, we have lost the ability to distinguish between the military danger posed by communist states to non-communist states, and the political danger of communist penetration in unstable and regressive states where the government has little popular support. Having failed to make this distinction, we have tried to prevent the collapse of our client regimes by our own military power—even against their own populations.

This is the logic of the "domino theory." It decrees that if communists come to power anywhere, they will come to power everywhere; that if the dominoes fall in South Vietnam, they will soon fall all the way to California. This was the basis of American policy in Southeast Asia during the long Dulles period and, despite protestations to the contrary from the State Department, it still continues to play a dominant role in our policy. If we did not believe that there is truth in the domino theory, we would not be involved in Vietnam to the degree that we are today. We could tolerate the possibility of a communist-led government in Saigon if we did not assume that this would necessarily lead to communist governments coming to power throughout Southeast Asia. We continue to play dominoes even though our vocabulary has become more sophisticated and Washington has sought to justify our involvement in Vietnam as a struggle against aggression, or as a fulfillment of treaty obligations.

Because President Johnson believed in the domino theory—that communism has to be stopped on the 17th parallel, as he told the troops in Korea, because "it is better to do it there than it is in Honolulu"—he expanded our commitment in Vietnam from the furnishing of military equipment and advisers into a full-scale war. Until the November elections of 1964 we had simply been aiding the Saigon government, corrupt and incompetent as it was, to defend itself against its own people. But in deciding to take on the major burden of the war, not only against the communist-led rebels of South Vietnam but also against North Vietnam, the United States turned a civil war among Vietnamese into an American war against Vietnamese. The administration did this because it believed that the preservation of an anti-communist government in South Vietnam was essential to the containment of China, that a victory by the Vietcong would show that wars of "national liberation" could be won and thus would inflate Chinese power and induce a series of such wars throughout the world.

The problem of applying this theory was not only the crudity of the analysis but its inapplicability to the unique situation of South Vietnam. South Vietnam was not simply a nation trying to maintain its independence against a foreign aggressor. It was rather the site of a civil war instigated by southerners who were allowed no other means of protest against a dictatorial government in Saigon. This civil war was then aided by the government of North Vietnam, which was determined to unify the country and thereby implement its understanding of the Geneva accords.

The participation of the North did not change the fact that this was a civil war among Vietnamese. The only truly foreign element in the war is the Americans, who have assumed the role of authority vacated by the Saigon government. The ruling regime in Saigon could not survive without American protection and has not been able to command the allegiance of its own people. This is why the communists have won so many sympathizers and why there has been such mass desertion from the Vietnamese army. As an American journalist who spent several years in Vietnam for *The New York Times* has written:

> In Vietnam only the communists represent revolution and social change, for better or worse according to a man's politics. The communist party is the one truly national organization that permeates both North and South Vietnam. The men who lead the party today, Ho Chi Minh and the other members of the Politburo in Hanoi, directed the struggle for independence from France and in the process captured much of the deeply felt nationalism of the Vietnamese people. Perhaps because of this the communists, despite their brutality and deceit, remain the only Vietnamese capable of rallying millions of their countrymen to sacrifice and hardship in the name of the nation and the only group not dependent on foreign bayonets for survival.[2]

If the assumption that we are defending freedom and self-determination by our presence in South Vietnam has been denied by the reality of a state which has not known freedom and where independence is a mockery, the further assumption that this is a "test case" for other wars of "national liberation" is equally false. The fact that communist-led rebels may topple an incompetent and unpopular regime in South Vietnam does not mean that there are going to be little Vietnams in all the unstable states of the Third World. What happens in Kenya and Bolivia and Ceylon will be determined by conditions in those countries and not by what happens in Saigon. There is no hydra in Peking, Moscow, or anywhere else master-minding world revolutions. The idea of revolution by example is a Trotskyite myth that Peking is promulgating and only Washington has been gullible enough to accept.

Even if the North Vietnamese are finally successful in unifying

Vietnam under a communist government, this could hardly be construed as a victory for China. Indeed, a strong unified Vietnam, even under communist control, would be a better barrier to Chinese expansion than a divided Vietnam prey to civil war and foreign intervention. The peoples of Vietnam have been engaged in resisting their powerful neighbor to the north for some 2000 years. They are not likely to stop now, even though both pay formal allegiance to Marxism. "The peoples of Southeast Asia," in the words of one highly placed American, "have, over the centuries, shown an obstinate insistence on shaping their own destiny which the Chinese have not been able to overcome." [3] This is true regardless of what kind of government the Vietnamese live under, and it is unfortunate that George Ball was unwilling, or unable, to act upon the logic of his own argument when he was Under Secretary of State.

This "obstinate insistence on shaping their own destiny" is true of the peoples of Vietnam, and it is true of the other nations of Asia. Their resistance to China has little to do with the fact that she currently has a communist government, and a great deal to do with the fact that China is a resurgent power seeking to play a world role that she believes is rightfully hers. The peoples of Asia will have a vital interest in restraining the Chinese even if, as seems highly unlikely, they should all pay formal allegiance to the same political ideology. The one problem all the nations of Asia face is that of preserving their independence against whatever power threatens it. In this effort the crucial consideration is how well they are able to guard that independence, not whether they have communist or anti-communist governments.

Anti-communism in Asia is not a policy; it is a stance. Most of Asia is not democratic, as we in the West define the term; it never has been, and it may not be for a long time, if ever. Parliamentarianism in the Western tradition is largely unknown, except in Japan and in the former colonies of Britain. Government by representation, however, has ancient roots at the village level and embodies principles which may be better suited to the emergent states of Southeast Asia. We are not going to be able to impose our style of government upon the Asians, or our style of economy either. Having known few of the benefits and most of the horrors of Western-style capitalism, the Asians tend to associate it with colonialism, misery, and exploitation. Instead, they pay allegiance to a socialism which strikes them as anti-colonial and more humane. In practice their socialism seems to run the gamut from the venture capitalism of Singapore to the collectivism of China. Behind the common label of "socialism" lies the confusion of Asian realities.

By now we should have learned the danger of attaching too much importance to labels. If the military juntas in South Korea and South Vietnam are part of the "free world," if the communist dictatorships in North Korea and North Vietnam are "people's democracies," and if the authoritarian regimes in Indonesia and Pakistan are "guided democracies," then a healthy skepticism may be the best attitude toward the political tags the new nations choose to wear. No matter what doctrines they profess, most of the Asian states are authoritarian in fact and likely to remain so for a long time. In some cases, such as Pakistan, this authoritarianism may lay the foundation for an eventual political democracy; in other cases, such as Indonesia, it has been a kind of social fascism. And in some cases, such as North Korea and North Vietnam, this authoritarianism may call itself communist.

All this, however, may be a good deal less important than we have imagined it to be, for the labels, in fact, describe very little. It may be that in the future a few more Asian nations may adopt the communist label to describe their particular brand of authoritarianism. Perhaps one day Laos or Indonesia or Burma or even India may "go communist," as the saying runs. What do we do then? Slit our throats? Retire into isolation? Drop the Bomb? Judging by the rhetoric coming out of Washington, the "fall" of one more Asian nation to communism would be a catastrophe for the United States. But the conventional wisdom, such as it is, was put together in the early 1950s, when everybody knew that communism was a conspiracy directed from the Kremlin basement. Today even the State Department has admitted the passing of that myth as Moscow and Peking feud not only for leadership of the communist world, but over the ownership of Central Asia. The communist victory in China, rather than increasing Soviet power, has reduced it—as Stalin feared all along. If there are those in Washington who still yearn for the return of an aging Chiang Kai-shek to Peking, there are those in Moscow who yearn for it even more.

Communism, then, is not an octopus with one head and a dozen arms, but a hydra with one trunk and a dozen heads, each of them ready to bite the other. Just as the medieval Christians slaughtered one another in the name of their common faith, and the nations of the West nearly destroyed their common civilization twice during this half-century, so the communists are split by national squabbles which are more important than the dogma of the secular religion they profess. This is a lesson we have finally learned in Europe, where we now recognize that such nations as Poland and Hungary are no danger to the West even though they may carry a communist label.

But if communism in Eastern Europe is not a threat to the West, why is communism a threat in Southeast Asia? True, the label may be offensive, but it is one we have learned to swallow elsewhere without ill effects. The communist nations of Asia, like those of Eastern Europe, are just as eager to guard their independence as are nations that are non-communist. We embrace dictators in many places—among them Spain, Saudi Arabia, and Iran—because we think it suits our interests to do so and because we pride ourselves on our "realism." Why draw the line at the communist dictatorships of Asia?

A major reason why we support the dictatorships in South Korea, Taiwan, and South Vietnam is not that they are "freedom-loving democracies" (which they are not), but that we think they are a barrier to Chinese expansion. But why not, by the same token, support North Korea and North Vietnam as well? If it is China we are worried about, we should be aiding whatever nations are best capable of resisting her. If North Vietnam can ward off Peking better than the incompetent military clique in Saigon, then it is Hanoi that should be receiving our blessings instead of our bombs, and our earnest hopes that Vietnam may become the Rumania of Southeast Asia.

The fact that Saigon or Seoul may be ruled by anti-communist regimes no more affects the power of China than the fact that Havana is ruled by a communist regime affects the power of the United States. The communist countries of Asia are dangerous only insofar as they allow themselves to be used by China for military purposes, just as Cuban communism became a danger to America only when it was used as an instrument of Russian military power. Yet neither North Korea nor North Vietnam has shown any indication of being China's servant. The government in Pyongyang has purged its pro-Chinese officials and sharply criticized Peking's attempts to define communist orthodoxy. Hanoi, despite its exposed position on China's frontier, has tried to maintain neutrality between Moscow and Peking. In terms of ability to resist Chinese power, unified, neutralist, self-sustaining governments—even if they should call themselves communist—are preferable to weak, divided, and discredited regimes which cannot survive without direct American support. Just as Eastern Europe is one of the few places in the world where the United States is actually popular—owing, by no accident, to the fact that it is almost the only place where we have no military bases or regular foreign-aid program—so the communist nations of Asia might offer unexpected opportunities for an agile American diplomacy.

If China is to be contained—and it is important that she be contained—it can be only through the creation of *viable* nations in Asia which can stand on their own feet economically and which are able to resist internal threats to their authority. If they can do this, we need not overly concern ourselves with what ideology they pursue or what forms of government they maintain. The containment of China cannot be accomplished by American soldiers fighting in the jungles of Vietnam for a puppet government, but by Asians who have a vested interest in their own independence and a willingness to defend it. This means containing China not through the weak little states along her periphery, but through the major nations of Asia: Japan, Indonesia, the Philippines, India, and Pakistan.

As for the small states of Southeast Asia, they are going to have to lie within China's sphere of influence, just as Chiang Kai-shek always said they must. This is unfortunate, but it is a fact of geography, and it is confirmed by several thousand years of Asian history. The peoples of Southeast Asia may not like to live in China's shadow, any more than the peoples of the Caribbean like to live in America's shadow. But being within China's sphere of influence does not mean that they must be, or will be, absorbed by China. Throughout her history China has shown a willingness to live at peace with her smaller neighbors so long as they are willing to respect the formalities of her dominant status. Even today China has friendly relations with such non-communist states on her frontiers as Burma, Nepal, and Pakistan. If this tradition is pursued, if there can be influence without domination, then we can be reasonably satisfied. Every great power demands a certain obeisance on the part of its smaller neighbors: the Russians do so, we do so, and the Chinese do so as well.

It is possible, though not really likely, that one day a major state such as India or Indonesia may turn to communism. But this might be more of a problem for Peking than for us, for a powerful communist rival in Asia would not only resist China's territorial expansionism but also dispute her claim to be the ideological leader of communism in the Third World—just as China has challenged Russia for the mantle of communist leadership. Even if one day India or Indonesia does claim allegiance to the principles of Karl Marx, she will have a vital interest in containing Chinese power. Indeed, the day may yet come when China has reason to fear the expansion of her powerful neighbors even more than they today fear hers. It was only a generation ago that Japan was the most powerful nation in the Pacific and China was an American-supported client. The next generation may be faced with the problem of containing an expansionist India or Indonesia. Stranger things have happened, and we need look back only twenty-odd years to be reminded of them.

Thus while China may today seek to instigate revolutionary ferment in Asia to reduce Western or Russian influence, it is highly unlikely that China herself will be the beneficiary, any more than Russia was the beneficiary of the Chinese revolution. China's influence in Asia is, to be sure, greater than it was twenty, or even ten, years ago. The reason, however, is not that she espouses communism, but that she is once again becoming a great power, and American intervention in Southeast Asia has given her the opportunity to pose as an anti-imperialist power. That advantage, which has been given to China by the shortsightedness of American policy, will diminish once our interventions in Asia cease. Then the major nations of Asia can turn from their current problem of trying to moderate American interventionism to the growing problem of how to contain China.

By defining the containment of China in terms of communism versus anti-communism we have alienated the neutral governments of Asia, which do not want to become involved in an ideological struggle. We have not been able to convince them that anti-communism has anything to do with the containment of China. And we cannot do so because we are not able to make the distinction ourselves between China as a communist nation and China as a potentially imperialist power. Our obsessive anti-communism has canceled out much of the natural sympathy many of them might otherwise have for our efforts to contain China.

Anti-communism is our own private crusade. The resistance to Chinese imperialism, on the other hand, is an issue in which every Asian nation, communist or non-communist, has a vital interest. It is as crucial to communist North Vietnam as it is to neutralist Cambodia and to right-wing Thailand. It is an issue on which we could have won universal support because it is not simply an American obsession but an Asian reality. And, unlike simple anti-communism, it is a goal for which the Asians themselves would be willing to make sacrifices.

Whatever their feelings about communism, the nations along China's frontiers have reason to fear her ambitions. It is not the United States which will suffer from Chinese territorial expansion, for China can claim nothing that is ours. It is the Russians, whose Central Asian lands were seized from China, who are worried by the growing threat on their Asian frontiers. It is North Korea and North Vietnam, whose struggle with anti-communist regimes in the South makes them more dependent on China than is either safe or prudent. It is India, plagued with monumental social and economic problems, and it is Indonesia, with the remnants of a Peking-oriented Communist Party and a resentful Chinese minority which has suffered racial and economic discrimination. These are the nations which have a vested interest in restraining China. They should be our natural allies. Unlike China, we have no territorial designs upon them, they are not within our sphere of influence, and they have nothing we need. Yet we have lost the benefits of their nationalism by trying to distort it into anti-communism.

Whether we like it or not the Chinese can no longer be ignored or kept in isolation. Capitalist or communist, under Chiang or under Mao, China has been aroused to the full measure of her enormous potential. It may be generations before she reaches that potential, and by that time Chinese leaders will probably think and behave very differently from the way they do today—whether for better or for worse may depend in large part on how we deal with China today, on whether we try to carry on a lonely crusade through our weak protectorates along China's frontiers, or whether we try to build a new balance in Asia based not upon the dying rhetoric of anti-communism but upon the realities of Chinese power and Asian nationalism.

9. New Balance in Asia

The central drama of our age is how the Western nations and the Asian peoples are to find a tolerable basis of coexistence.
—WALTER LIPPMANN

❧ ❧ ❧ THE chaos that is the hallmark of today's Asia stems directly from the breakdown of the world power structure that existed until 1939. With the Second World War came the collapse of the European colonial system, the destruction of Japanese power in the Pacific, and the confrontation of America with a revived China. Everything that has happened in Asia since 1945 has been an attempt to come to terms with the breakdown of the old order. The American interventions in Korea and Vietnam, the war between India and Pakistan, the continuing hostilities in Indochina, the "confrontation" between Malaysia and Indonesia, and the new cold war between Washington and Peking—all these are part of the effort to create a new equilibrium to replace the one that was destroyed more than two decades ago.

This effort to build a new Asian balance has been particularly painful and violent because it has involved the clash of three powerful forces: nationalism, communism, and imperialism. Alone, any one of them would have proved troublesome. In combination they have been explosive. The replacement of the European colonial empires by a collection of rabidly nationalistic new states would in itself have been enough to strain the most stable political order. Inflamed by the nationalism that has nearly destroyed Europe twice since 1914 and which seems to be the lot of all new states, as well as of ambitious older ones, the nations of Asia have also had the misfortune to be swept into the cold war. The communist powers, led by Russia and more recently by China, have tried—although so far with little success—to induce the new states, by both persuasion and subversion, to convert to their secular religion. The anti-communist powers, led by the United States, have tried to ensure the membership of these new nations in what is called the "free world." The result has been a competition for influence that has raged throughout Asia and has turned Korea and Vietnam into battlegrounds. Caught between communist penetration and American military intervention, these states have had the misfortune to be on the firing-line of the cold war.

To add a third element to their tragedy, they are plagued by something older than communism or nationalism: the imperialism of powerful nations toward weaker neighbors. This imperialism has taken many forms, from Indonesia's "confrontation" of Malaysia to India's domination of Kashmir to China's recapture of Tibet. But imperialism, like nationalism, is one of the prices the new nations have had to pay for casting off colonialism. As colonies they were protected by their European overseers, until Japan swept these away during the Second World War. Now, with the retreat of Japan and the achievement of their own independence, the nations of Asia find themselves facing the problem they had before the Europeans arrived, and long before America existed: how to guard against the imperialism of their neighbors.

Thus communism, while it is *an* Asian problem, is not the only one, and not even the most important one. Asian governments which have the support of their own people have shown a heartening immunity to communist subversion. Even those in an exceedingly vulnerable position, such as Cambodia, Burma, and Nepal, have shown an ability to retain their independence and to resist communist penetration by maintaining strict neutrality in the cold war. Communism has been an American preoccupation—indeed, even an obsession. But to the nations of Asia it is only one of the problems they must face in working out a new balance between East and West, between individualism and collectivism, between America and China.

The new balance in Asia, therefore, cannot be built upon the simplistic equation of communism versus anti-communism that has been the foundation of American cold-war diplomacy. It can be achieved only by addressing ourselves to the realities of an Asia in which nationalism and resistance to foreign imperialism are more important than the ideology of communism. Indeed, it is possible that other nations of Asia may eventually embrace some form of communism, no matter what we do. An Asian balance requires the containment of aggressive threat, from whatever source it comes. Today the threat is China. Tomorrow it may be Indonesia or perhaps even India. These nations may be communist, they may be fascist, or they may be somewhere in between. But chances are that they will probably be authoritarian, paying allegiance to democracy by pronouncement rather than by practice. If we are looking for democratic governments to defend against Chinese totalitarianism, we may have an even harder time finding them in tomorrow's Asia than we do in today's. And we are already having trouble enough.

Judging from the record, the prognosis for either democracy or stability in Asia is not very promising. With the notable exceptions of India and Japan, the major governments of the continent are authoritarian to one degree or another, ranging from the benevolent monarchy of Cambodia to the harsh totalitarianism of China. This does not mean that many of these governments do not enjoy a considerable degree of popular support, but rather that democracy as we understand it in the West has not taken root. It may not do so for a good many decades to come—if ever. Nor have we any reason to expect tranquillity in the area, even if China can be persuaded that it is dangerous to rock the international boat too much. The equilibrium of power which now seems to have been, at least temporarily, reached in Europe has not even begun to show itself in Asia. The undeclared wars between India and Pakistan, China and India, Indonesia and Malaysia, may be only a preview of the troubles that lie ahead.

Most populous of the non-communist nations of Asia and the leading recipient of American aid is India. More a geographical expression than a nation, India is a place of residence for people with a dazzling diversity of religions, races, and languages. In many cases these people have little in common other than that they were once conquered by the Moguls and later ruled by the British. These tribes, which have been at war with one another for centuries, form not a common civilization, like the peoples of China, but a mosaic which has never been put together into a coherent pattern. India itself, as we know it today, does not conform to any historic boundaries but is the accidental product of the disintegration of the British Empire in 1947. Rather than moving to independence as a unified state, British India was split apart by the inability of Hindus and Moslems to agree and by the collapse of British power on the subcontinent. Unable or unwilling to hold on until a compromise was reached—if, indeed, one was possible once religious passions had been inflamed—the British partitioned India and transferred power to the nationalist leaders within the incredibly short period of two months. "India," in the words of Lord Ismay, one of those responsible for carrying out the transfer, "was like a burning ship in midocean, with fire on its deck and ammunition in its holds." From this panic the nations of India and Pakistan were born.

Since the trauma of that separation, the two nations have been at swords' points not only because of their past, but over the status of Kashmir, which lies divided between them like a parody of the Indian subcontinent in miniature. Pakistan, originally embraced by the United States as a bulwark against communism as well as against Indian "neutralism," has, with the help of $3.5 billion in American military and economic aid, made considerable progress in coping with the needs of her 100 million people. Although she is geographically split in two by India, and has no appreciable natural resources, Pakistan, as a result of hard work and intelligent leadership, is approaching the point where her economy may be self-sustaining. In their foreign policy the Pakistanis moved away from their former tight embrace with the United States when they discovered that Washington had no intention of lining up with them against India, and have shown a remarkable ability simultaneously to balance off Russia, China, and America, while maintaining friendships with each, and to forge new links with the Afro-Asian states.

India is a land of infinite promise and spotty fulfillment, a land of nuclear reactors and advanced technology, together with sacred cows and people still deemed "untouchable." Despite an intelligent civil service, an industrial superstructure, and an extraordinarily patient population, India has had enormous difficulty in meeting her grave social problems. Although she receives more money in foreign aid than any other nation, including $6 billion from the United States, not to mention help from Western Europe, Russia, and Japan, plus a variety of UN technical-assistance programs, India has not been able to industrialize fast enough to become economically self-sufficient. Her galloping population, already at 525 million and increasing at the rate of 15 million a year, devours her economic gains and leaves little for capital accumulation. India is also torn between Socialist reformers like Madame Gandhi and arch-conservatives intent on retaining ancient privileges. One day India will be a great power, but for the time being she is consumed by internal troubles. She cannot, and should not, be distracted by efforts to play a major role on the world stage.

Indonesia, the third of the large nations of Asia, is no better equipped at the present moment to contain China than is India. One day Indonesia may be a great power, for her natural resources are extraordinarily rich and her people gifted. But the flamboyant exhibitionism of the Sukarno era has taken a heavy toll of the Indonesian economy, the carnage that followed the destruction of the Indonesian Communist Party has left a heritage of bitterness that may yet lead to a new round of retribution, and the internal problems of society are so great that it will be some time before Indonesia is ready to play a major role in Asian affairs. By the time China is a real threat to the security of her neighbors— if she should turn out to be so—Indonesia may serve as a powerful barrier to the south. For the time being, however, she is absorbed, and rightly so, in the recuperation from Sukarnoism and the problems of her own economic development.

India, Pakistan, Indonesia: democracy dubious, stability uncertain among the major competitors of China. Yet one more remains, a nation so pacific she is often forgotten, so prosperous she is scarcely considered Asian at all: Japan, the bloodthirsty demon of the Second World War, the scourge of Asia, "the only enemy of the peaceful peoples whose shores overlook the Pacific Ocean," in Ambassador Grew's memorable words of 1942. Another time, another world. Japan, once our sworn enemy, is now our faithful ally in the struggle against China—which was lately our faithful ally and is now our sworn enemy.

Perhaps Japan alone will remain democratic and capitalistic in Asia, alone demonstrating that political tyranny need not be the price of industrial progress and political justice. Perhaps it is Japan which will be able to exert a positive influence on China, on India, and on the smaller states of Asia, leading them to some more hopeful middle ground between anarchy and despotism.

We had best hope that Japan will do so, for if she does not, Asia's future may be even stormier. Already the world's third industrial power, Japan is an economic giant whose political, and even military, power will be felt increasingly. Dependent on foreign trade and access to the markets of the industrialized nations, Japan could suffer a severe shock if those markets were diminished by higher tariffs or a world recession. Then she might once again be tempted to an expansionist policy. Having urged Japan to rearm and assume her Asian "responsibilities," the United States may yet come to fear an aroused, and perhaps nuclear-armed, Japan. The prognosis is optimistic, but a wise diplomacy hedges its bets on the future.

As an American protectorate, Japan has been endowed with a democratic government for the first time in her history, and, with her usual genius for adaptation, has made it work remarkably well. She has been restored to a place of honor in the world, her culture is admired, her people are respected, and her industrial products are sought everywhere. This has been a triumph both for the United States, which has done so much to guide a reformed Japan back into the community of nations, and for Japan herself, which has shown an extraordinary ability to shed her old skin and to achieve a political maturity which a good many Western nations might well emulate. But Japan's honorary incorporation into the West has not necessarily been a good thing for Asia, where her example and her·influence are sorely needed.

Japan's isolation from the rest of Asia, understandable in the early postwar period, has lasted unduly long. This is partly the result of American policy, which has prevented Japan from establishing closer ties with the Asian mainland, and which institutionalized her military dependency through the mutual defense treaty of 1960—a treaty that resulted in such an eruption of anti-American feeling that President Eisenhower was forced to cancel his scheduled visit. This isolation is also the result of a Japanese reluctance to play power politics once again after the tragedy of her last attempt. It is a reaction with which all Japan's friends can sympathize, but it is not one that should be maintained much longer, either for Japan's sake or for Asia's.

Japan has a very close and special relationship with the United States, resulting from an occupation that was transformed into a friendship. Yet the United States cannot be both father and mother to Japan; she cannot be a substitute for the Asia to which Japan belongs both geographically and culturally. Nor should she try to be. The Japanese are now beginning to stir with the desire for closer ties with the Asian mainland, and particularly with China. This desire is not simply part of their "guilt complex" toward China, nor can it be explained by cultural ties or a desire for increased trade. Beyond all this there is, as George Kennan has explained, "a perfectly natural desire among the Japanese to escape at least partially from the cloying exclusiveness of the American tie, from the helpless passivity it seems to imply, from the overtones of 'anything you can do we can do better,' which so often accompanies American friendship, and to throw open a sector of the international horizon where Japan could have a set of relationships and an importance of her own, not dependent on American tutelage, perhaps—who knows?—even helpful, ultimately, to the

United States in an area where we seem to have difficulty help-ing ourselves." [1] It is a possibility that may not have occurred to us, but which is well worth pondering.

A new Asian balance thus must ultimately rest on the ability of the Asians themselves to create and sustain it. It cannot be a bal-ance of the communist states against the anti-communist states because this is not an issue which interests the Asians or which they consider their own. The attempt of outside powers to create such a balance in Asia has broken down more than once. As Viet-nam has shown, it leads to foreign interventions which dev-astate the country involved, play into the hands of the Chinese, and threaten to ignite a clash between America and Russia. The failure to enlist Asia in an anti-communist crusade with the United States against China, despite twenty years of impassioned and costly effort, indicates that firmer ground will have to be sought. That ground can only be Asian nationalism, whatever its political tint.

The long-term containment of China can be accomplished only in Asia and by Asians—as President Nixon declared at Guam. For some time the United States—preferably in cooperation with Russia—will have to stand by as the guarantor of an Asian military balance. We clearly have an interest in dissuading overt military aggression by one Asian nation against another. We must not, how-ever, allow ourselves to interfere in internal Asian affairs, such as insurrections and civil wars, for these are beyond our interests and beyond our competence to resolve.

Insofar as she plays a role in Asia, the United States does so as a power bordering on the Pacific, not as a Western power defend-ing common Western interests. Our European allies, having never felt our particular attachment to China, or our current revulsion against her, are not going to help us build a wall around China. They do not even share our assumptions about China's aggres-sive intentions. As Konrad Adenauer once said, speaking candidly for many Europeans, "If we had our hands free politically, we would have recognized the Chinese People's Republic long ago." [2] For the Europeans, China was always a market to be exploited, through the opium trade, territorial enclaves, and economic treaties forced on the hapless emperors. Now that she has ceased to be exploitable in the old way, Europe is shopping around for more normal ways of doing business with China. The fact that China is today governed by a communist despotism is of little interest to the Europeans. They are used to dealing with despotisms and they have come to take for granted the communist regimes in Europe itself. That there is another one halfway around the world does not particularly alarm them.

Nor are the Europeans overly concerned by the threat that China, reverting to her old imperial habits, may pose to Southeast Asia. When they lost their Asian colonies, they also lost most of their investments. The relatively small amount of trade they carry on in the area today is unlikely to be affected much by politics one way or the other. The Dutch, having lost their billion-dollar oil investments in Indonesia, and the French, having watched the Americans take their place in South Vietnam, cannot be expected to come thumping down on Washington's side now that the American presence in Southeast Asia is in danger. Except for Britain, with her shopping center at Hong Kong and her military outpost in Malaysia, the Europeans are largely indifferent to Chinese hegemony in Asia. The more prosperous China becomes, the better customer she will be for European wares. America's effort to arouse her allies to a crusade against communist China has been a failure, not because the Europeans are naïve or because they want to spite the United States, but because they see the world differently. Their stake in the tranquillity of Southeast Asia went out the window with the loss of their colonies. The containment of China is not their problem. They have about as much interest in containing China as the young American republic had in containing the European ambitions of Napoleonic France.

The Europeans are, on the other hand, becoming aware of a peculiar community of interests with the Chinese—a community of interests that centers around the containment of Russia. For the Europeans, the major threat to their security comes not from China, which is too distant to cause them any harm, but from an imperialist Russia on their doorstep. The Chinese, by the same token, have no quarrel with Europe, now that the colonies have been mostly shut down and the enclaves are but a memory. They do, however, have a running grievance with Russia, the giant with whom they share a frontier running for thousands of miles across the steppes of Asia. Two imperial powers facing each other before a disputed border, China and Russia are natural adversaries. By forcing Russia to guard her eastern frontiers, thereby reducing Russian pressure in the West, China inadvertently serves European interests. So long as Russia poses a danger to her western neighbors, China will be Europe's natural ally. To expect the Europeans to be hostile to China because Washington is shows a profound misunderstanding of Europe's own interests.

The European allies have too much sense to say so directly, but they have already made it obvious that they have no great stake in Chinese expansion and no vital interests in Asia. Nor can the burden be carried by such client states as South Korea, Formosa, South Vietnam, and Thailand. With the single exception of Thailand, these nations are artificial products of the cold war, and their independence depends almost entirely on the willingness of the United States to defend them.

If neither our European allies nor our weaker Asian clients can help us contain China, who is left? Most obviously there is Russia; Russia, which sits nervously on Central Asian lands seized by the Czars in the last century; Russia, which is the inheritor of the traditions of Catherine the Great and also of Lenin and Stalin; Russia, which fears that leadership of world communism will pass from her cautious hands into those of a revolutionary China. Given their growing fear of China, it is likely that the Russians, despite their ritual propaganda, are actually pleased by an American military presence in Asia, for they know it is directed against the Chinese and not against themselves. Without this American-backed counterbalance in Asia, Russia might be left alone face to face with an expansive China. It is this fear which has no doubt inspired the Russians to build up India and to seek the friendship of Japan. An essentially European power possessed of enormous and sparsely populated Asian territories, Russia is almost certainly doomed to a long conflict with China over the vast frontier they share, and on which Peking has already staked its claim.

Will Russia, then, become the new ally of America in the containment of China? There are already signs, in Vietnam and in the India-Pakistan war, that such an alliance of convenience may be taking place. The striking parallelism between American and Soviet interests in Asia will likely lead to an even greater cooperation. But, considering the sudden shifts our foreign policy is prone to—comradeship with Russia in the middle 1940s, bitter enmity by the late 1940s and throughout the 1950s, and now back toward cooperation—we would do well not to exaggerate this parallelism. We must maintain and expand our détente with Russia. But its purpose should not be a joint holy war against China, as some have suggested (many of them the same people who ten years ago were preaching a holy war against Russia), but rather an attempt to restrain China so that an accommodation may be reached peacefully, just as one is now being worked out between Russia and the West.

While we need Russia's help in the effort to restrain China— help that was dramatically tendered during the India–Pakistan war—we should resist the temptation to take Russia's side in the great quarrel now shaking the communist world. Moscow would naturally like us to view Peking as the scourge of the universe, eager to plunge the world into nuclear holocaust. There is perhaps some truth in this, but we would be unwise to take Russia's word for it. Simply because Moscow now finds it convenient to seek Western support in its feud with China does not mean that such support should be automatically given. Russia has changed enormously in the past decade, and there are places where her interests converge with those of the West. But her motives are not pure and her conversion to peaceful coexistence is too recent for us to look on her with anything less than a healthy suspicion.

Russia has an ideological as well as a national interest in isolating China. The more power she is able to assert against China, the more she will be able to secure her own hegemony within the communist camp and thus dominate the smaller communist nations. The so-called "Togliattism" under which national communist parties enjoy a growing degree of independence from Moscow is at least in part a result of the Sino-Soviet dispute. The new cold war between Moscow and Peking has given such nations as Rumania and Hungary a freedom of maneuver they might not enjoy if they had to depend solely on Russian generosity. It is no accident that the small communist nations have tried to avoid choosing sides in the great dispute. They know that the longer Russia and China are at odds, the more freedom they will have to pursue their own interests. They enjoy being wooed, and they fear that they may be the first to suffer if Moscow regains undisputed hegemony within the communist world.

The West can have no interest in serving Russia's desire for ideological conformity, nor need it take her side in the territorial dispute with China. Whatever government sits in Peking, the Russians are going to have to look to their defenses where China is concerned. And it is in our interest to keep them looking there. The more the Russians are worried about China, the less of a menace they will be to Europe, the greater will be the disarray within the communist camp, and the more amenable they will be to compromise with the West. Although the Sino-Soviet split has been an established fact since 1960, until lately there has been little interest in Washington in exploiting the shattering of unity. If anything, our policies—bitter hostility toward China and the intervention in Vietnam—may have had the effect of postponing an even sharper break. It is questionable whether the Sino–Soviet alliance would have lasted as long as it did if Washington had given Peking an alternative to its ties with Moscow.

Instead of playing Russia's game where China is concerned, the United States has an opportunity to encourage the Chinese to detach themselves from Russia and to give them a reason for taking a less provocative attitude toward the West and toward their neighbors. This road lies in establishing some kind of diplomatic and economic communication with China. Ever since the Russians struck China from their foreign-aid list in 1960 for political disobedience, the Chinese have been almost entirely dependent on their own efforts to meet their staggering economic problems. What they have done is remarkable; what they have left to do virtually defies the imagination.

If China is forced to feed 700 million people, while simultaneously trying to build a modern industrial state—all by her own efforts—she may be tempted to turn to foreign aggression to relieve mass hunger, if for no other reason. Is it to the interests of the West to drive China into a situation of such desperation? Is it not more politic, as well as more humane, to offer China a stake in cooperation with the West, a stake which would cost us nothing and might win a great deal? We have tried to intimidate China with our nuclear weapons, and we have failed. We have tried to contain her by building a rim of anti-communist states around her southern frontiers, and it has collapsed. We have practiced a policy of uncompromising hostility, and it has only brought us more hostility in return. It may be that China would be totally unreceptive to an American initiative. Peking almost certainly does not want to exchange ambassadors with us at the present time, and may find it advantageous to keep us as an enemy. But it is at least worth finding out, and if we fail, the onus will be on the Chinese and not on us. It is a hopeful sign that the Nixon administration has now begun to explore paths toward more normal relations with China and in 1970 reopened the ambassadorial discussions in Warsaw.

American businessmen are now openly speaking of the advantages of restoring trade with China in non-strategic goods. Some observers would even go beyond trade to economic aid. "Communist China today," Harry Schwartz has written,

is the only important underdeveloped country receiving no economic aid from any source. Might it not be worthwhile to explore what easing of political tensions with China we might obtain by agreeing to normalize trade or even, if Peking is willing to pay the price, to extend economic aid? Those who share the Soviet-painted image of a China ruled by madmen hell-bent for war will dismiss such ideas immediately. Those who have watched the careful and clever way in which China has mended its relations with Ceylon, Burma, Nepal, and Pakistan may feel more charitably inclined toward such explorations. . . . If we now view China as a national state serving its national interests rather than as a part of an implacable conspiracy dedicated solely to our extermination, the possibility of accommodation for mutual advantage cannot be excluded. We have already granted such possibility in the case of the Soviet Union. Why must China be regarded as so much more evil than its former partner and ally?[3]

This is not to say that aid, or even trade, is any panacea. Aid does not buy friends, or even stability. But trade is another matter. Our European allies are trading with China in a wide range of non-strategic items. This means that our present embargo on all trade is symbolic and serves little purpose other than self-delusion. We should be willing to carry on the same normal trade relations in non-strategic items with the Chinese that we conduct with the Russians. Maybe the Chinese will not want to trade with us. But it is worth keeping the door open so that we can offer some hope to China other than total isolation.

The goals of our policy toward China should be no different from those of our policy toward Russia: to break down accumulated hostility, to separate emotion-laden rhetoric from our real national interests, and to probe continually for areas of mutual agreement. This means maintaining a scrupulous neutrality in the Sino–Soviet quarrel, resisting the temptation to "final solutions" of our temporary frustrations, and viewing China with the same realism and understanding that we now apply to Russia. It should not, after all, be an American objective to drive China deeper into an isolation that breeds desperation, but rather to use all the political and economic means at our disposal to bring her back into the world community. The policy of military containment, as Professor Fairbank has written, is only half a policy. It tries to negate the use of force and subversion against other peoples, but it requires the holding out of feasible alternatives to aggression, and it must be balanced and accompanied by programs of peaceful intercourse, by non-containment. Mr. Dulles' prescription of military containment and economic-diplomatic isolation was a recipe for producing an eventual explosion.[4]

We cannot hope to establish a rapport with China overnight, perhaps not even within the next decade. The rancor is so deep on both sides, the interests are so at odds, that no single change in behavior can possibly provide a solution. Each finds in the other the mirror of its own anxieties. The Chinese distrust our motives and fear our actions. We fear their motives and do not believe their actions. It is a dialogue of the deaf. Even if the United States were immediately to withdraw from Southeast Asia, the Chinese would probably continue to find us a convenient whipping post. Even if China were to drop her claims to Taiwan and cease preaching world revolution, the United States would still feel a sense of betrayal because China is no longer our friend.

But there is a difference between recognizing that a certain degree of hostility will exist, and actually stimulating such hostility. The Chinese have stimulated it by trying to subvert their neighbors, as revolutionary powers feel obliged to do, and by preaching a virulent anti-Americanism. The United States, however, has given them some reason for this campaign of anti-Americanism by pursuing policies which the Chinese can reasonably interpret as deliberately hostile: keeping China out of the United Nations, denying her right to Taiwan, and surrounding her territory with military bases.

We may not sympathize with the desire of the Chinese communists to regain control of Taiwan. We may regret that we ever told the Chinese, then ruled by Chiang Kai-shek, that they should regain sovereignty over the island Japan seized from China at the turn of the century. We may feel that we have a moral obligation to Chiang, if not to the Taiwanese who live under the rule of his refugee army. But we can at least understand China's point of view by imagining how we would feel if, after our own Civil

War, General Lee had sought refuge in Puerto Rico and continually threatened to invade the mainland with the help of the British Navy. The analogy may be far-fetched, but it is not totally inapplicable.

This is not an argument for turning Taiwan over to Mao Tsetung or his successors. Rather, it is to say that we should try to extricate ourselves from the dregs of the Chinese civil war by recognizing that Taiwan is not China. It is not even a "second" China. It is an island off the coast of China, which may or may not belong to China, as its inhabitants—who have never been asked—may decide, if they are ever given the opportunity. But we can no longer afford to indulge ourselves in the myth that there are two Chinas, one of them *ours*, the other *theirs*. There is one China and there is one Taiwan. The choice is not ours to make, but only ours to accept.

We have assumed an obligation to the people of Taiwan that we cannot ignore. It is, however, an obligation, not to make them permanent prisoners of Chiang Kai-shek's exile army, but to allow them to choose what kind of government they want to live under. If the Taiwanese want to be independent, then they have every right to be so and deserve our support. If they want to join the mainland government of China, that too is their right, and we must respect it. But it is their decision. Let there be one China, including Taiwan. Or let there be one China and an independent Taiwan. But let the myth of two Chinas be buried once and for all.

And let the myth that Chiang is going to return to the mainland be buried with it. The communists control China and they are going to control China for a long time to come, no matter what we think about it. We can recognize China or not recognize China, and it won't make any difference as far as the authority of the communist government over the Chinese people is concerned. There is a case for recognizing Peking, since the communist government is here to stay. There is also a case for not recognizing it, since its leaders seem to have little, if any, interest at the moment in exchanging ambassadors with the United States. But we have no right to continue blocking its admission to the United Nations, to keep a quarter of the world's population out of the supposed forum of mankind. "If the communist government of China in fact proves its ability to govern China without serious domestic resistance," one daring commentator wrote in 1950, "then it, too, should be admitted to the United Nations." [5] The author of those heretical lines was John Foster Dulles.

Our policy toward China has been a weird compound of hurt pride, fear, and incomprehension. We have not been able to come to terms with the reality of China's new place in the world because we are still in a state of trauma over the fact that China has a communist government. We cannot deal rationally with the problem China poses because we are too much prisoners of our own anxieties and misapprehensions. The Chinese, emerging from a century of humiliation and foreign domination, see themselves surrounded by enemies and have behaved accordingly. America, the most powerful nation the world has ever known, has trembled before the bluster of China's verbal aggressiveness without being able to sense her deep-seated insecurity. China, bordered on the north by a hostile Russia, rimmed from Japan to Pakistan by American military bases, her coastal waters controlled by the American Seventh Fleet, and her territory under continual surveillance by American planes, may have some reason to feel apprehensive. If she is afraid and takes out her fear in verbal belligerence, it should not be beyond our comprehension to understand why. Nor should it be an excuse to justify an obduracy and a narrowness of spirit on our own part. As the world's richest and most powerful nation, we can afford to meet China somewhat more than halfway. Perhaps the Chinese will reject our overtures; perhaps they will reject them for a long time to come. But we have nothing to lose by making the first step, and perhaps a great deal to gain by breaking down the barrier of hostility and misunderstanding that may yet lead both our countries into a tragic and wholly unnecessary conflict.

Asia is in turmoil, and China is seeking the redress of her former humiliations at the hands of the West. The attempt to contain China without provoking or unnecessarily appeasing her will be a long and agonizing process. It will require the greatest restraint and the highest discrimination. The United States has an important role to play in this effort to contain China. But the major role can be played only by the Asian powers themselves, as they strive to work out a new balance in which China may take her rightful place as a great power among other nations, not dominating, but not being dominated. This is a task that demands compromise, patience, tolerance, and, perhaps above all, modesty—modesty in letting others forge their own destiny, and modesty in accepting the diversity of a world that does not care for our solutions.

This is a challenge we have not met noticeably well on the distant shores of Asia, and one which is now confronting us much closer to home in the turbulence of Latin America.

10. Pan-American Illusions

The United States appear to be destined by Providence to plague America with misery in the name of liberty.

—SIMÓN BOLÍVAR

❦ ❦ ❦ THERE was a time, and not very long ago at that, when Latin America was considered to be a kind of rest home for tired American diplomats. It was a place where nothing of much importance ever happened, where friendly natives and a colorful folklore were the only compensations for a life of stultifying political boredom. While there were, to be sure, the usual quota of military *golpos* and peasant uprisings, nobody in Washington—or anywhere else, for that matter—took them very seriously. The Latin American revolutionary, with his smoking pistols and twirling mustaches, was a kind of joke, better material, it was thought, for Hollywood than for the State Department. For a diplomat to be assigned to Latin America was to go into a political purgatory from which he might never again emerge into the real world.

It was not that Washington didn't care about Latin America, but rather that there seemed no reason to take it seriously. The Second World War had plunged the United States deep into the affairs of Europe and Asia, and no sooner was that war over than the cold war with Russia had begun. There was no time to worry about Latin America while the United States was busy fighting communism in such places as Greece, Lebanon, and Korea. Just as it was the role of the United States to fight communism, so it was the role of Latin America to stand on the sidelines and cheer. Those who did so the loudest, such as dictators Batista in Cuba and Pérez Jiménez in Venezuela, were rewarded with medals for themselves and military equipment for their armies. To say that Latin America was taken for granted is to say that it was carrying out the role it was supposed to play.

What a shock, then, to have the students of Caracas spit, hoot, and throw rocks at Vice-President Nixon in 1958—a preview of the treatment other United States politicians were to receive on their rare goodwill trips to our sister republics in the south. Why didn't somebody tell us the Latin Americans were angry at us? But the shock Nixon received in Venezuela was nothing compared to the shock all Americans suffered when Fidel Castro raised the banner of revolution in Latin America, shook his fist at Washington, and marched Cuba into the communist camp. For Americans it was a rude awakening from a long sleep. Fidel brought the cold war into the western hemisphere, and whatever else his revolution may have accomplished, it revolutionized Washington's attitude toward Latin America.

Suddenly money started flowing from the coffers of the Treasury, the Alliance for Progress was solemnly proclaimed and $20 billion pledged for development projects, crash programs were launched to teach Spanish to United States diplomats, Latin American research institutes sprang up at scores of universities, professors of Latin American studies were yanked from oblivion and called to Washington for consultation, bookshelves rapidly filled with analyses of the perplexing problems south of the border, and President Kennedy dutifully declared Latin America to be the most crucial area in the world today.

North Americans have become aware that something strange and even ominous is going on south of the border. The acquiescent little states of the Caribbean are brimming over with violence and an increasing resentment over Yankee dominance. On the continent of South America itself there is resistance to the United States and a determined effort to seek new outlets to the outside world: to the booming markets of Western Europe, to Japan, to the unaligned states of the Third World, and even to the communist countries. And underlying all, like distant claps of thunder approaching from over the horizon, is the prospect of revolution—not a revolution for political independence, for that was won more than a century ago, but a revolution for political equality and social justice. Like all revolutions, it threatens to overthrow the established order. And part of that order has been the United States, which dominates Latin America's politics just as it does the economy of the entire hemisphere. We thus find, a bit to our astonishment, that we are the target of a new nationalism in a Latin America that totters on the brink of revolution.

All this is unfamiliar and vaguely shocking to most North Americans because until lately we have thought of Latin America as part of a loose family of which the United States is the *paterfamilias*, or at least the elder brother. The vision of the nations of the two Americas as one big, though not necessarily happy, family is one of the most vigorous and enduring fables of United States diplomacy. It is a powerful fable, rooted in the common revolt against European colonialism, nourished by the ambiguities of the Monroe Doctrine, and perpetuated by the economic and political imbalance that has made the United States more powerful than all the Latin American nations combined. Rich and strong, with no rivals worthy of the name throughout the entire hemisphere, enjoying stability and democracy while the other nations were torn by violence and dictatorship, we developed a proprietary attitude toward Latin America that was more than just a little patronizing. We saw ourselves as the benevolent protector of a host of little brothers whom, if they would behave and not make excessive demands, we would instruct in the ways of democracy. The image has not, however, been one which either we or the Latin Americans have been able to live up to. "In our own century," as Louis Halle has observed,

we have striven to realize the legend of an inter-American community of nations distinguished from the rest of the world and bound together by a common New World ideology. But the Latin American nations, with a different cultural background, have not been able to live up to this legend. Our own attitude toward them, consequently, has been quixotic and unstable, varying back and

forth between an eager fraternalism, whenever the legend dominated our thinking, and an impatient or outraged paternalism whenever the reality has become too vivid for us.[1]

At the core of our complex, and often contradictory, attitude
toward Latin America lies the belief that our geographical loca-
tion in the same hemisphere creates special bonds between us.
These bonds, we believe, should be stronger and more important
than the bonds with nations in the "other" hemisphere. But, when
examined closely, this turns out to be a rule that is to apply only
to the Latin Americans. Like a pasha with many wives, we think
that *their* world should revolve around us, but we want to be
free to set up families elsewhere. We assume that their gaze should
be confined to the western hemisphere, but it goes without saying that ours should stretch across the oceans, embracing Europe,
Asia, and even Africa. We feel sentimental about our "inter-
American family," but that feeling doesn't prevent us from pledging allegiance to the "Atlantic community" or from taking over
the role of policeman in Asia. In practice, the fable of the pan-
American family turns out to be a very flexible one. But it is no
less strong on that account, and it dominates our thinking about
Latin America.

We see ourselves as members of one big family partly because
we are all located in the same hemisphere, and partly because we
all at one time or another won our freedom from European colonial powers. These common experiences are a good beginning
for brotherhood, but are they enough? They certainly have not
been enough in Asia, where India and Pakistan have been at each
other's throats ever since they gained independence, even though
they both share the same subcontinent and were lately colonies
in the British Empire. Nor have they been enough in Africa,
where such nations as Ghana and Nigeria, the two Congos, Mo-
rocco and Algeria, are barely on speaking terms, although they too
share a common geographical and colonial heritage. Proximity and
ex-colonialism have not been conducive to brotherhood outside the
western hemisphere, and not even among the Latin American na-

tions themselves. Is it a very serious bond between the United States and her Latin American neighbors?

One of the problems is that even in a geographic sense we are not really neighbors with most of South America. New York is closer to Paris than it is to Lima; closer to Athens than to Buenos Aires. Seattle is nearer to Tokyo than it is to Santiago. Geographically, most of South America might as well be in another hemisphere, which indeed it is. And since it is in the southern hemisphere, its crops, its culture, and even its temperament are different from ours. The United States, although a melting pot, has managed to stamp upon peoples of every kind the same Anglo-Saxon mold, whatever their color, religion, or national origins. Latin America, however, is what its name implies: it is Latin. Its European culture came not from the rainy, Calvinistic lands of the north, but from the hot, Catholic countries of the south. Rather than being dedicated to work and progress, it is preoccupied with sin and redemption. This cultural gap was captured by the Mexican poet Octavio Paz when he wrote: "The North American considers the world something that can be perfected . . . we consider it something that can be redeemed."

Racially as well as culturally, Latin America is different from the United States. Only four nations—Uruguay, Costa Rica, Chile, and Argentina—are predominantly European in origin. The others are all multiracial societies, ranging from the Negro-white *mélange* of Brazil to the Hispano-Indian fusion of Mexico to predominantly Indian Bolivia and to almost totally Negro Haiti. These countries feel little enough affinity with one another. What they feel toward the United States, with her white Anglo-Saxon Protestant image and her WASP prejudices, may be a good deal less brotherly than we imagine. While our society is a multiracial one, its whole texture, tone, and problems are different from theirs, just as theirs are different from one another's.

Culturally the two Americas, North and South, could hardly be more different. The United States, like Canada, was originally settled by Anglo-Saxon immigrants who brought with them a Calvinistic religion that preached salvation through work (and work itself as a kind of salvation), an ingrained sense of guilt about the pleasures of the flesh, a social ethic that recognized human and political equality even when it did not always practice it, and a political orientation resistant to autocratic rule. The nations of Latin America, on the other hand, were founded not by those who sought haven from political or religious oppression, but by soldiers in arms and soldiers of fortune. They are products not of the age of enlightenment but of the age of discovery, and of Iberia's obsession with gold as a source of easy national riches, the obsession which ultimately destroyed the empires of Spain and Portugal and reduced those countries to a torpor from which they have not fully recovered to this day. The settlers of Latin America were not pilgrims but *conquistadores*, who ransacked the continent for riches, destroyed the great Indian civilizations, and imposed their political feudalism on the societies they conquered. To the virgin territories of the New World, these armies brought the social structure of seventeenth-century Iberia: the *auto-da-fé* rather than Newtonian skepticism, the hacienda rather than the mill, the slave system rather than the Rights of Man.

When the Latin American nations were later settled by a more permanent type of colonist, they were exposed not only to some of the glories of southern European culture and manners, but also to some of the burdens under which the mother countries of Spain and Portugal themselves labored. From the very beginning of their existence as nations they had to contend with a feudal social order supported by a powerful Catholic Church, with a priesthood still caught in the grip of a Counter-Reformation that stifled independent thought, and with a hacienda system of land ownership which enriched the few through the suffering of the many. In addition, they suffered from a concentration on mineral wealth at the expense of agriculture, a political tradition that preached acquiescence and inequality, and a provincial ruling class closed to the ideas and forces that were remaking northern Europe during the age of enlightenment.

Beyond the infirmities they inherited, the Latin Americans had to try to build a political tradition from scratch. Unlike the

United States, which used the arguments of the British political philosophers to justify her independence from the crown, the nations of Latin America did not so much win their freedom as have it thrust upon them. While their history books relate the heroism of brave and stalwart patriots, the fact nonetheless remains that there was never anything approaching a mass or popularly supported uprising against colonial rule. The revolutions were to come later, after independence was gained, and they were to be social rather than political in inspiration. Whereas the young United States already possessed a sense of national identity by the time she revolted against Britain for her independence, the states of Latin America became independent because Spain was weakened by the armies of Napoleon.

Thus independence was more of a historical accident than an act of rebellion for equality or social freedom. This is not to denigrate the heroism of Latin American patriots but simply to put their struggle into perspective. The rich landowners did not defy the Spanish (or Portuguese) crown from a burning desire for liberty so much as from a burning determination to retain their feudal privileges. The armies they recruited to throw off colonial rule stayed on to impose a new tyranny on the hapless Indians and the politically impotent settlers. Independence did not shatter the old feudal order; it merely perpetuated it under a different label. Uninterested in democracy and hostile to any system that would weaken their privileges, the landowners ruled through a succession of figureheads and *caudillos*. Today the same families live on, four hundred years after the colonial conquest, to control many of the governments of Latin America—the oldest surviving political Establishment in the Western world.

Latin America may have been a child of Europe, but of a Europe already dying and reduced to a few crumbling redoubts in Iberia. The United States, on the other hand, was the child of the new age of reason that was sweeping the north of Europe. She was born skeptical of natural law and defiant of authority. Blessed by fortune, geography, and a power struggle in Europe that kept Britain tied down on the Continent, the young American republic began as a new society which deliberately sought to break with everything it found oppressive in imperial Europe. The North Americans were able to build this new society without the problem of assimilating the Indians (whom they nearly exterminated and then herded into reservations), without the chains of a feudal social order, and without the restrictions of a politically reactionary landed aristocracy. They drew upon the wealth of the world's richest continent, sold their agricultural and mineral resources to an eager European market, and built up their economy through massive European loans and investments—the nineteenth-century version of foreign aid. America came into being just in time to pluck the fruits of the Industrial Revolution, and just late enough to avoid some of its worst excesses.

The Latin Americans were not so fortunate. In addition to the man-made difficulties they inherited from their mother countries, there were the problems they inherited from a continent that had often been cruelly used by nature, a continent with only a fraction of the arable land enjoyed by North America, cut down one side by a mountain wall, much of its land covered with jungle and swamp, and so unfortunately shaped that its bulk is in the torrid zone of the equator and its narrowest parts are in the temperate zones. South America is a continent where most of the land is either too dry or too wet, where the temperature is either too hot or too cold, and where nature forms nearly impassable jungle and mountain barriers. To add to these natural difficulties, Latin America has been split up into a collection of sovereign states, most of them cut off from one another by nature as well as by culture and instinct. The size of these barriers can be seen through one statistic: only a handful of countries in Latin America carry on more than 10 per cent of their trade with their neighbors; the bulk of trade is with the United States and, to a lesser degree, Western Europe. To this day it is easier for Ecuador to ship goods to New York than to Bolivia, for Argentina to ship to Italy than overland to Peru.

With this heritage imposed upon them, it is not surprising that the peoples of Latin America have had such difficulty in building viable economies and democratic governments. Too often democracy has been a slogan rather than an object of action, and in its name oligarchies and military juntas have enjoyed unlimited authority. Liberty is in the heart and on the tongue of every Latin American—not, however, because it is an achieved fact but because in many places it is still little more than an ideal. The rich vocabulary of Latin America's preoccupation with democracy has tended to obscure the realities of a more ancient tyranny. Between the dream of Latin American liberty and the reality of a political and social oppression still predominant in the continent lies the abyss of ideals betrayed and goals unachieved. Beneath the fervor and idealism of so many Latin Americans lies a skepticism and even a despair that has defeated so many attempts at reform. It is a skepticism that can be traced back to Simón Bolívar and his famous statement that "treaties are pieces of paper, constitutions are books, elections are fights, liberty is anarchy, and life a torment." This is a profoundly Latin declaration. But where this kind of nihilism combines with an equally fervent idealism, there are bound to be conflicts which the pragmatic northern mind can understand with difficulty, if at all. Nor is it easy for the Latin American to bring together the vision of his ideals with the crassness of reality.

Thus it is not uncommon for the Latin American reformer to engage in a verbal extravagance that reveals his own emotional ambivalence. He damns the United States for her power and materialism, while damning himself for envying her success. He preaches revolution at home to sweep away intolerable injustices, yet shrinks from the violent consequences of such a revolution. Even the vocabulary of revolution is a qualified one, for such reformers do not want to destroy the past so much as to recapture the values of a civilization which an oppressive social order has perverted. Between the hierarchical world of the past and the tempestuous industrial world of the present, the Latin American feels an undefinable tension and ambiguity.

Latin Americans are torn within themselves as to what kind of societies they want to achieve. They demand radical change and declare the present situation to be intolerable. Yet they have not been able to work together to pursue such change, or to form a consensus that would make it possible, or even to be sure that the changes they want are likely to be achieved by the methods they have chosen. Latin America is on the verge of a political explosion, one which so far, at any rate, promises to be without direction and often even without any clear sense of purpose. This is an explosion meant to create, but which has been pent up for so long that it is likely to destroy a good deal before it can begin to rebuild. There is so much to be swept away, so little to build on, so many who stand in the way of change, and so few who are capable of leading what are in fact sick societies. A continent rich in human and material resources, and infinite in its possibilities, Latin America is caught in the grip of a deep social malaise.

The ambivalent motives of Latin American reformers are reflected in actions that are often hesitant, in policies that are contorted, and in pronouncements burdened with defeatism. Wanting the best of both worlds, the reformers frequently end up with much of the worst: the rigid feudalism of their hierarchical societies without its dignity and grace; the destructive ugliness of the industrial world without its economic compensations. In such a world the anger of the intellectual is joined to the cynicism of the slum-dweller and the despair of the peasant. Yet without a clear sense of purpose, the forces which could bring about desperately needed changes tend to be dissipated. In much of Latin America there is a political impasse among Left, Right, and Center that borders on paralysis.

Whatever their political orientation, the Latin Americans are fiercely nationalistic, and nowhere more so than among the reformers of the middle class. Like the aspiring elites in other nations of the Third World, many of whose economic and social problems they share, articulate Latin Americans tend to seek refuge in chauvinism, to condemn the foreigner for everything that is wrong at home, and to take offense where none is intended.

Hypersensitive to the slightest criticism—perhaps because they are so aware of their failure to achieve their own national potentials—they are engaged in a constant quest for scapegoats. Further, they are plagued by an envy of others that takes the form of a burning resentment.

In Latin America these emotions are usually directed toward the United States, for it is the colossus of the North that dominates the economies and pervades every aspect of political life. Feelings toward the United States are complex, ambivalent, and often conflicting. Latin Americans envy us our wealth, our power, and the openness of our society. They resent us for having achieved so much of what is still unattainable to them. They begrudge us the position we hold as autocrat of the western hemisphere. And they fear us for the way our power has been used against them in the past and may again be used in the future. For the states of the Caribbean, that power means military occupation by the Marines; for the larger nations of South America, it means economic power exerted through American corporations and political power exerted by the United States government. We dominate Latin America in a way that few North Americans realize. "With respect to the peoples of South America," de Tocqueville wrote more than a century ago, "Americans of the United States find themselves in exactly the same position as their English fathers with regard to the Italians, the Spaniards, the Portuguese, and all the peoples of Europe who, being less advanced in civilization and industry, receive from them most of their consumer goods." [2]

In addition to this great economic power we wield over our Latin neighbors—which is greater than that Britain exerted over the poorer nations of the Continent in the nineteenth century—there is the enormous military superiority of the United States. Behind the pieties of the "good neighbor" policy and the idealism of such programs as the Alliance for Progress, they have seen—and often felt—the raw boot and the unsheathed bayonet of American military power. It is a power which, despite all the solemn vows of nonintervention subscribed to in the charter of the

Organization of American States, we have applied against them twice within this decade alone: in 1961 and again in 1965. It matters little that we have done so for causes which we declared to be for their own good. In their eyes what is important is that no nation in Latin America is safe from United States intervention. To many Latin Americans the image of the United States is not that of a big brother who will protect them from the evil nations lurking outside the western hemisphere, but that of an imperial power ready to send the Marines whenever her good neighbors threaten to step out of line. From the days of the Monroe Doctrine the United States has roped off Latin America as a private domain in which she would not tolerate any interference, even by the Latin Americans themselves. It should not be surprising that the Latin Americans, who never wanted to be our little brothers in any case, should greet our embrace with something less than enthusiasm. "The often-used metaphor of an inter-American 'family,'" as one observer has written,

> permitted the United States to consider itself as big brother, rich uncle, or even head of the family. Historically, we asserted, under the Monroe Doctrine, the right and duty to protect the junior members of the family, and under the Theodore Roosevelt corollary, to chasten them as necessary. Such an attitude was perhaps accepted in the early years, but it became increasingly galling to junior members as the disparity of wealth and power widened, and as the United States grew more patronizing and assertive and the Latin Americans more sensitive of their lag. This sensitivity was aggravated by suspicions that—contradictory but mutually reinforcing— on the one hand that North American exploitation was to blame for the slower progress of the Latin peoples, and on the other that they themselves had failed, that perhaps in some way they *were* inferior to the *gringos*.[3]

All these powerful, if ambivalent, emotions of fear, envy, and resentment combine into a pervasive anti-Yankeeism that is lodged deep in the soul of many Latin Americans. It is the one common denominator of all the diverse societies from the Rio Grande to Cape Horn, and it runs through the entire social scale, from the peon at the bottom to the landowning aristocrat at the top. It is strongest of all among the middle-class reformers and intellectuals—the very group, ironically enough, in which Washington has placed such high hopes for peaceful change through the Alliance for Progress. An opposition to Yankee dominance is the cement that holds together—or at least the veneer that embellishes—virtually every Latin American political party, right, left, or center.

To dismiss this anti-Yankeeism as immature or mistaken is beside the point. Perhaps it is exaggerated, perhaps it is wrong. But it is real and it is powerful, and it is getting stronger all the time. It has nothing to do with communism, for it existed long before the Russian revolution and even before Karl Marx. It is not recent, for it can be traced all the way back to Bolívar. Rather, it is a home-grown American product which has flourished in the rich soil of misunderstanding between the two radically different continents of the western hemisphere. Anti-Yankeeism is rooted in the enormous disparity of power between the United States and the various-sized nations of Latin America, a disparity which the Latins have found humiliating and occasionally dangerous. It has been fed by the long history of United States military intervention in the Caribbean, an intervention which in the early decades of this century placed five nations under United States military occupation. And within the past few years it has been fanned into a passion by the landing at the Bay of Pigs and the occupation of Santo Domingo.

This policy of intervention began harmlessly enough with the declaration of the Monroe Doctrine in 1823. It was harmless because there was no way to apply it. In a splendid gesture the young United States peremptorily told the imperial powers of Europe to keep their hands off the western hemisphere, and in return the United States promised to refrain from interfering in European affairs. If the first part of the Doctrine was presumptuous, since the United States lacked the power to prevent the Europeans from returning to their American colonies if they were so inclined, the second part was sheer impertinence. For the United States of 1823 to promise to refrain from interfering in European affairs was as though Egypt today were to tell us that she would not interfere in American affairs if we kept out of Africa. As an expression of real power exercised by real nations, it was irrelevant. What gave the Monroe Doctrine its teeth was not official warnings from Washington, but British sea power operating to prevent the Continental nations from re-establishing their colonies. Even if the new states of Latin America were in danger from imperial Europe, the young American republic of 1823 was not in a position to do very much about it. The Monroe Doctrine—which has since become one of the most important, and most misunderstood, declarations of American foreign policy—was not much more than a bold gesture.

Nor was the exaggerated language of the Doctrine related to any legitimate security interest of the United States. While it swept up the entire western hemisphere in its embrace, it offered no convincing reason why the United States should take a proprietary interest in the affairs of the distant republics of South America. The largest nations of the southern continent, Brazil, Argentina, and Chile, are twice as far from the United States as Europe is, and not half so important. What happened in these nations—whether they were independent or whether they were tied to Europe as colonies—might be significant on some scale of political morality. In terms of the security of the United States, however, it was irrelevant.

Didn't President Monroe and his advisers know this? Of course they did. They did not intend the Doctrine to be taken at face value, and in fact they knew it would not be. For all its windy presumptuousness about hemispheric unity, the Monroe Doctrine was not meant to be taken literally. Rather, it was an expression of intent, a declaration that the United States wanted her interests to be taken into account in any European claim upon the Americas. Above all, it was designed to focus attention on the one area where United States security was involved and where the European powers were still active: the Caribbean. Stripped of its more sweeping presumptions, the Monroe Doctrine was essentially a Caribbean doctrine, affirming the vital interest of the

United States in the tranquillity of what it considered to be its inland sea.

Even cut down to size, the Monroe Doctrine remained little
more than a dusty and half-forgotten state paper throughout the
remainder of the nineteenth century. It had no effect whatsoever
on the island colonies that Britain, France, Spain, Holland, and
Denmark maintained from one end of the Caribbean to the other.
Nor was it of the slightest use at the single time it was seriously
challenged: when the French tried to recapture an empire in the
New World by sending Maximilian to claim the crown of Mon-
tezuma. Napoleon III's imperial efforts in Mexico collapsed ig-
nominiously, but if the Monroe Doctrine had anything to do with
this collapse, nobody was aware of it at the time. While it showed
the sympathy of the United States for her sister republics of the
hemisphere, and her concern for her own security interests in the
Caribbean, the Doctrine was not taken particularly seriously during the first six decades of its existence. Nor, whatever its care for
the territorial integrity of the republics to the south, did it prevent
an expansionist United States from seizing nearly half of Mexico's territory—an act of open imperialism which United States
history books gloss over, but which Latin Americans have never
forgotten.

It was not the Mexican war, however, which marked the turning-point in the relations between the United States and Latin
America, for the territory between the Rockies and the Pacific,
and including Texas, could, by a stretch of the imagination, be
considered a kind of no man's land. Rather, it was the new policy
of intervention that erupted so explosively in the war of 1898
against Spain. Intoxicated by the new spirit of Manifest Destiny,
convinced by Mahan's dictum that the United States must be supreme in the Caribbean, we launched a crusade to expel the
Spaniards from Cuba and Puerto Rico. Spain, whose authority was
already disintegrating, would be taught a lesson at relatively little
cost, and the United States would proclaim its role as defender of
the Americas. A war fever swept the nation. The press wanted

war, the Congress wanted war, and presumably even the public wanted war. Everybody wanted war except the Spaniards, who made things difficult by complying with most of the demands served upon them by Washington. They were not, however, to get away that easily. The USS *Maine* conveniently exploded in Havana harbor under mysterious circumstances, a *casus belli* was miraculously furnished, the Rough Riders swarmed across the straits into Cuba, and the last outposts of Spanish authority in the New World were duly snuffed out.

The Spanish-American war marked the translation of the rising sense of American power into the vocabulary of an American mission. If this was imperialism, it came swathed in the colors of a new morality. It was the age of Manifest Destiny, an era when the United States felt herself under the historical compulsion to spread the blessings of liberty to less fortunate peoples everywhere. The spirit was willing, but the fleet was weak, and American power had to be confined mostly to the Caribbean area. There American capital had its greatest stake, and there American security was most involved. To a vigorous and expansive United States, which was feeling her new political and economic muscles, the old policies of self-restraint seemed too limiting. In fact, under the emerging ground rules of Manifest Destiny, they could even be considered irresponsible. The United States, it was believed, had an obligation to bring democracy to her sister republics of the hemisphere.

Despite all our good intentions, things did not work out that way. Cuba and Puerto Rico were successfully detached from Spain, the latter becoming a colony of the United States and the former only narrowly escaping annexation. Despite the belief of many Americans that, in Senator Stephen Douglas's words, the destiny of the United States "was to possess Cuba," the island retained its formal independence. Its freedom of maneuver, however, was sharply limited by the Platt amendment, under which the United States reserved for herself "the right to intervene" in Cuban affairs "for the preservation of Cuban independence [and] the maintenance of a government adequate for the protection of life, property, and individual liberty." The reasons for such intervention clearly had less to do with political guardianship—for Cuba suffered a succession of incompetent and brutal dictators even under America's watchful eye—than with the demands of trade and defense. American investments were flowing into Cuba—investments which, under a businessman's administration, had to be protected by force if necessary. Equally important, Cuba guarded the naval approaches to the Caribbean, and the Caribbean had suddenly become the gateway to the Pacific for the American Navy. As a rising naval power, the United States became acutely aware of the need for a canal through Central America, offering a short-cut to the Pacific. Under the guiding hand of Theodore Roosevelt, Panama was pried loose from Colombia, the canal was built, and the United States informed infant Panama that she was retaining permanent sovereignty over the land adjacent to the canal.

It was also under Theodore Roosevelt that the long-moribund Monroe Doctrine was dusted off, revived, and put into clothing more suitable to the new sense of Manifest Destiny. What had formerly been a declaration of America's desire to guard the independence of the Latin American nations from predatory Europeans, now became a manifesto of Washington's right to intervene as the peace-keeper of the hemisphere. In the famous corollary that bears his name, President Roosevelt told Congress in 1904 that:

> Chronic wrong-doing may in America, as elsewhere, ultimately require intervention by some civilized power, and in the western hemisphere the adherence of the United States to the Monroe Doctrine may force the United States, however reluctantly, in flagrant cases of such wrong-doing or impotence, to the exercise of an international police power.

This was a radical transformation in both the scope and the intent of the original doctrine. Instead of being the guardian of the independence of her sister republics, the United States appointed herself the policeman of their behavior. She was, through a self-assumed "international police power," to punish such evils as "chronic wrong-doing" and political instability. And what did such "chronic wrong-doing" consist of in the context of the times? Not in any threat to the security of the United States—for the Latin American nations were too weak, and the Europeans had long since discarded their old dreams of empire in the New World —but in political instability which might threaten American investments and invite outside intervention. The United States believed she had a moral obligation to bring political tranquillity to the Caribbean; she also felt that it was necessary to a favorable climate for business.

Thus trade and a desire to keep the lid on the anarchy that was sweeping the immature states of the Caribbean led the United States to intervene with her military forces in half a dozen countries during the early decades of the twentieth century. Not only was Panama seized from Colombia and the Canal Zone placed under permanent United States sovereignty, but Nicaragua was occupied more or less continuously by American troops from 1912 to 1933, Haiti from 1915 to 1934, and the Dominican Republic from 1916 to 1924. In addition, the United States intervened repeatedly in Cuba until the repeal of the Platt amendment in 1934.

Even Mexico was treated to incursions by the United States Army when Woodrow Wilson, in an excess of misguided morality, decided to punish the Huerta government for conduct unbecoming a neighbor within easy reach of American power. Unlike his predecessors Roosevelt and Taft, President Wilson did not intervene in Latin America to defend American business interests so much as to punish immoral governments. He sent troops to Veracruz and General Pershing chasing after Pancho Villa because he thought this effect would be good for the Mexicans. But whether economic or moral in their inspiration, what is significant about all these interventions is that not a single one of them was launched to ward off European encroachment on the Americas, for by that time there was none. The original Monroe Doctrine had been completely swallowed by the Roosevelt corollary and the conviction of the United States that she had a special duty to punish "chronic wrong-doing," however defined by her, in the western hemisphere.

But even under Wilson, the idea of the United States as policeman of the Americas began to seem like a dubiously glorified responsibility. It was a messy, frustrating business at best, and it opened the United States to charges of imperialism that did not sit well on the American conscience. As a result Wilson, followed by Harding and Coolidge, tried to convince the Latin Americans that the Monroe Doctrine was also to their interests. It remained for Herbert Hoover to announce the "good neighbor" policy and in 1930 detach the Roosevelt Corollary from the Monroe Doctrine. The policy was carried on by Franklin D. Roosevelt, who had the Platt Amendment repealed and at the Montevideo Conference of 1933 accepted the principle of non-intervention. A pan-American council was set up, and the nominal emphasis shifted from unilateral action by the United States to collective action by all the American republics.

The power structure in the hemisphere, however, remained exactly the same as it had been before the good neighbor policy went into operation, and the United States was still free to act as she pleased. But the vocabulary was different, and with it came the belief that American power should be limited in its application by the will of at least some of the nations involved. At Bogotá, Colombia, in 1948, the Organization of American States was set up as the guiding body of hemispheric action. Intervention by one state in the affairs of another was ruled out, and defense against aggression, whether from inside or outside the western hemisphere, was to be dealt with by collective action of all the American states. On paper it was a formidable repudiation of intervention. According to Article 15 of the charter of the OAS,

No state or group of states has the right to intervene, directly or indirectly, for any reason whatever, in the internal or external affairs of any other state.

And according to Article 17:

> The territory of a state is inviolable; it may not be the object, even temporarily, of military occupation or of other measures of force taken by another state, directly or indirectly, on any grounds whatever.

The declaration issued by the OAS was clear and it was forceful: no state has the right to intervene in the affairs of another state *for any reason whatever.* It would be impossible to draw the line against intervention any more sharply than that. For the states of Latin America the agreement reached at Bogotá marked a new departure in relations with the United States. For the first time it seemed to free them from fear of the big stick which had been applied against them so often in the past. For the United States as well, it was a radical break with the past, a final and explicit repudiation of "gunboat diplomacy" and a recognition that the Monroe Doctrine could no longer be used as an excuse for unilateral interventions designed to punish or intimidate recalcitrant states.

It was a noble declaration of intent, but it completely neglected to take into account the cold war with communism which was just coming up over the horizon. In fact, had the Bogotá conference come a year or so later, it is quite likely that the United States would not have accepted the declaration of nonintervention. The trouble with nonintervention, from Washington's point of view, was that it failed to deal with the problem of a communist government's coming to power. If such a thing happened, it would come not by Russian invasion—which, despite all the military equipment the United States was funneling into Latin America, nobody took seriously—but by a seizure of power from the inside: a communist *coup d'état*, a take-over of a legally elected government, or perhaps even a communist victory in a free election. It was clear that the United States, locked in a cold-war battle with Russia, had no intention of observing the ground rules of nonintervention where communism was involved.

Nor was the problem merely an academic one. By 1954 the government of Guatemala, legally elected and popularly supported though it was, seemed to be falling under the influence of radical left-wing reformers, perhaps even communists. President Jacobo Arbenz nationalized the United States-owned electrical company and told the United Fruit Company that it would have to release some 200,000 acres of land it was holding in reserve. To American policy-makers, scarred by the trauma of the Korean war and still in the grip of McCarthyism, the prospects seemed ominous. Something had to go, and nonintervention was it. At a meeting of the OAS in Caracas in 1954, John Foster Dulles took back much of what had been granted at Bogotá and by a bare majority obtained an OAS declaration that:

> The domination or control of the political institutions of any American state by the international communist movement . . . would constitute a threat to the sovereignty and political independence of the American states.

Thus was anti-communism written into the definition of pan-Americanism. Having obtained the green light, the CIA then proceeded to overthrow the Arbenz government with an invasion launched from neighboring Honduras, and Guatemala returned to its traditional pattern of dictatorial rule. It had been "saved" for the free world. Thanks to Dulles's agile arm-twisting at Caracas, the United States intervention even seemed to carry the stamp of approval of the OAS—although the major democracies of Latin America voted against it and the most enthusiastic support for the Caracas declaration came from the military dictatorships and right-wing oligarchies.

Nonintervention became a casualty of the cold war. In face of the communist peril, it seemed outdated and even dangerous. The legacy of the Monroe Doctrine decreed that in no case should an outside authority, in this case "international communism," be allowed to seize power in the western hemisphere. To Washington the danger clearly outweighed allegiance to an abstract principle. But to most Latin Americans the situation appeared very different. Communism seemed largely an abstract danger, distant and improbable. Intervention by the United States, on the other hand, is something Latin Americans have had to contend with as long as they can remember. For the nations of the Caribbean who have had the big stick used against them, and for all those who fear that their turn may be next, the possibility of American military intervention is a good deal more real than the remote danger of a communist take-over.

Thus Washington's efforts to rally the nations of Latin America into defiantly anti-communist postures has been either unsuccessful or irrelevant. Those regimes controlled by military and extreme right-wing oligarchies have, to be sure, enthusiastically seconded our anti-communist declarations—not, however, because they love liberty, but because they fear any changes in the status quo that might threaten their authority. In such countries it is convenient to label the opposition, however moderate it may be, "communist," in order to convince Washington that the regimes are firmly on the side of the United States. In fact, they are on nobody's side but their own, and simply use anti-communism as a convenient tool to discredit their opponents. For the relatively democratic governments of Latin America, those which depend upon some serious degree of popular support, Washington's anti-communist appeals have posed a terrible dilemma—again, not because they have any affection for communism, but because they recognize the dangers they run among their own people by obediently voting for the anti-communist declarations decreed by the United States. In Latin America the political kiss of death is not to be called a communist, but to be labeled a lackey of the Yankees.

Washington's attempts to enlist the OAS in the cold war have been unsuccessful where the democratic governments of Latin America have been concerned, and have had the effect of dividing the OAS and weakening the fragile spirit of pan-Americanism which had been built up so laboriously since the early 1930s. The Latin Americans have tried to keep out of the cold war because they believe, with considerable reason, that it is none of their affair and that to meddle is get their fingers burned. They have been willing to go along with the United States on issues that do not hurt their interests, voting obediently at the United Nations and, for the most part, providing a favorable climate of investment for American business. But Washington's insistence on linking anti-communism with pan-Americanism has roused the fear of Yankee intervention which they thought they had put to rest at Bogotá in 1948. For Latin Americans the principle of nonintervention is one that overrides party and class, for it involves the very question of national independence, a cause Latin Americans care a good deal more about than they do about anti-communism. And in their eyes, the two are not identical.

This has posed a serious dilemma for American foreign-policy-makers. On one hand, they would like the United States to be a "good neighbor" to the Latin Americans, encourage them to replace dictatorship with democracy, help them raise their standard of living through such devices as the Alliance for Progress, and observe the rules of nonintervention solemnly sworn to in the charter of the OAS. They want, in short, to assure the Latin Americans that the days of "gunboat diplomacy" are gone forever, and that we are all members of one big happy inter-American family.

On the other hand, Washington officials fear that the nations of Latin America may fall into the hands of one of the various "international communist conspiracies" directed from Moscow, Peking, or Havana. Looking at Latin America, they see a continent ripe for revolution: a feudal land-holding aristocracy which refuses to give up its ancient privileges, a politically impotent middle class without the middle-class values that normally support Western-style democracies, a tradition of violence and military dictatorship, an alienated industrial proletariat, and an impoverished peasantry beginning to be roused to political consciousness.

While Washington officials do not consider themselves to be hostile to revolutions *per se*, they are deeply antagonistic to any revolutions in which communists may play a role, or even which communists support. They assume—although more from fear than from experience—that communists, be they ever so few, will

immediately seize control of any popular revolution. By such rea-
soning they come close to believing that any revolution is inherently dangerous for the United States because communists tend
to support revolutions. During the Kennedy administration the
United States tried to channel revolutions along paths of peaceful
reform by using cash and persuasion through such programs as
the Alliance for Progress. But for all its noble ambitions, the Alliance has not been able to bring about the sweeping social reforms
its advocates hoped for, and the pressure for revolution is just as
great as ever in much of Latin America.

Faced with the prospect of continuing revolutionary agitation,
the United States has swung away from her support for democratic
reform movements and is returning to a policy of direct military
intervention, as was displayed at Santo Domingo in the spring of
1965. In doing so, the United States has tended to treat nonintervention as a concession to Latin American sensibilities rather
than as a principle of diplomacy—and as a fairly expendable concession at that, to be ignored or pushed aside whenever the demands of the cold war seem to dictate. Taken in the abstract,
this change is a perfectly normal, if regrettable, fact of international life. Nations are often forced to swallow their promises,
and even their principles, where their own security is at stake.
Nobody could expect them to do otherwise in cases where, to re-
peat, the national security is in question. But this is precisely
where there has been the most difficulty, for beginning with the
intervention in Guatemala in 1954 the United States has had
difficulty in distinguishing a real question of American security
from peripheral considerations of national pride and influence.
Above all, she has tended to confuse communism as a social and
economic doctrine with communism as a form of Russian-directed
imperialism. This confusion has been the source of most of our
recent troubles with Latin America and has involved us in a succession of interventions which have had the perverse effect of rein-
forcing the very communist penetration we have been trying to
combat.

What has gone wrong with our policy in Latin America is basically an exaggerated version of what has gone wrong with it in Southeast Asia and throughout the twilight zone of emerging states in the Third World. We have confused our real security interests—which most recently have been threatened by Soviet Russia, just as they were threatened by Germany and Japan before that—with an aversion to the political-economic system under which the Russians happen to live. We have made anti-communism into the guiding principle of our diplomacy and in doing so have lost the ability to differentiate between the kind of communism that threatens our security and the kind that is simply a nuisance. By viewing any action involving communists anywhere in the western hemisphere as a threat to American security, we set the stage for a policy of permanent intervention without any definable limitation. It is not surprising that such a policy should arouse apprehension in Latin America, for it makes any nation a potential target for a landing of Marines whenever communists are involved in any political upheaval—no matter how few the communists or how remote the upheaval.

The belief that the United States has a special obligation to save the Latin Americans from communism, or perhaps even from their own revolutions, is implicit in the whole pan-American myth. We began our career of intervention in Latin America with the Monroe Doctrine in a desire to protect our sister republics from the evil colonial powers of Europe. We later moved into the Caribbean in an excess of zeal to "liberate" Cuba and Puerto Rico from Spain, and stayed on to provide a wholesome climate of political stability for our own economic interests. Now we are embarking on a new type of intervention, one designed to protect the Latin Americans from communism—not a communist invasion from abroad, which is mostly science fiction, but communist threats from within—through an inter-American gendarmery and, if necessary, our own troops. We are, as President Johnson declared, not going to "let the communists set up any government in the western hemisphere."

To many in Washington, this is merely proof of our deep concern and affection for our southern neighbors. We so loved the

Latin Americans, it can be said, that we sent them our Marines. It is the least a big brother can do. But the Latin Americans, who are perhaps more naïve than their well-wishers in Washington, can be excused if their image of big brother tends to be obscured by the shadow of his big stick. To those who have felt that stick, and there is scarcely a nation in the Caribbean that has not, the prospect of a new round of Yankee intervention brings little joy —except, of course, to the communists, who argue that the United States will try to stamp out even democratic revolutions, and who hope to profit from our crushing their democratic rivals. Is American military intervention the only way to prevent the communists from taking over Latin America? Does it hurt the communists or does it help them? Is it necessary to be anti-revolutionary just because we are anti-communist? Is there, for that matter, any hope for reform in Latin American without revolution?

11. The Millionaire and the Beggars

*The Alliance for Progress is an alliance between one
millionaire and twenty beggars.* —FIDEL CASTRO

❧ ❧ ❧ IT has now become a truism, and a tired one at that, to
say that there are no easy solutions for what ails Latin America.
But the observation remains valid. The problems caused by political feudalism, social repression, and economic stagnation are so
deep and their effects so widespread that chances for orderly and
peaceful change in Latin America are not very bright. It is not
simply that conditions are intolerable for the vast majority of
Latin Americans, but that they are getting even worse. Today
food consumption per inhabitant is less than it was twenty-five
years ago. A good part of the continent is living on the edge of
starvation and, as population growth takes its toll, prospects for
the future are blacker still. With the highest birth rate in the
world, Latin America is expected to double its population within
thirty-five years, creating twice as many mouths to feed on the
same inadequate resources. By the end of the century, if current
birth rates continue, the continent's present population will have
grown to 450 million. Figures like these transform such vaguely
abstract terms as "population explosion" into a social catastrophe
which could well be beyond the ability of even the most stable
governments to contain. And there are not many stable governments in Latin America.

The uncontrolled rise in population, disturbing enough in itself, has been complicated by the relative paucity of good arable

land. What decent farm land there is lies for the most part in the hands of a few wealthy proprietors; or in some cases it is parceled out into thousands of minuscule plots too tiny to be productively farmed or to earn their owners a decent living. Between the big estates, the *latifundia*, and the tiny plots, the *minifundia*, there is little on which to build a stable agricultural base capable of feeding and supporting the continent's growing population, most of which is dependent on the land for a living. With a few notable exceptions, land distribution is based upon patterns inherited from the Spanish and Portuguese. Thus, in Venezuela, for example, 2 per cent of the population owns 75 per cent of the land; in Brazil 5 per cent of the population owns 95 per cent of the land; while on the continent as a whole 5 per cent of the population owns 70 per cent of the arable land. Except in Cuba, Bolivia, and Mexico, there has never been any comprehensive agrarian reform. The United States has urged the Latin American governments to push through land-reform programs. But since in many countries the governments are run by the land-owning oligarchs, these pleas have been met with indulgent smiles. The Latin American oligarchy has no intention of relinquishing its land, because land is the basis of its political and economic power, not to mention its social prestige. To ask it to share some of its wealth is to seek a degree of social responsibility and political awareness which is rare in any oligarchy and virtually unheard of in Latin America.

Shackled by a rigid social structure, a feudal land pattern, and the demands of a galloping population increase, the nations of Latin America are also victims of underdevelopment. Like many other countries of the Third World, they are dependent on a primary product, whether it be a crop or a raw material, for their livelihood. The product varies from country to country—bananas in Panama, coffee in Brazil, copper in Chile, oil in Venezuela, tin in Bolivia—but the problem of a one- or two-crop economy is the same. These products account for the bulk of the foreign currency earned, currency needed to feed the population, buy essential imports, and capitalize industrialization. Yet such products are subject to wild fluctuations in price, depending on the size of the crop, the foreign competition, and the demands of the market. Sugar, for example, during a single recent two-year period fell from 12 cents a pound on the world market to 3 cents a pound. Fluctuations like that can spell catastrophe for nations that are trying to achieve some sort of orderly economic development. They can mean the difference not only between industrialization and stagnation, but also between subsistence and starvation. To take another example, in a recent year the fall in coffee prices on the world market resulted in a loss of revenue for Colombia that was three times greater than all the funds she received from the United States under the Alliance for Progress. World market prices are subject to wild jumps upward as well, resulting in short-term bonanzas for the producing countries. But these do not help the process of orderly development. For this reason the Latin American nations have favored international agreements on commodity prices (already worked out for such products as coffee and sugar) that will protect them from precipitous changes in world prices for their primary products. Even with relatively stable prices, the income they receive for their raw materials has not, for the most part, kept pace with the steadily rising prices they must pay for imports of manufactured goods from the industrialized nations. This means, in technical language, that they are suffering a serious deterioration in the terms of trade. In everyday terms, they are going broke.

Stable commodity prices could make economic planning a good deal easier. These should, the Latin American nations agree, be supplemented by diversification of their economies into other crops and industries. But such diversification takes time, money, and specialized skills, all of which are in short supply in Latin America and throughout the underdeveloped world today. It also takes the cooperation of the industrialized nations and their willingness to remove the trade barriers they impose on Latin American exports. Even the United States, despite the enormous amount of American private investment in the Latin nations, imposes trade barriers. They are even more pronounced in the case of Europe, where such countries as Britain give preferential tariff treatment to the nations of the Commonwealth, while France and her Common Market partners favor the former French colonies of Africa, many of whom produce the same export commodities as do the nations of Latin America.

Diversification can be speeded through large-scale private investment from Europe and the United States. But because of Latin America's past instability and discouraging prospects for the future, foreign corporations have been interested in investing only in those areas where a fast and high return on capital seems likely: in the oil industry of Venezuela, the copper mines of Chile, the banana plantations of Central America. In most cases this is precisely the kind of investment which does Latin America the least good because it is concentrated in those very areas on which the economies are already overdependent. Further, since the corporations are owned largely by foreigners, most of the profits leave the country to pay off shareholders in North America and Europe, rather than being reinvested in other Latin American businesses. Some countries have tried to deal with the situation by nationalizing key industries or putting a ban on the export of capital. But all too often they have only scared off investors and reduced even further the scarce supply of foreign capital.

The economic crisis faced by many Latin American nations has served to reinforce a social crisis resulting from the breakdown of the feudal order. Virtually every Latin American society is going through a period of sustained social tension that inspires searches for radical solutions. The oligarchies feel the rumble of popular discontent, and even the democratic governments face social and economic ordeals they may not be able to surmount. It is generally assumed that much of Latin America is ripe for a social revolution. Whether or not the communists will benefit from such a revolution is difficult to say. But some kind of revolt, whether it be inspired by Castroism or by social fascism, seems likely in a number of countries.

It is wishful thinking to imagine that private enterprise may be able to stave off revolution by gradually raising the standard of living over the decades. Latin America will not wait. It may even be asking too much of democratic government to channel such a revolution. Unless democracy is somehow able to find a way to feed the masses, provide jobs for the unemployed, introduce radical agrarian reform, redistribute income, and achieve a meaningful degree of political equality, it is likely to be rejected for one of the totalitarian formulas which are exerting an increasingly powerful appeal. Indeed, it is surprising that democracy has fared so well, considering that, to the landless peasant and the slum-dwelling urban proletarian, political democracy as practiced in much of Latin America has not meant more than the freedom to be hungry and ill. To sacrifice that kind of freedom is not going to be a difficult choice.

Although Latin America has had hundreds, if not thousands, of revolts, coups, and insurrections, only three times has a fundamental change in the social order been achieved: in Mexico in 1910, in Bolivia in 1952, and in Cuba in 1959. All the rest, the uprisings, the *golpos*, the interchangeable *caudillos*, was simply a change of characters within the same basic plot. Only these revolutions destroyed the power of an oppressive oligarchy, redistributed the national wealth, and achieved a system of social equality which gave the poor, usually for the first time in their lives, economic opportunity and political dignity. And in each case the revolution was achieved only by violence. Considering their own history, and looking at the stagnation and paralysis around them, it is not surprising that Latin American reformers are becoming increasingly pessimistic about peaceful change and are turning toward the extremes. In a continent where military coups are the norm and where elections have been little more than charades, even the best-willed reformers think in terms of revolution.

The Latin American radicals are virtually a class unto themselves. Never having experienced a viable democratic government, they are concerned less with formal constitutional guarantees than with breaking the grip of the oligarchy and launching a social revolution that will remake their societies. These radicals of the "Jacobin Left," as Professor Robert Alexander calls them,

favor not only extreme nationalism, but also rapid social change. They want to get rid immediately of the old institutions of large landlordism and other legacies of the semi-feudal and semi-servile past. They are little concerned with the cost of this change, in terms of human suffering, disorganization of the economy, or individual liberties. The Jacobin Left have little regard for political democracy. At best they feel it to be ineffective; at worst, they look upon it as a means by which the supporters of the status quo defend their property and their interests.[1]

Despairing of the prospects for peaceful change, disgusted with the ineffectuality and incompetence of the middle-class reformers, skeptical of the ability of liberal democracy to break through encrusted centuries of social privilege, they are ready to seek radical solutions, even if these can be achieved only by violence.

Their hero, needless to say, is Fidel Castro. To the Latin American intelligentsia, rabidly xenophobic and instinctively anti-Yankee, Fidelismo represents their own idealism carried out in practice. That Castro has turned his revolution into a political tyranny is less important to them than the fact that he has remade Cuba from top to bottom. While most North Americans may consider Cuba an oppressive communist police state, to the Latin American radicals it is the example of a social revolution that succeeded, and all the more admirable because it did so by defying the giant of the North. To have smashed the Batista dictatorship and broken the power of the Cuban oligarchy with Uncle Sam's big stick only ninety miles away—that is a source of inspiration for many Latin Americans. Even those who have little sympathy for Fidel admire his defiance of Washington, for, when confronted with the power of the United States, they cannot help thinking of themselves in Cuba's shoes.

Latin American radicals are less alarmed by the excesses of the Castro regime than are most North Americans. They do not compare Cuban economic conditions or Cuban methods of justice with those in the United States, but with the situation as it existed in Cuba under Batista, or as it exists in many of their own countries today. By this yardstick, Fidel does not come off so badly as many North Americans might imagine. While the governments of Latin America form committees to discuss new housing, schools, and hospitals for the poor, the Cubans have already built them; while the others muse over the problems of agrarian reform, the Cubans have put it into practice. Despite the American blockade, severe shortages of food and equipment, and bad economic planning, they are surviving on Russian help and slowly growing trade links with Western Europe and Japan. It is not Fidel's domestic reforms that Latin American radicals question, but a foreign policy which has become almost totally dependent on the Soviet Union. He is frequently criticized for turning Cuba into a Russian dependency, but most Latins are convinced that the United States drove him to it.

The Cuban example is one, although not the only, choice open to Latin America if reform does not come fast enough to stave off violent change. In addition, there is the possibility of an insurrection by young army officers determined to push through social reforms opposed by the oligarchy and by their own generals. This could lead to a military dictatorship, perhaps with vaguely democratic aspirations, such as the one that Nasser led in Egypt or Ayub Khan in Pakistan—authoritarian, radical, but non-communist. Peru provides a current example. In Latin America young military officers are imbued with a desire for economic progress, and they resent a feudal social order which provides no outlet for their ambitions, nor any future for their country but economic stagnation. A third possibility is a national socialism of the kind espoused by Juan Perón during his heyday in Argentina: a fascist dictatorship. A fourth choice, of status quo, does not exist. Even in the most repressive and primitive backwaters of Latin America, such as Paraguay, Haiti, and Nicaragua, the archaic and dictatorial one-man states cannot hope to survive indefinitely the ferment that is sweeping the rest of the continent, any more than Batista survived it in Cuba or Trujillo in the Dominican Republic.

Latin America today has gone beyond the point of maintaining the status quo—through either economic injections from Washington or minor political reforms at home—because there is no viable status quo to maintain. The problem has now become one of choosing revolutions: of deciding whether they must be bloody and convulsive or whether they can be gradual and relatively nonviolent. It is a question in which the United States has a serious and abiding interest, but far from a controlling one. What we do or do not do can have an enormous impact on the future of Latin America. But in the long run what happens to these countries, whether they become democratic or authoritarian, free-enterprise or socialist, depends upon the people themselves —what they are willing to fight for and what they are willing to endure.

And they are becoming less and less patient. Where the ballot box is rigged, where reform is blocked by powerful oligarchies, and where misery is offered no relief, it is not surprising that the recourse should be to rioting in the streets and eventually to guerrilla warfare in the hills. In some cases violence is the only way of forcing change, and we can expect a good deal more of it throughout Latin America.

Although the Fidelista revolution dates all the way back to 1959 and the Alliance for Progress to 1961, there has been little significant improvement in the Latin American social structure. Nearly everywhere the oligarchy remains in tight control, the democratic process has broken down in a number of countries, and the recourse to violence becomes increasingly compelling as the only realistic hope for early change. The rhetoric has been impressive, but behind it the fundamental ills of Latin America remain unchanged. Except for Chile, Peru, and Venezuela, there has been little reform in the key areas of land holdings, tax revision, and income redistribution. Yet it is precisely in these areas that the architects of the Alliance for Progress placed such faith for peaceful change.

It was neither charity nor a guilty conscience but Fidel Castro who provided the inspiration for the Alliance for Progress. By bringing the cold war into the western hemisphere, by forcing

Washington to realize that it could no longer take Latin America for granted, he galvanized United States policy-makers into a flurry of action and terrified the Congress into voting $20 billion over a ten-year period for the economic development of Latin America. Promulgated by the Kennedy administration, the Alliance for Progress might never have seen the light of day, let alone grown into childhood, had Fidel not injected the fear of communism into official Washington. Castro is, as Latin Americans are the first to admit, absolutely indispensable, for he keeps the coffers of the Alliance primed. If he did not exist, he would probably have to be invented.

Castro's brand of revolution was exactly what the Alliance was designed to prevent. Essentially a device for the abortion of revolutions, the Alliance sought to do with American dollars that which Castro had done with rifles and communist manifestoes. The idea behind the Alliance was that since revolution of some kind in Latin America was virtually inevitable, it should be led along peaceful and democratic lines. The reformers would not have to turn to the extremes because they would be able to achieve their goals by the consent of the oligarchy. Far more than a simple foreign-aid program, the Alliance would use economic assistance to prod the Latin American governments into pursuing a social revolution. This would demonstrate that democracy can provide economic progress and political justice far better than communism. Fidelismo would be discredited by making it seem irrelevant.

In its analysis of the problems facing the Alianza, the administration mingled its idealism with a heavy dose of realism. "Political freedom," President Kennedy told the Latin American ambassadors in the spring of 1961, "must be accompanied by social change, for unless necessary social reforms, including land and tax reform, are freely made—unless we broaden the opportunity of all our people—unless the great mass of Americans share in increasing prosperity—then our alliance, our dream will have failed." To bring about this social change, United States officials counted heavily on the reform-minded elements of the middle class—on the journalists, the professors, the students, the lawyers, and the liberal intelligentsia. These are the most outspoken voices for change in Latin America, and these, it was assumed, would be the natural allies of the Alianza. They, in the name of self-interest even more than idealism, would make its cause their own because its aims were essentially theirs.

Frighten the oligarchy and woo the intelligentsia, this was the program of the Alianza. Yet neither the bogyman nor the bait seemed to work. The Latin American reformers—and particularly the left-wing radicals, who are most outspoken against the oligarchy—proved incapable of swallowing any program that bore the fatal stamp MADE IN USA. The fact that it might be for their own benefit, that through North American help the oligarchy's power might be broken, was less important to them than that it was Yankee in inspiration. Their traditional *anti-yanquismo* was too strong, their own demagoguery too compelling, their inbred suspicion too overwhelming, and their preference for talk over action too inbred, to permit them to adopt the principles of the Alianza as their own. They chose to damn it as corrupt before they knew what it was, ignore it when they had a chance of controlling it, and disown it when it failed to achieve its high ideals without their active support.

If the reformers turned their back on the Alianza, the oligarchy proved to be indifferent. In most countries the land-owning rich were less worried by Fidelismo than by the loss of their privileges through Alianza reforms. Washington's gory picture of imminent revolution seemed exaggerated, while its prescription for reforms horrified them. If revolt were to break out, they were convinced that the army would quickly suppress it, and the army, they believed, was in their pocket. As for Washington's bribes, they were convinced that the United States would have to keep pumping dollars into Latin America in any case, not to encourage reforms, but to protect the economic investments of her own private corporations. American business, they reasoned, would never allow the administration to tolerate another Cuba. And even if Wall Street were willing to write off its investments as a bad gamble, the American public could surely be counted on to oppose any revolution that could be labeled, rightly or wrongly, as communist-inspired. The oligarchy's assessment turned out to be more or less correct.

Faced with the hostility of the business groups, the conservatism of the urban middle class, the refusal of the oligarchies to be frightened or bought off, and the reluctance of the radical left to have anything to do with the Yankees, the Alianza has been politically paralyzed. It has spent a good deal of money and in some countries spurred economic growth. But mostly it has had to dispense aid on the basis of promises offered rather than on performance rendered and to content itself with the usual jobs of technical assistance: building roads, hospitals, and schools.

For the region as a whole, the balance sheet of the Alianza has been depressing. A survey completed in 1969 by the United Nations Economic Commission for Latin America revealed that problems of urban poverty, rural unemployment, inequality of income, lagging industrialization, dependence on foreign capital, and slow expansion of foreign markets were in some respects more critical at the end of the decade than in 1961. The external debt of governments and private borrowers doubled since 1960 to close to $20 billion. Outflow of profits and interest to foreign investors rose in 1968 to 36 per cent of Latin America's export income, as against 25 per cent a decade earlier. This drain reached $2.4 billion in 1968 and is continuing to grow, devouring loans and credits meant for economic development, and forcing Latin American governments to cut back essential imports. Restrictive trade practices by the industrialized countries have seen Latin America's share of world trade shrink from 11 per cent in 1950 to 5 per cent in 1968. The region's share of the United States market plummeted from 21.2 per cent in 1962 to 13.2 per cent in 1968. During the decade the annual growth rate averaged 4.8 per cent, compared to 5.1 per cent during the 1950s. Even more remarkably, the share of domestic savings devoted to investment was higher in the 1950s than it has been since the formation of the Alianza. Sluggish growth rates have intensified unemployment, reaching the level of 23 million out of a labor force of 83 million. In the rural areas, where some

70 million people live, per capital income averages less than $90. Perhaps the most dramatic statistic of all is that nearly a third of Latin American income goes to the wealthiest five per cent of the population, and that these extremes of income distribution have scarcely been touched by taxation or redistribution of property.

The United States was not entirely responsible for the failure of the Alianza to project a compelling mystique. Much of the blame must fall on the Latin Americans themselves, and particularly on the left-wing reformers, who often prefer the pleasures of *anti-yanquismo* to the harsh realities of social change. But the Alianza was also hobbled by its preoccupation with communism. When the chips were down, the oligarchies and the generals who backed them up knew that Washington's fear of communism was even greater than its desire for reform. If reform could be connected with communism and social stability made to seem a bulwark against communist penetration, then structural reforms could be quietly dropped by the wayside. The lesson was easily drawn and, in the wake of the Bay of Pigs, it was soon applied. Encouraged by Washington's fear of communism and by its preference for verbally anti-communist regimes, would-be *caudillos*— usually trained and equipped by the United States—moved in to depose a number of legally elected governments. Their charge: civilian reformers were soft on communism. Between 1962 and early 1970, army coups toppled ten of Latin America's twenty-four governments, some twice. The military now controls three of the continent's four largest nations—Brazil, Peru, and Argentina— with half of Latin America's 276 million people.

The record has shown that the kind of government that creates a favorable climate for business investments under the Alliance for Progress, and that can be counted on for anti-communist votes in the OAS and the UN, is not the kind of government likely to win popular support. President Kennedy realized this and tried to back the democratic progressives. But in the end his determination to punish, and if possible to topple, the Castro regime led him to align United States policy with the very oligarchies he detested, and served to neutralize his enlightened attitude toward Latin American reformers. Because it needed their votes to expel Cuba from the OAS and enforce economic sanctions, the administration found itself wooing dictatorships such as those in Paraguay, Haiti, and Nicaragua, while at the same time declaring its allegiance to reforms that such regimes had no intention of undertaking. The result of this policy was a double failure: it neither brought about the weakening, let alone the downfall, of the Castro regime, nor succeeded in instigating social change in Latin America. The implementation of the anti-Cuba policy tended to cancel out the ambitions of the Alianza.

The Cuban revolution thus is in the anomalous position of having inspired the Alianza and also in large degree of having been responsible for the failure of its reformist ambitions. Without Castro there would have been no "vast, cooperative effort, unparalleled in magnitude and nobility of purpose, to satisfy the basic needs of the American people for homes, work and land, health and schools," as President Kennedy described the Alianza to Congress in March 1961. Without Castro, however, there might also not have been the assumption that insurrection in Latin America automatically involved the danger of a communist take-over, and thereby required direct military intervention by the United States. The equation "insurrection = communism = peril to the United States" is rooted in the tragi-comedy of the Cuban revolution.

Whether Castro jumped into Russia's arms or whether he was pushed by Washington is a point likely to be argued for years to come. Some believe that Fidel sprang, like a bearded Athena, full-blown from the brow of Karl Marx and had been determined to turn Cuba into a communist state ever since he was old enough to tell the proletariat from the bourgeoisie. Others assume that, like Topsy, he just grew into a communist, a little bit more every day, until the old agrarian reformer was transformed into the militant red revolutionary. Perhaps Castro was determined to lead Cuba into the communist camp from the very beginning, and thus he would not have been amenable to compromise after seizing power. Yet in an interview with Herbert Matthews in October 1963, Castro said that in outlining his plans for "a very radical revolution" he initially "thought it could be done under the Constitution of 1940 and within a democratic system." His conversion, he explained, was "a gradual process, a dynamic process in which the pressure of events forced me to accept Marxism as the answer to what I was seeking." It was, he said, the American reaction to his "agrarian reform" of May 1959 that "made me realize that there was no chance to reach an accommodation with the United States. So as events developed, I gradually moved into a Marxist-Leninist position. I cannot tell you just when, the process was so gradual and natural." Perhaps Castro was fabricating an elaborate story in explaining his conversion to Marxism-Leninism. But since there is no convincing reason for fabricating such a story, it is equally possible that he was telling the truth.

Hostile to the United States by instinct as well as by conviction, and imbued, like most Latin American radicals, with a vaguely Marxist vocabulary and frame of reference, the Fidelistas sought to crush two enemies: the Batista dictatorship, and the hold of the United States, which, in tacit cooperation with the Cuban oligarchy, seemed to support it. The connection they made between the United States and the Batista regime was not entirely fanciful. Without the cooperation of American government and American industry, the Batista regime probably could not have survived. It served American business interests well, and Washington found the regime expedient, however distasteful its internal politics. Politically and economically, Cuba was an American dependency, its fate decided in Washington and New York. President Kennedy, in an interview shortly before his death, indicated a profound awareness of the causes that inspired the Cuban revolution. "I believe there is no country in the world," he told a French journalist, ". . . where economic colonialism, humiliation, and exploitation were worse than in Cuba, in part owing to my country's policies during the Batista regime." [2]

Despite its high per-capita income for Latin America, Cuba before the Castro revolution was the very model of economic colonialism in action. Every light bulb that was bought, every kilowatt of electricity consumed, every telephone call that was made, every razor blade that was used, and even nearly all the food that was eaten could be traced back to an American corporation and to American shareholders. As Wall Street financiers controlled the Cuban economy, so Miami racketeers ran the elegant gambling casinos of Havana that catered to the North American vacationers, the Pentagon supplied the Cuban army with its military equipment, and the State Department instructed it in the diplomacy it was to follow toward the rest of the world. Even the famous sugar quota, under which the United States guaranteed to buy the bulk of Cuba's sugar crop at prices well above those quoted on the world market, did not benefit the Cubans. Rather it was a disguised subsidy for the American owners of the Cuban sugar plantations and for the sugar-beet industry in the United States itself, which could compete only if prices of Cuban sugar were kept artificially high. As an economic colony of the United States, Cuba did better than most of the Caribbean republics. Or at least those Cubans on the top of the social pile did well, while the others lived in the misery which is taken for granted throughout most of Latin America.

Castro's struggle for power was aided by the widespread hatred for the Batista dictatorship, by the low morale of the army, and by his own moderate program for social reform, which attracted support from the Cuban middle class and even from some of the industrialists. After gaining power, as we know, Castro dropped his liberal reformism, dispensed "revolutionary justice" by firing squad, and began a wholesale expropriation of foreign-owned industries, combined with the systematic destruction of the Cuban middle class. The development of the proletarian aspect of the Cuban revolution marked the turn toward Moscow for inspiration and support. Yet there are those who believe that this was more of an impromptu decision than a deliberate choice—one imposed on the Fidelistas by their own economic ignorance and their determination to break the hold of North American business on their economy. "There is evidence to suggest," the British economist Barbara Ward has written, that Castro chose a Marxist pattern not because he had drawn his support from embattled peasants and workers—in fact, middle-class disgust with Batista was his strongest suit—but because it was the only pattern he knew to help him to exercise the power he had un-expectedly achieved. Faced with the multitudinous uncertainties of responsibility, he grabbed the only pattern which seemed likely to preserve his leadership and deal with his difficulties.[3]

Rather than trying to avoid a fight with the United States, the Fidelistas seemed almost to relish it. They enjoyed the publicity which transformed the Cuban revolution into a symbol of virtue for radicals everywhere, and they appeared to see themselves in the role of David going into battle against the Goliath of the North. During the months following his seizure of power, Castro enjoyed a favorable press in the United States and conducted a veritable triumphal tour in the spring of 1959. Washington showed considerable forebearance and seemed willing to put a good face on what it saw as a rather dubious turn of events. Even after the seizure of United States-owned investments in Cuba, it is far from certain that Washington would have tried to inter-vene against the Castro regime. The nationalization of foreign business is not new in Latin America. The United States accepted Mexico's nationalization of her oil industry and Bolivia's seizure of the tin mines without trying to overthrow their governments, even though heavy American investments were involved. The Bo-livian revolution, which occurred in 1952, even managed to win economic support from the Eisenhower administration.

Yet the Fidelistas assumed the hostility of the United States and, by behaving as though intervention were a foregone con-clusion, tended to encourage the very reaction they feared. Had Castro been content with nationalizing United States-owned property and pushing through social reforms within Cuba, he could probably have had his revolution and, if not American friendship, at least American acquiescence. But, as ideologues, the Cuban revolutionaries were not content with simple Marxism. They had to make a dramatic spectacle of leading Cuba into the communist camp. Fidel had to declare his undying faith in the secular dogma of Marxism-Leninism and embrace Soviet Russia as the guide and defender of the Cuban revolution. Once having done this, he became dependent on Russia for economic and military support.

It was here that Washington drew the line, for while it was willing to tolerate a revolutionary Cuba isolated within the safe confines of the United States-dominated Caribbean, it was outraged at the prospect of Cuba as a center of subversion and as a Soviet outpost in the western hemisphere. The former involved a matter of pride; the latter seemed to entail the security of the United States herself. By failing to recognize that difference, the Fidelistas not only lost the American goodwill they enjoyed when they first came to power, but unleashed a complex of cold-war emotions in the United States that has made any accommodation between the two countries exceedingly difficult. Fidel waved the red flag, and the United States came charging into the bull ring.

Why did he do it? Why was he not content to fashion a Tito-style communist dictatorship in the Caribbean, one which would proclaim all the half-truths of Marxism-Leninism but which would carefully avoid entanglement with the United States? Above all, why did he allow (or persuade) the Russians to turn Cuba into a missile site directed against the United States? The answer is open to speculation, but it may be more practical than ideological. It may be that the Cubans turned to Russia because, having decided to defy the Yankees and become the paladins of Latin American revolution, they needed Soviet protection. To be anti-Yankee and vaguely communist would be to suffer the fate of Guatemala in 1954. But to be a protégé of the Soviet Union would be to enjoy a prominent role in the duel of the giants, and thus to put the Russians in the position where they would have to defend a fellow communist regime. Cuba has ostentatiously made itself a communist state, it has been suggested, "because the United States itself has made it plain that a communist role is the one an *anti-yanqui* Latin American state is expected to play—and because this is the only role Cuba can play if it expects *safely* to defy the United States." [4]

As a result of their decision to jump into Moscow's arms, the Cubans today are almost totally dependent on the Soviet Union for their military and economic survival. Whereas they were once in a state of abject dependence on United States industries and the American sugar quota, they are now even more dependent on Russian planners and the Soviet sugar quota. They have replaced one kind of colonialism with another. The Cubans have had to turn to Moscow for everything from toothpaste to tractors, and in so doing have managed to cut themselves off from the nation that both geography and economics have decreed to be their natural trading partner: the United States.

Yet it is a tribute to Castro's remarkable political skill that, despite a near-total dependence on the Soviet Union, he has managed to avoid having the island turned into a Russian satellite. He has cleverly used the Sino–Soviet split to his own advantage, blackmailed the Russians into furnishing far more foreign aid than they would like to give, and given virtually nothing in exchange. Not only has Fidel resisted satellization, but he has twisted the Cuban Communist Party to his own purposes, using it in 1961 to set up a new Castroite political party, and then expelling the Communist Party organizer from the country the following year, leaving the party, in Theodore Draper's words, "dismembered, dishonored, and discarded." Castro's Cuba is a communist state because Fidel has declared it to be so. But its communism bears more resemblance to traditional Caribbean *caudillismo* than to Moscow-organized conspiracy. It is Latin American authoritarianism with a Marxist veneer, *anti-yanquismo* enveloped in the protective armor of communism. As Draper, one of the most serious and reliable of the observers of the Cuban revolution, has written:

> Castroism is not a peasant movement or a proletarian movement any more than it was a middle-class movement. The déclassé revolutionaries who have determined Cuba's fate have used one class or another, or a combination of classes, for different purposes at different times. Their leader functions above classes, cuts across classes, or maneuvers between them. He belongs to a leadership

type, not unprecedented in this century, which establishes a direct, personal, almost mystical relationship with the masses that frees him from dependence on classes. It also frees him from what Lenin thought was indispensable for a communist revolution—a party. If Castro had happened to make his revolution in a much larger and stronger country, preferably far removed from the United States, he might not have needed to attach himself to an older movement or to place himself at the mercy of its greatest national power. He belongs to the new revolutionary wave for which it is more important to go than to know where it is going.[5]

This is why the real problem of the Cuban revolution is not communism as an ideology. The kind of government the Cubans live under is their business: President Kennedy said so, and President Johnson reaffirmed it. Whether this pledge would be honored in case of "another Cuba," however, remains open to speculation. After Santo Domingo, one might have good reason to be dubious. But it has become American dogma that every nation has the right to self-determination—even, perhaps, in the Caribbean. The Cubans, therefore, presumably have the unalterable right to practice communism, cannibalism, or nudism at home. They do not, however, have the same right to let their island be used as a Russian base against the United States, or as a center of subversion against the other governments of Latin America. Professional revolutionaries may consider this unfair, but it is a fact of life within the sphere of influence of any great power. There is a clear line between self-defense and subversion, and the Fidelistas are quite aware of it, even though they do not choose to observe it. If the Russian Bolsheviks could learn to live with revolution in one country, so can the Cuban *barbudos*.

As far as American security interests are concerned, a communist regime in Cuba is irrelevant. It may be a nuisance. It is certainly an embarrassment. But it is hardly a threat to our safety. It became so only when the Russians committed the folly of trying to turn the island into a missile-launching platform. The Russians had their fingers burned badly and are exceedingly unlikely to make the same mistake again. President Kennedy's demonstration that the United States would not tolerate a Soviet military presence in the Caribbean was an adroit, restrained use of American power. Not only did it help bring an end to an adventurous phase in Russian foreign policy and thereby pave the way for the present détente, but it also caused a sharp drop of Russian and Cuban prestige in Latin America. It showed the Latin American radicals that Russia could not be counted upon as an instrument to achieve their dream of breaking the power of the Yankee colossus, and it discredited the Fidelistas among those who still had ideals about their intentions. It was a turning-point of the cold war and, had it been wisely exploited, could have put relations between the United States and the Latin American republics on a more solid footing.

Instead, Washington has remained mesmerized by the communist orientation of the Cuban revolution and has exaggerated Cuba's role as a cheerleader of world revolution out of all proportion to its real importance. Isolated within the western hemisphere, only ninety miles from the shores of the most powerful nation in the world, and five thousand miles from their nearest ally, the Cubans are bound to search for and encourage political friends wherever they can find them. Considering the troubles she has at home and the perils she faces abroad, a Trotskyite Cuba is virtually inevitable. To expect her to preach "communism in one country" is asking too much of an island bobbing precariously in America's inland sea. But so what? The United States has been preaching democracy at the Latin Americans for two hundred years with infinitely greater resources and rewards to offer, but with little noticeable success. The Cubans, for their part, have been preaching since 1959, yet their prestige and their influence have dropped precipitously over the past few years. Fidel Castro is unlikely to talk any government out of existence. Indeed, among younger Latin American radicals one can see a sharp disenchantment with the Cuban example and a turning toward Maoist extremism—and even beyond that, toward a vague left-wing anarchy that seems to defy any organized direction. Latin America may be ready for revolution, but it is exceedingly unlikely that Fidel will lead it, or even play any major part in it. Cuba is

too small, its record too shabby, and the price it has had to pay
—economic and military dependence on the Soviet Union—too
high for most Latin American revolutionaries.

We can afford to let Fidel talk without suffering high blood
pressure and visions of *barbudos* springing up all over the continent. The Egyptians, the Algerians, and even the Albanians continue to preach revolution as the cure for all ailments, yet we have
managed to contain our anxiety about them. The reason is that
we know this is little more than talk, useful for keeping the
crowds at home in a high state of agitation, and for demonstrating one's revolutionary credentials, but not particularly useful for
stimulating real insurrections. Considering our strength and
Fidel's unimpressive record of conversion, we can afford to be as
indifferent to his propaganda as he is to ours. If we did so, then
we might discover not only that the influence of the Cuban
revolution on the Latin Americans is a good deal less than we
imagine in our tormented nightmares, but also that the lingering
obsession with ideology is impeding our understanding of the real
problems facing Latin America.

We have allowed ourselves to become obsessed with Cuba, in-
flating Fidel from a minor irritant into a source of torment. Thus
we have imposed an embargo on Cuba, withdrawn diplomatic recognition, and encouraged anti-Castro subversion. The result has
been a near-total failure. Our policies have made the Cuban people suffer, but they have not forced the Castro regime to capitu-
late, or even weakened it. If anything, they have helped to
strengthen Fidel's hold on the people and to instill in them a
sense of pride for successfully defying the Yankee colossus. Despite the embargo and the severe shortage of hard foreign currency, the Cuban revolutionaries, after some disastrous mistakes
in planning, have achieved striking progress within the country.
They have built homes for the slum-dwellers, schools for the illit-
erate, and hospitals for the sick, and have provided equality of
opportunity for the Negroes. The middle class may have been virtually wiped out as a class, but the vast majority of Cubans are
incomparably better off today than they were under the Batista

dictatorship, and it is they who are Fidel's most fervent defenders. The revolution has remade the Cuban economy and even Cuban society, and if Fidel were deposed tomorrow, the reforms he has pushed through could not be easily undone.

By our own actions we have made Castro a hero in the eyes of many Latin Americans, and perhaps even pushed Cuba further into the communist camp than it would necessarily like to be. By blacklisting foreign ships that trade with Cuba, by exerting diplomatic pressure on our allies and on the neutrals, and by our own trade embargo, we have made Castro more economically dependent on Moscow than is good for him. Thus our policy suffers from a logical inconsistency: we declare the Castro regime to be intolerable because it is a tool of "international communism," and yet we have so barricaded Cuba off from the Western world that she has been dependent on the communist nations for support. Thus we tend to stimulate the causes for our own complaint.

Even the complaint is exaggerated, for Fidel has shown an extraordinary ability to steer between the twin perils of Peking and Moscow and has followed an iconoclastic approach to Marxism that drives his mentors to despair. His is a do-it-yourself communism that combines a Spanish zest with an African torpor and bears about as much relation to the brand preached by the Russians as the merengue does to the mazurka. The Cubans are nobody's abject servant, as both Moscow and Peking have discovered to their displeasure. Nor are they the hod-carriers of revolution to Latin America. Where conditions are ripe for revolution—where the rich are insensate, the poor are desperate, and peaceful reform is impossible—revolution will break out of its own accord, just as the Castro revolution succeeded with virtually no help from the Cuban communists or from Moscow. Havana may distribute Che Guevara's yellowing pamphlets on how to make a revolution, but if, as Al Smith used to say, no girl was ever corrupted by a book, no revolution has ever been exported by mimeographed instructions on guerrilla warfare.

To ponder American policy toward Cuba is to become convinced that our pride has been wounded even more than our interests. If we examined our reactions calmly, we would discover that we are not really worried about being invaded by seven million Cubans; nor do we seriously believe that Fidel and his companions can subvert the other nations of Latin America with their manuals and their Marxist formulas. Even if Castro were to disappear tomorrow, even if we were to invade Cuba, bring Batista back from exile, and annex the island to Florida, Latin America would be just as shaken by agitation and revolt as it is today—and perhaps a good deal more so.

Castro has understood these problems and he has capitalized on them, but he did not create them. What he has done is to say to our face what most Latin Americans whisper behind our back, and in doing so he has hurt our feelings. We have always had a paternal feeling toward the Cubans, and now we feel, somewhere down deep in our national soul, that they have let us down; even worse, that they have betrayed us. We are like a parent with a child who has not only grown up and left home but actually joined forces with his father's competitors. This is hard on our collective ego. It is why the super-patriots of the extreme Right have scoured the State Department in a search for scapegoats who could be blamed for Castro's rise to power, why the liberal Left has gagged itself and gone into contortions to prove that it cannot be duped where Caribbean communists are concerned, and why a climate of unreason has developed which to this day makes it virtually impossible to discuss the Cuban revolution rationally and without emotion.

In addition to this gnawing irritation that the Cubans have rejected us, there is a feeling of indignation that they have turned to our arch-rivals, the communists. We are mesmerized by the fact that the Cuban revolutionaries call themselves Marxists-Leninists. Indeed, it seems to be the label that bothers us most, for the kind of Marxism they practice is not much different from the various brands of socialism of the rest of the Third World. If the Cubans had only called themselves "revolutionary socialists" or "progressive democrats," life would probably have been much easier for them, and for us too. But there they are, shamelessly proclaiming their communism right in our own back yard. That such a foreign ideology as communism, such an *un-American* ideology, should be allowed to enter the western hemisphere, *our* hemisphere, has struck us as an insult.

It is this absorption with communism as a doctrine and the refusal to distinguish between ideology and national interest that has forced us into such a self-defeating policy in Latin America today. This confusion has been intensified since the death of Kennedy and the by-passing of the social-reform goals of the Alliance for Progress. Even under Kennedy there was a tendency to compromise with the oligarchies and to let a preoccupation with Cuba override some of the more ambitious political goals of the Alliance for Progress. Lyndon Johnson displayed more of a tolerance for dictators, as in Argentina and Brazil, and favored political stability over social reform. This now seems to have become the official policy of the Nixon administration. The report released in late 1969 by Nelson Rockefeller, whose concern for stability in Latin America is fortified by his family's extensive holdings in shipping, banking, oil, real estate, and commerce, warned that the spread of Castroism to the mainland "would present the gravest kind of threat to the security of the Western hemisphere." The Rockefeller report urged more aid to the Latin American military and a lowering of tariff barriers "to provide a vast market for our manufactured goods." Beset by fears of "another Cuba," Washington provides military aid and counter-insurgency training to Latin military regimes that promise "stability."

Lip service to the ideals of the Alliance for Progress remains, but behind it is a tendency on the part of our policy-makers to be satisfied with formal avowals of anti-communism. The vocabulary of the new policy still speaks of the inter-American "family," of good neighborliness, and the hallowed principles of the OAS. But its instruments have been the big stick, the Monroe Doctrine, and that recent refinement of the Roosevelt corollary—the Johnson Doctrine.

12. Whose Hemisphere?

The government of the United States is not entitled to affirm as a universal proposition with reference to a number of independent states for whose conduct it assumes no responsibility, that its interests are necessarily concerned in whatever may befall these states simply because they are situated in the western hemisphere. —LORD SALISBURY, 1895

We don't propose to sit here in our rocking chair with our hands folded and let the communists set up any government in the western hemisphere. —LYNDON B. JOHNSON, 1965

❦ ❦ ❦ "REVOLUTION in any country is a matter for that country to deal with," President Johnson declared on May 2, 1965, as he sent the Marines to Santo Domingo. "It becomes a matter for hemispheric action only when the object is the establishment of a communist dictatorship." This, in essence, is the guiding principle of what has come to be known as the Johnson Doctrine, a formula that would justify the dispatch of United States troops to any country in the hemisphere threatened by a communist take-over. Harking back to the Monroe Doctrine and the Theodore Roosevelt corollary, it asserts the right of the United States to provide order in and exclude unfriendly influences from the Americas—and very sensibly too, according to most people in the United States. What could be more tolerant than our willingness to allow revolutions in other countries, so long as they do not fall into communist hands? What could be more responsible than our determination to keep communist regimes from seizing power in the western hemisphere? Is this not a combination of power and idealism in which all North Americans can take pride and all Latin Americans find encouragement?

Perhaps there are many in Washington who think so, but they are having a hard time defending their views against the Latin American democracies that the Johnson Doctrine is ostensibly meant to benefit. The reason is not that the democratic governments of Latin America like communism, but that they are opposed to a unilateral police power exercised by the United States, and they fear that such interventions as the one at Santo Domingo may actually aid the long-range ambitions of the communists. Further, they have been alarmed by the manner of the Dominican intervention, which was totally contrary to the principle of nonintervention written into the charter of the OAS, and which was launched without the prior consent of the other Latin American governments. Instead of inter-American cooperation to encourage democracy and social reform, the Johnson Doctrine puts the emphasis on a unilateral police action by the United States.

This approach to the problems of social unrest in Latin America rests upon the belief, expressed by President Johnson at Baylor University shortly after the Dominican landings, that "the old distinction between civil war and international war has already lost much of its meaning." Consequently, if the line between internal and external danger is obliterated, then it is possible to treat any serious disturbance of the established order as a justifiable cause for military intervention "by some civilized power," as Theodore Roosevelt said in his corollary. Such threats to order include not only armed insurrection, but even subversion and infiltration, for, as the President explained, "when a communist group seeks to exploit misery, the entire free American system is put in deadly danger." While the President did not indicate how much "deadly danger" the mere presence of a communist group involves, or who would determine when a potential danger had become a deadly danger, it was clear that he was giving the United States *carte blanche* in deciding when, where, and to what degree she chose to intervene with troops in Latin America.

President Johnson went to considerable trouble to demonstrate that he was not breaking new ground but simply affirming an old principle. While the scope of the Doctrine leaves the President's interpretation open to question, it is true that the guidelines for United States intervention against communist regimes in the western hemisphere were laid down by his predecessor. "Let the record show," President Kennedy declared on April 20, 1961, shortly after the Bay of Pigs,

> that our restraint is not inexhaustible. Should it ever appear that the inter-American doctrine of noninterference merely conceals or excuses a policy of nonaction—if the nations of this hemisphere should fail to meet their commitments against outside communist penetration—then I want it clearly understood that this government will not hesitate in meeting its primary obligations, which are the security of this nation.

While the extravagance of President Kennedy's language can be attributed to some degree to his embarrassment over the Bay of Pigs fiasco, it nonetheless implied that military intervention in the Caribbean would not be ruled out even where communist regimes come to power by peaceful means. Perhaps Kennedy did not mean to go that far; perhaps he was simply relating intervention to instances where foreign powers might try to use indigenous communist groups to threaten the security of the United States—as Khrushchev attempted to do eighteen months later by installing missiles in Cuba. Nevertheless, Kennedy set the stage for the Dominican intervention of his successor by linking American security to the suppression of communist regimes within the hemisphere. He was never able to distinguish clearly between the kind of communism in Latin America that was a threat to American security and the kind that was simply a nuisance. Or if he did make the distinction, it was never translated into policy.

Consequently, when President Johnson sent the Marines to Santo Domingo, he was not so much plowing new ground as deepening a furrow dug by his predecessor. Communism in the hemisphere was declared to be inimical to American security, and therefore intervention against it was justified. "Our goal," President Johnson said in an address to the nation early in May 1965, "is to help prevent another communist state in this hemisphere." This statement was based upon the assumption that communists controlled the Dominican revolution. Yet the administration was never able to prove this, nor did it even seem to believe that it was necessary to prove it. It knew there were communists in Santo Domingo, as there are everywhere else in Latin America, and it simply assumed they would gain control of the revolution. For President Johnson, the diplomatic correspondent of the *Wall Street Journal* has written,

> it was never necessary to satisfy himself that the revolution was communist-controlled, or that it *would* produce another Cuba. The point was that it *might*. That risk he found unacceptable. In this conclusion he was strongly reinforced by Dean Rusk, who tended to see the Dominican Republic not in isolation, but as part of a global communist conspiracy and therefore a factor affecting the United States position everywhere in the world, and above all in Vietnam.[1]

In its feverish determination to prevent "another Cuba," with all the internal political embarrassment it might involve, the administration acted as though the two situations were the same, and convinced many people that the United States is the enemy of all revolutions. Today, thanks to the American intervention, the Dominican Republic once again has a right-wing regime offering a safe haven for American investments.

Johnson and his advisers were unsympathetic even to popularly based revolutions in the Caribbean, for they believed that radical reforms would threaten not only American investments but American political control of the area. Washington could accept nationalization of American investments on the South American continent, as it was forced to do in Peru, because direct military intervention would have been extremely difficult. But within the confines of the Caribbean, expropriation of American-owned properties and an embrace of communism are often considered to be synonymous, particularly by key policy-makers and Congressmen with extensive economic interests in such commodities as sugar.

With the landing of the Marines, the United States turned the clock back thirty years in her relations with Latin America. It was not the handful of Latin American communists—most of them isolated and ossified—who suffered from the American intervention. On the contrary, it is the reformers of Latin America who have been harmed, the democrats who have tried to walk the delicate line between military dictatorship on the Right and communist totalitarianism on the Left. The middle ground has been drastically narrowed, and reformers driven to extremes of violent action. By her intervention the United States has given powerful support to the Fidelista argument that there can be no hope for serious reform by anything short of a communist revolution. Unless our policy is drastically revised, we ourselves will have helped stimulate the revolutions we most fear.

Thus, while it is ostensibly directed against communism, the Johnson Doctrine is an invaluable boon to revolutionaries. It supports their argument that the United States is the bulwark of the oligarchies and will not tolerate any change in the status quo. If Latin Americans, as a result of the lesson at Santo Domingo, accept this argument, they will have nowhere to turn but to the revolutionaries for the social changes they are determined to bring about. If the door to reform is closed, the door to revolution will be blasted open, because almost everywhere in Latin America the status quo is not good enough. Today the radicals are listened to in the impoverished areas of Latin America by people who have no interest in Marxist dialectics or in the cold war, but who have despaired of finding in their present societies food for their families, land they can till, schools to educate them, houses in which they can live, jobs to employ them, and medical care to keep them alive. If the middle-class reformers are driven to the same despair as the poor, if they abdicate their role of democratic leadership or turn to extremist solutions as the only alternative to stagnation, there may be little hope for nonviolent reforms.

The problem of communism in Latin America is a serious one,

but not in the way it is generally conceived by official Washington. Since we have virtually no domestic communist problem, most North Americans see communism as a conspiracy nourished by hostile foreign powers and thus totally alien to the societies that individual communists are trying to transform or subvert. But the Latin Americans, who have real communists of their own, view their problem rather differently. For them communism is not an abstract "international conspiracy" directed from a distant Politburo, but a specific reaction to social conditions within their own countries. It is not an abstraction to be fought with another abstraction—be it an Alliance for Progress or theories of welfare capitalism. Even less is it a Russian (or Chinese) plot to turn them into satellites. Rather, it is an extreme response to a desperate situation.

We North Americans, who have the fortune to live in societies where democracy is a living reality and not a cheap form of rhetoric, where change can come through the ballot box rather than by the sword, where the law is a generally respected standard of justice and not an instrument of oppression, cannot begin to understand why Latin Americans turn to rebellion and even to communism. But the Latin Americans understand, and it is the democratic reformers who are the most opposed to the simplistic approach of Washington toward Latin American communism. They recognize that it cannot be stamped out by bayonets, that by being driven underground it only becomes more powerful, and that the only viable alternative to communism is a democratic revolution. The dangers posed by United States policy were made clear by Chilean President Eduardo Frei when he told an American journalist:

> The problem of communism is entirely different when seen from the perspectives of the United States and Latin America. In the United States communism is a problem of power, a problem of relative military and economic strength among the United States, Russia, and China. But in Latin America communism is an internal, not a foreign, problem. Communism is a danger in Latin America because it has found roots in the soil here. It thrives with or without Castro because he is not the important element. The

strength of communism in Latin America is born and resides in the masses, among peasants and marginal people without land, slum-dwellers, and workers with low salaries—in other words, in the poverty and more than that in the misery of the people. They seek in communism a way to change their lives, and that is what communism and sometimes communism alone offers them.

Second, communism also has great ideological appeal. The young people in Latin America are restless and searching for answers to our problems. They look to politics to supply some of these answers. Thus in Latin America communism is also a problem of philosophy, of ideas. It is not a police problem to be dealt with by repression. The first weapon against communism in Latin America is economic development and social justice—social justice in particular because many times economic development favors only a small group. It is very important for the United States to understand this.[2]

It is on President Frei's Chile, where a resurgent Christian Democratic Party subdued the military and crushed a powerful Marxist group in the 1964 elections, that liberals pinned their hope for non-violent reform in Latin America. With the support of a progressive Catholic Church that was one of the first to teach the encyclicals of Pope John XXIII, with the aid of young people and a reform-conscious middle class, the Chilean Christian Democrats tried to outflank the oligarchy and the Castro-inspired Left. Promising reforms as sweeping as those advocated by Moscow-line communists, and with a record free of compromise with the oligarchy or dictatorships (unlike the communists in Cuba under Batista, in Brazil under Vargas, and in Argentina during the early days of Perón), the Christian Democratic Parties of Latin America offer a possible alternative to Marxist authoritarianism. Further, they promise reform without cutting themselves off from the trade between Latin America and the United States on which Latin American markets depend. But Frei's daring experiment to achieve "revolution in liberty" produced no revolution and not enough reform to satisfy the radicals. His party was torn by ideological differences, and the country became increasingly polarized between extreme Left and Right. While Chile has had a long democratic tradition, this is the kind of situation that provoked military intervention in Argentina, Brazil, and Peru. In Peru the army has been reform-minded and has won wide popular support by such nationalistic measures as expropriation of American-owned sugar holdings and Standard Oil properties. In Brazil and Argentina right-wing military regimes stress economic growth and political repression.

It may be unrealistic to expect both stability and democracy in much of Latin America within the near future, considering its severe economic problems and its weak democratic traditions. The creation of Western-style democracies will be the work not of decades, but of generations. Latin Americans, faced with the enormous problems of economic development and social reform, are also the inheritors of a political tradition where change is usually brought about by violence. Only in such countries as Costa Rica, Uruguay, and Mexico has the military been brought under control and democratic procedures established. These countries are not in danger of a social revolution because there are institutionalized procedures for reform. Such countries as Chile and Venezuela, which are trying to achieve a peaceful social revolution, may also be able to find an alternative to violent change. But nearly everywhere else the right-wing oligarchy has dug in its heels, the Center is paralyzed by doubt and indecision, the liberal Left is a prisoner of its traditional factionalism and preference for rhetoric over action, while the young radicals flirt with violence and fanaticism on the Chinese model. It may be that in many countries social reform can be achieved only by circumventing democratic procedure.

One alternative, of course, is popular revolution on the Cuban model—an uprising of the peasants and the urban proletariat, led by the alienated middle-class intellectuals. It is the fear of this which has so galvanized official Washington, and in certain countries the political climate shows signs of being favorable to such a prospect. But more likely over the short run is the possibility of direct intervention by the Latin American military —not always a reactionary intervention in support of the oligarchy, but at times an intervention against it. While the Latin American military establishments have shifted to the right since the Castro revolution, they are not necessarily committed to playing a reactionary role. Nor are they strangers to politics, *une grande muette*. On the contrary, the army in Latin America is a political instrument with a rich tradition of direct intervention in civilian affairs.

To most North Americans and Europeans the first aim of any democratic government should be to keep soldiers out of politics. In politically developed countries, where there is a variety of powerful political and social groups, this is a reasonable ambition. But in Latin America to keep the army out of politics is to evict it from its natural habitat. During the past twenty-five years only three nations, Mexico, Chile, and Uruguay, have enjoyed uninterrupted civilian government; the others have been rocked by a succession of *revolucións* and *golpes de estado*. It is estimated that Venezuela has had 50 revolutions since independence, Bolivia 150, Mexico perhaps 1000. Some of these have been little more than change of faces in the presidential palace; others have been more serious. By any standard the record is formidable. The reason, however, lies not in any special Latin American propensity toward violence, but in the absence of a solid political tradition of civilian government and of strong political institutions to resist the military. The army is powerful because every other group is weak. Apart from the Catholic Church, it is virtually the only organized group in Latin America. The political parties—with the exception of the populist forces in Peru, Venezuela, and Bolivia, and more recently the Christian Democrats in Chile and Peru —have tended to be weak and often corrupt. "In many of the republics," the historian S. E. Finer has written,

> notably those in Central America . . . politics is largely a struggle between rival urban elites over the heads of a predominantly passive and hermetic native peasantry. It is a strife of personalities, powerful by virtue of their social or economic position, to broaden and consolidate their power at the national level. . . . The traditional parties with their various names—Radicals, Conservatives, *Colorados, Blancos*—are usually little but highly personalized cliques with few and shallow roots in the countryside. Again, over most of the subcontinent, representative institutions are tarnished by over a century of massive corruption, manipulation, peculation, and fraud.

. . . By contrast, the armies are powerful. They are strong by virtue of their necessarily hierarchical and disciplinarian organization, as well as by their monopoly of modern arms. But they are strong, also, by reason of moral factors. The republics are in fact the endowments of their armies. Their founding fathers were *caudillos*—the Bolívars and San Martíns, the Sucres and the Paezes; and the armies have never suffered their population to forget it. Again, in the highly stratified society of the various republics . . . the army has traditionally provided the means of social mobility. The highest military office (as the *dicho* goes) is the Presidency of the Republic.[3]

With this rich tradition of participation in politics, any facile generalization about "putting the military in its place" tends to break down. In most of the Latin American republics its place is square in the middle of politics. There it has exercised power as well as toppled it, and the role it has played has varied enormously, depending on the country involved and the situation at the time. Some of the Latin American military establishments have been reactionary, some have been progressive, some have been Center-moderates, and all have been opportunistically pro-military. In Argentina the military has on various occasions allied itself with the ranchers, with labor, with the middle class; and may yet switch Left again. In Brazil the army has consistently intervened in politics, but as the self-appointed protector of constitutionalism from its enemies on the extreme right and the extreme left. In Venezuela the army a decade ago suppressed the socialists and welcomed the support of the communists, while today it does the reverse. Even Batista's army in pre-Castro Cuba forged a liaison with labor and accepted communist help. The military regime in Paraguay is perhaps the most reactionary and oppressive in Latin America, but the military government in Brazil has reformist elements, while it is the generals in Peru who are pushing the oligarchy to accept social reforms.

The modern Latin American army is, first of all, no longer merely an instrument of the ruling oligarchy. It is a powerful force in itself and conceives of its role as that of guardian of the national interest. In this sense it can find, and frequently has found, itself at odds with the oligarchy—and in some cases even the instrument of its repression. Second, these armies are not directed by either bandits or idle aristocrats. Increasingly the younger officers are being recruited from the rising middle class, whose interests in democratic reform they tend to express. These officers have been trained in Northern technology (usually in the United States) and exposed to Northern ideas. They are not against social reform and are often passionately in favor of it. It was the young officers, for example, who overthrew the dictatorship of the older generals in the Dominican Republic in April 1965 and tried to return the nation to constitutional rule.

Third, these armies are no longer simply gold-braid window dressing, useful only for parades, dress balls, and *coups d'état.* They may not have to defend their borders against their neighbors, although they do it nonetheless, but they are becoming preoccupied with the effort of pacification in their own hinterland. There guerrilla bands have sprung up in profusion, some of them led by bandits, others by religious fanatics, some of them calling themselves communist—and all a potential threat to political stability. There are Fidelista-inspired guerrillas in Venezuela and Colombia, in Honduras and Guatemala, in Peru and in Bolivia. In trying to suppress these guerrilla bands, the army has discovered that they only spring up again if the causes of discontent are not dealt with and the support of the peasants is not won. As the Latin American armies become enmeshed in the pacification of the countryside, they find themselves playing the role of reformers, building roads, hospitals, and schools. Consciously or not, they are agents of social change, or at least in those countries with leadership wise enough to realize that rebellion cannot be stamped out by repression.

Fourth, the Latin American military is becoming highly politicized. Young officers tend to admire such leaders as President Nasser and Colonel Boumedienne. They pore over the revolutionary manuals of Mao Tse-tung and Che Guevara. They know their Karl Marx perhaps even better than their Thomas Jefferson, and they often speak in the loose vocabulary of Marxism—which naïve North Americans too easily equate with communism—of "neo-colonialism" and "imperialism," the stock phrases of the Left in all developing countries. This does not mean they are communist—usually quite the opposite—but that they are becoming politically conscious and are not necessarily opposed to the ambitions of the radical reformers. Younger officers often find common cause with radical student and labor groups in denouncing "foreign intervention" and "economic colonialism." Many even have an admiration for Castro in his defiance of the United States and his rapid climb to world fame.

All of these forces working together have changed the role of the Latin American armies, making them more like the armed forces in the other developing states of the Third World. From self-interest, professional pride, and patriotic nationalism, they are developing a vested interest in modernization. And in traditional societies modernization is impossible without social reform. Thus, almost unconsciously, the Latin American armies are becoming instruments of change. In this new role, their natural allies are not the established oligarchies, whose thinking and whose methods younger officers often find reactionary, but the middle-class reformers—the students, the journalists, the teachers, and the new generation of technocrats. Products of the same background and moved by similar aspirations, these discontented reformers of the middle class are discovering that the army is not necessarily their enemy.

As the army becomes more politically conscious, more eager for the modernization that is the hallmark of contemporary nationalism, more drawn into the problems of social reform, it is likely to assume an increasingly important political role. A Latin American brand of Nasserism is developing, in which the army will have to plunge even deeper into politics in order to carry out the reforms that the middle-class Left is incapable of putting through by itself. The pattern must obviously vary from country to country: in places such as Costa Rica and Mexico reform has such firm roots and the role of the army is so restricted that military intervention is unnecessary and unlikely. In countries such as

Chile, Colombia, and Venezuela the army can be a powerful ally of the reform-conscious governments of the Left-center. But in much of Latin America the democratic Left is so disorganized and ossified, so corrupt and so ineffectual, that the main burden for social change must fall on the army simply because there is no one else. Thus it may well be possible that in some of the more repressive and dictatorial countries a politicized military elite will ally itself with the restive middle-class reformers, the urban proletariat, and the dispossessed peasants to break the stranglehold of the oligarchy, implement social reforms, and push the society headlong into the technocratic revolution of the mid-twentieth century. This now seems to be happening in Peru.

It would be an irony if social reforms should be carried through by the military brass, but it is one which has already taken place in a good many other underdeveloped states. Even if the political parties of the Left-center should take heart from the Christian Democratic experiment in Chile, they cannot hope to push through essential reforms over the opposition of the army. They need its cooperation, or at very least its neutralization. This is why the liberal's predilection to look on all military intervention as a bad thing by definition is confusing and unhelpful in Latin America. In some countries the only serious alternatives to Castro-style revolutions may be military regimes on the Egyptian model, espousing one of the varieties of "basic democracy" or "progressive socialism" that are such specialties in the new states of the Third World. Nasserism may not seem to us a particularly inspiring political doctrine, nor is it the solution we might prefer for our Latin American friends. But in countries where the democratic tradition is weak, where the oligarchies are strong and the pressures are reaching the explosion point, it may be the best that we, or the Latin Americans, can hope for.

The Latin Americans are saddled with problems that have no easy answer, many of them, perhaps no answer at all within a democratic context. In their frustration, Latin American reformers berate the United States for not doing what they have been unable to do themselves. Overestimating the purposeful exercise of

American power, and identifying the role of American business with that of the American government, Latin Americans see the heavy hand of the United States even where it is not necessarily present. Just as they assume that it is entirely our fault that they live under tyrannical governments, so they imagine that we can dismiss the tyrants at will. They criticize us for interfering in their affairs, and then complain that we do not use our power to achieve objectives which they consider desirable. They want us to solve their problems but to do so without interfering.

Often without realizing it themselves, Latin Americans have an ambivalent attitude toward the United States. They want us to protect them from foreign enemies, to coddle them, to develop economically their backward societies, and to feel responsible for them—as long as we ask nothing in return. The oligarchies applaud our intervention against left-wing regimes such as those in Guatemala, Cuba, and the Dominican Republic, while the left-wing radicals urge us to condemn the current rightist dictatorships in Haiti, Paraguay, and Guatemala. They want us, in other words, to intervene where it suits their purpose, and not to intervene where it doesn't. They seem to need the United States to rail against as much as to emulate, to provide solutions for their problems and to blame for their own shortcomings.

This is particularly true of the left-wing Latin American intellectuals, who have a tendency to compensate for their own political incapacity and their abdication to the oligarchies by engaging in a shrill anti-Americanism. This allows them to rationalize their own impotence and to retain the purity of ideals unsullied by the responsibilities of power. These intellectuals are in a state of rebellion against themselves as well as against their own societies, and, rather than face the truth of their predicament, prefer to blame the United States. They are the true dispossessed of Latin America, too educated to accept the feudal social structures of their societies, too imbued with the stock phrases of elementary Marxism to be objective, too politically frustrated to be fully rational, and too weak and hesitant to lead the struggle for social reform. They are, as Frank Tannenbaum has written,

really caught in a world where their major role is that of critic.
. . . They would have the best of both worlds; the patronal, sen-
orial society and the egalitarian and industrial one, and will not
recognize that they cannot have them both. There is no way out of
the dilemma by a deliberate act of will. They cannot reject either
of the two worlds or remain content with one. The schizophrenic
world they live in is beyond their control; and we must accept that
for the next generation or longer the intellectuals will be possessed
by a restless, bitter, and turbulent mood. America will be the major
target of this inability to square the circle; to make an agrarian
feudalism fit in nicely with an industrial egalitarianism, for fortune
has cast the United States as the major symbol of their dissatisfac-
tion with both worlds.[4]

It would be a mistake to attach too much importance to this
emotional anti-Americanism, just as it would be a mistake to ignore it. The exercise of power rarely elicits affection, and we live
in a hemisphere where the United States is by far the greatest
power. We have to expect a certain amount of anti-Americanism
from those who are confined to our back yard. But by the same
token, we would be wise to do what we can to restrain or deflect
it. Because we assume that there should be such a thing as an
inter-American "family," under our direction, we have tried to
bind the Latin American nations to us in a tight organizational
embrace, ranging from military-aid pacts to such hemispheric political bodies as the OAS. This tight embrace, which is not required by United States military security, stems from our patronal
tendency to shepherd the Latin Americans and insulate them from
other parts of the world. But to Latin Americans this embrace has
been more stifling than comforting. They resent our patronizing
attitude and they want to break loose from abject dependency
on the United States, simply to assert their own political identity.
In a continent where gestures are sometimes more important than
actions, the ability to resist the United States is extremely important. As we have seen, one of the major appeals of Fidel Castro,
even among those who oppose much that the Cuban revolution
stands for, is that he dared defy the colossus of the North.

Among people who feel trapped and dominated, this is a perfectly understandable reaction, and it is one we can sympathize with. It is also one which we can help relieve, for it is of no benefit to us to have the Latin Americans tied to our apron strings and to be responsible for every military coup and peasant revolt. It is to our interest, as much as to the interest of the Latin Americans, to loosen our organizational ties, to downgrade the military provisions of the OAS, and to encourage the Latin Americans to strengthen their ties with one another. Above all, we can urge them to open links with the big world that lies beyond the western hemisphere—with the countries of Europe they look on as their cultural parents, with the new states of Africa and Asia whose problems of underdevelopment and instability they often share, and even with the communist countries that can provide the markets and the materials they need. It is to nobody's advantage to have the Latin American nations cooped up in the western hemisphere, with the United States holding the jailer's key.

There is a great deal that we can do to help the Latin Americans, but there are also sharp limits to our ability to solve their most basic problems for them. We can, and indeed should, wish them well in their efforts to break the grip of their feudal oligarchies and achieve some real measure of social democracy. We can aid them by loans and grants through such bodies as the Inter-American Development Bank and the Alliance for Progress. We can buy more of their primary commodities, work out agreements to regulate the widely fluctuating prices of these commodities, and reduce our tariff barriers on their manufactured projects. We can continue to send our technicians where they are requested, furnish advice where it is solicited, and encourage the self-help that is essential to any healthy relationship between the two Americas. We ought to be exceedingly restrained in our relationships with dictators and lend a hand to the social reformers and democrats who share our ideals.

All this, of course, is also a form of intervention, and it would be foolish to deny it. Every time we make a loan, demand a reform, receive an emissary, or sign a commodity agreement, we are intervening in Latin American affairs. We cannot help it. So great is our economic and military power that we can intervene simply by doing nothing, by letting a country subside into economic stagnation or refraining from the support of a reform-oriented regime. With a gross national product more than ten times that of all Latin America combined, we are bound to be the dominant force in the hemisphere, regardless of what we do. We cannot help intervening in societies where both our presence and our absence are equally critical—and, in many cases, equally resented.

The problem, therefore, is one not of intervention versus non-intervention, but of what kind of intervention best serves our interests and those of the Latin Americans we are ostensibly trying to help. In this effort it is essential to distinguish between military intervention with American forces, and economic intervention under the Alliance for Progress. Overt military intervention is neither immoral nor unjustified in the abstract. The decision depends upon the facts of the situation and the stakes involved. There was nothing immoral about the United States intervention in Western Europe to defeat the Nazis or contain the Russians. Nor, for that matter, was there anything immoral in principle about the United States intervention in Santo Domingo. It was merely stupid. Had there been a direct threat to the security of the United States, as there was in the Cuban missile crisis, few would have criticized the Dominican landings. The mistake, however, was to use American military power in the Caribbean—with all the loss of prestige inevitably involved—against the mere *possibility* that communists might ultimately seize control of a reformist regime. Most Americans seem to fear that this nation would be threatened by "another Cuba." But even if Caribbean communism should pose a danger to the United States, there is an even greater danger in panicking over it. In contemplating the problem of military intervention in the Caribbean, as a former State Department official has written,

> all that is urged is that we be prudent, that we pay a decent respect to the opinions of mankind. If indeed a communist regime emerges, we are emphatically on record that we will not permit its survival,

and we can move strongly against it. If we cannot tell whether a regime is communist or not, then let us act on the assumption that it is not; it will pose no threat to our security. Above all, let us not conclude automatically that because known communists are associated with popular movements, even movements sired by violence out of desperation, that the movements are ineradicably tainted. Had our intelligence services been as ubiquitous and as susceptible to cold-war criteria in 1930 as they are today, Romulo Betancourt would never have reached the Venezuelan presidency to put his country firmly on the march toward effective democracy.[5]

This is a rule of thumb the United States can live with, and one that will serve her interests far better than Pavlovian reactions to communism. United States military intervention must be confined to legitimate threats to American security. If ever anything proved that the principle of nonintervention is basically sound, the disastrous interventions at the Bay of Pigs and at Santo Domingo did. They accomplished nothing except to provide fodder for the communists and convince most Latin Americans that the United States is opposed to any social reforms that might lessen her traditional political and economic hegemony. While it is possible to defend military intervention in the Caribbean because the area lies within the United States sphere of influence, it is not logically possible to defend such intervention when it defeats the very purpose it is designed to advance.

Nor is the Pentagon's current infatuation with "counter-insurgency" tactics and the creation of an inter-American police force of OAS members likely to serve any interests but those of the Latin American oligarchies. A United States-financed brigade of Paraguayans, Brazilians, and Peruvians parachuting in to suppress communist-inspired revolutions in other countries is a prescription for twenty Vietnams. Small wonder that the idea has been greeted with contempt by the democratic governments of Latin America.

If we could bring some kind of order to Latin America, if we could ensure the triumph of democracy in countries where it is scarcely more than rhetoric, then there might be some reason for our desire to play schoolmaster to the other nations of the hemisphere. But where we tried to enforce order, as in Mexico during its civil war, we only ensured continued anarchy; where we tried to topple a communist government, as at the Bay of Pigs, we assured the survival of Castroism in Cuba; and where we tried to suppress a revolution for fear communists might be involved, we only increased the stature of the communists and assured continuing chaos from which only they can profit. We are such incompetent imperialists, such naïve Machiavellis, that we would do better to leave off such activities entirely and instead concentrate on areas in which we have some competence and where our presence is, if not welcomed, at least not looked upon with fear and disgust.

We shall be tempted to continue plunging into the maelstrom of Latin America with military force. We shall do so, of course, for noble motives: to advance democracy, or speed modernization, or punish tyrants, or defeat communists, or suppress revolutions. Some of these military interventions will come from habit, others from a desire to help others in spite of themselves, and not a few from a misguided sense of national interest. There are those who believe that such interventions are essential, that we must bring democracy and the (North) American Way of Life to our Latin neighbors, or that we have some kind of divine right to decree what kind of governments other nations should be allowed to have, or that a handful of communists in Guyana or Paraguay represents a mortal threat to democracy in the western hemisphere. This is, to be sure, one way of looking at our relations with the Latin Americans. But it is not one that is likely to do them, or us, any good.

The real problem in our relations with Latin America is not how we can bring democracy by the sword, but how we can aid the Latin Americans to achieve economic development and social reform. The Alliance for Progress tried to stimulate such reforms by demanding them as a condition of American aid. The attempt was a noble one, but it failed because the Alliance was never able to penetrate the barrier of the Latin American oligarchies and secure the allegiance of the middle-class reformers. Shorn of its more idealistic ambitions for achieving social change, the Alianza has now been transformed into a subdivision of the foreign-aid program.

In the long run no American economic-aid program can force the Latin Americans to pursue social reforms. If the nations of Latin America are to become progressive and democratic societies, they will have to do so mostly by their own efforts. We can make the going easier for governments that have demonstrated a willingness and a capacity to push through the changes that are needed to achieve economic growth. Such governments exist today in Chile, Brazil, Colombia, Venezuela, Costa Rica, Peru, and perhaps two or three others. For the rest, there is little we can do for them until they show some signs of being willing to help themselves. All things considered, we would do best not to worry overly about whether or not, or to what degree, these regimes are democratic. First comes economic development. Democracy, if it comes at all, will follow later. The former offers a field in which we can be of some assistance; the latter is a task that the individual Latin American societies can work out only for themselves. Perhaps the best we can do for the Latin Americans at this time is to step back a bit, so that they may resolve their own social problems, without trying to impose a North American image upon them. We have labored over the Latin Americans too long and intervened too often in their internal affairs. We have been made the scapegoat for their economic deficiencies and political shortcomings. But we have asked for it by our interference and have no one to blame but ourselves.

The problem of our relations with Latin America has been compounded by the mischievous legacy of the Monroe Doctrine and its various misapplications. But it also furnishes a dramatic example of our efforts to remake whole societies by infusions of money and advice—a program of economic intervention never before attempted by any nation, and one that has involved us deeply, and often unwittingly, in the mounting political disorder of the Third World of emerging states.

13. White Man's Burden

It is annoying to be virtuous to no purpose.　　　—OVID

❦ ❦ ❦ FOR the past two decades the United States has been engaged in a massive program of technical, military, and economic aid to other nations. Much of this goes to the support of client states, some of it to indigent friends, and a good deal to self-declared neutrals. Since the launching of the Marshall Plan in 1948 we have injected some $120 billion into building up the armies and developing the economies of some one hundred nations. Born of the cold war and perennially justified to Congress and the taxpayers as a weapon in the arsenal against communism, foreign aid has been one of the least understood and most maligned forms of American intervention. Unloved by those who pay for it, misconceived by those who support it, and distrusted by those who receive it, the aid program has been subject to skepticism and abuse that continually threaten its survival.

To some, foreign aid is a giveaway program that pours American dollars down foreign rat-holes from which they never again emerge —except perhaps in the form of air-conditioned Cadillacs and marble palaces for heads of new nations. To others, foreign aid is a way of buying cold-war allies and, in the process, stimulating American exports by creating potential customers. Others see foreign aid as a kind of antidote by which the backward states can be immunized against communist blandishments and by which representative government and free enterprise can be achieved. Many assume that foreign aid, by stimulating economic development, can help overcome some of the instability to which the backward nations are prone. Finally, there are those who consider foreign aid as basically a charity, an obligation of the rich to help ameliorate some of the misery of the poor.

Whatever attitude we now take toward it, foreign aid in its present form grew out of the cold war, was nourished by it, and is almost totally dependent upon it for survival. Every year since 1948 the President has gone before Congress with a foreign-aid request which he has defended as being absolutely vital to the national interest. Every year the Congress nips away at the aid budget, never quite convinced of the argument, never sure it is totally wrong, and grudgingly passes a hacked-up aid bill in the belief that it is helping to fight the cold war. But the growing belief in continued "peaceful coexistence" between America and Russia has undermined much of the support for foreign aid as a cold-war weapon, and the disappointing experience of the new nations has dampened enthusiam for aid as a cure-all for instability. The aid program is foundering in Congress, which has grown increasingly skeptical of its goals, and also among Americans in general, who do not see its achievements and are dubious about its necessity. Even liberals who have been long-time defenders of foreign aid have begun to ask, like Senator Fulbright, "if aid is just a tool and part of a new policy of manifest destiny in Asia."

The old justifications for foreign aid have worn thin, and the survival of the program itself is in doubt. The need for a foreign-aid program has not diminished. If anything, it has grown. But the reasons are no longer what they were, or what we thought they were. The world has changed radically within the past decade, but the old arguments for dispensing aid continue to be sounded by the administration, in Congress, and in the press. The gap between rhetoric and reality has grown to serious proportions. For our own sake we urgently need to rethink the purpose of foreign aid and what we hope to accomplish by it.

The concept of foreign aid became linked with the question of national security beginning with the Lend-Lease Act of 1940, by which Franklin Roosevelt stretched the definition of nonintervention to help a beleaguered Britain resist the Nazis. This link was reinforced during World War II, when we sent massive shipments of military supplies to our allies. In 1947, to help combat the danger of communism in the war-weakened democracies of Western Europe, Secretary of State George Marshall proposed a massive program of economic assistance. The Marshall Plan was an enlightened and extraordinarily successful act of self-interest and philanthropy that helped Western Europe get back on its economic feet and put to rest the fear that communism would come to power there from within.

Following the outbreak of the Korean war in June 1950, the foreign-aid program was expanded from a recovering Europe to the underdeveloped and poverty-stricken nations that seemed most susceptible to communist penetration. This aid took two forms: the Point Four program, which was basically a humanitarian effort to raise living standards through economic and technical assistance, and the military-aid program, which sought to bolster a select number of nations around the rim of the communist empire. In many cases the two programs overlapped; countries which received the lion's share of military aid—Iran, Pakistan, Thailand, South Vietnam, Taiwan, and South Korea—were also high on the list for economic and technical assistance. For convenience, and also to make the program more attractive to Congress, both military and economic assistance were lumped together under the single category "foreign aid."

This has been a source of confusion for many Americans, who believe that all the money appropriated for "foreign aid" goes into grants and loans for economic development. Yet, in any given year, about half the aid funds go for military purposes. In 1966, for example, President Johnson asked Congress for $3.4 billion in foreign aid "in the deep conviction that we must use foreign assistance to attack the root causes of world poverty." But of that sum, $917 million was earmarked for "direct military assistance" to a select group of states bordering Russia and China, while another $747 million was to be spent on "supporting assistance" to countries—such as South Vietnam, Laos, Thailand, and South Korea—which spend more on their military forces than they can

afford. The bulk of our military aid goes to nations whose inhabitants have an average income of less than $200 a year—a condi-
tion which led John Kenneth Galbraith, our former Ambassador
to India, to tell a Senate committee that "there is something in-
trinsically obscene in the combination of ill-fed people and well-
fed armies."

Obscene or not, it is a familiar feature of our aid program and
it is what induces Congress to justify such a strange thing as giving money away to foreigners. Without the military-assistance program as the tail to wag the foreign-aid dog, it is quite likely that
Congress would vote even less money for economic assistance to
the underdeveloped nations than it already does. Sophisticates in
Congress and in the administration secretly scoff at the naïveté of
those who conceive of foreign aid in purely cold-war terms. But
they are themselves often the victims of a cold-war mentality.
They unquestioningly assume that the economic development
of the poor countries will serve America's cold-war interests, and
they seem to believe that such development will help bring about
political stability. Their motives are not selfish, and they sincerely
want to help the less fortunate peoples emerge from stagnation
and misery. But they have a propensity to view the ills of a world
torn by rival ideologies, tribal passions, racial tensions, cultural
breakdowns, and virulent nationalism as basically an engineering
problem. As we imagine that our own social problems—among
them the alienation of the Negro, the disintegration of the family structure, and the decay of urban society—can be ameliorated
and even solved by money, so we approach the world from a similar point of reference.

Poverty is conceived of as being the spawning ground of communism: if poverty is somehow eradicated in the world, there will
be no more communism and, beyond that, perhaps even no more
violence. What self-determination was to President Wilson, so a
healthy gross national product is to our generation: the assur-
ance of universal justice and peace. Thus President Johnson has
told us that by eradicating the poverty on which such pernicious
doctrines as communism feed, we can eliminate war itself. "Only

when we root out the very causes of war—the poverty of man's body, the privation of his spirit, the imprisonment of his liberties —will there be a final surrender of violence itself. That is our aim in Asia as it has been our aim twice this century in Europe." [1]

The fact that this aim has twice failed in Europe has not prevented it from being pursued in Asia. It does not seem to matter that it has failed in Europe or that it is failing in Asia. And it does not matter because it is basically an act of faith, an expression of America's image of herself, not a program relevant to the world at large. It is an acting-out of the American Dream on a global scale —a dream that all human struggle can be defined in terms of poverty, that political consent rests upon economic advancement, that nations, like individuals, will always act in terms of their economic self-interest, that money is the root of all human endeavor. This is why President Johnson, taking note of the problems of poverty in North Vietnam as well as in most of Asia, did not understand why Hanoi refused to negotiate with him, why, indeed, it referred to his policy of napalm today and foreign aid tomorrow as the policy of "the broken stick and the rotten carrot."

To one who believes that violence can be defined in terms of poverty, the offer of a vast program of economic development in exchange for communist capitulation in South Vietnam seems like an eminently reasonable exchange. To President Johnson and his advisers it was inconceivable that Hanoi would fail to respond to such an offer—particularly when it was combined with the pressure of our aerial bombardment. It is inconceivable in an American frame of reference, but it is happening nonetheless. The reason is that nationalistic and ideological struggles cannot be bought off with bribes of economic assistance. Money can buy many things, but not political stability in countries shaken by rebellion, nor tranquillity in a world plagued by anarchy. Poverty is only one of many causes of instability, and even if we were, by some miracle, able to do away with poverty in the backward nations, they might well continue to be unstable, prone to violence, and tempted to commit aggression against their neighbors. It was not poverty that caused the civil rebellion in Vietnam, the communal violence in Cyprus, the tribal wars in the Congo, and the revolts of the Kurds in Iraq, the Ibos in Nigeria, and the Nagas in India. Poverty may be *a* cause of instability, but there are other causes, some of them far more powerful, and taking the edge off poverty may even bring those other causes to the fore.

The struggle against poverty as the cause of internal instability in the developing nations is, in a sense, replacing the old struggle with Russia as the basic justification for a policy of global intervention. Although we initially intervened to halt communism, we have more recently become entranced by the vision of a global Great Society in which the United States would serve as an international social worker, applying the balm of surplus grains, second-hand tanks, and dollar grants to a disturbed world. The effort to contain communism has now been translated into an obligation to arrest the forces of violence in human society. "Indeed," as President Johnson has said, "we know that so interwoven is our destiny with the world's destiny, so intricate are the bonds between us and every continent, that our responsibilities would be just as real in the absence of the communist threat." [2]

Thus has the containment of communism in Europe, which was a realistic program essential to America's own security, been magnified into a project for the protection of mankind from instability and violence. This is certainly an ambitious goal, but it is also an arrogant and even a dangerous one, for it could well involve us in a series of military interventions to support the client governments that are dependent upon our economic and military assistance for survival. This responsibility for the world's destiny may flatter our national ego, but it is not within our capacity to perform, and it certainly cannot be brought about by any foreign-aid program. Economic assistance to the poorer nations is necessary, but this has little relation to the cold war, or to the quest for political stability. It is, rather, a matter of narrowing the chasm between the privileged, mostly white, minority living in the industrialized nations of the northern hemisphere and the fringes of Oceania and southern Africa, and the impoverished, mostly nonwhite majority roused to political consciousness in Asia and in the southern hemisphere.

The problem is a pressing one because the majority of mankind has become aware that its poverty, its hopelessness, and its economic exploitation are not decreed by the stars and beyond man's control. The problem has been intensified by the falling death rate due to the introduction of public-health services in the backward nations. This has led to a population explosion that is swelling the overcrowded cities and putting enormous pressures on already inadequate food supplies. And the problem has been pushed to the level of crisis by the great revolutionary doctrines of our time, which preach radical remedies for intolerable conditions of misery and injustice.

The poor nations have to be helped, to be developed, and to be offered hope for the future, not only for their sake, but for ours. This effort will make great demands on the political resources and the patience of the developed nations. It will be even more trying for the backward nations, for it will demand both economic revolution and transformation of their societies in every respect. It means a rejection of age-old ways and a wholesale adoption of new, confusing, and deeply resented foreign customs. This transformation can probably not be achieved without turbulence, confusion, and even a recourse to violence. "It may very well be," economist Robert Heilbroner has observed,

> that in choosing the road to industrialization the underdeveloped lands are preparing for a period of distress and disorder far greater than any they have heretofore known. It is almost certain that industrialization will force upon leaders and underlying population alike trials and disappointments of such magnitude that the past, softened by distance, will often appear more attractive than the future, and the whole long march pointless and hopeless. And yet, given the realities of underdevelopment today and the overwhelming likelihood that under the population flood conditions can only worsen unless drastic remedies are tried, the decision is beyond possible dissent. For there is no possible alleviation for the hunger of the majority of the world, no possible replacement of its hovels, no manageable redress of its misery, short of a prolonged and profound economic reorganization of their lives.[1]

Thus foreign aid has become a burden which is unlikely to bring happiness, yet which cannot be avoided because the alternative is even worse. It is an obligation incumbent upon the rich nations from simple humanity, and also from an elementary regard for their own self-interest. For the industrialized nations the real problem is not whether they ought to furnish aid, but *how* to furnish such assistance intelligently to nations which can use it efficiently. Even more important, it is how to furnish aid without becoming involved in the instability in the developing countries resulting from the unfulfilled promises of national leaders, and how to prevent such instability from leading to the intervention of the great powers. Aid can theoretically lay the groundwork for eventual military intervention either by committing the donor nation to the political survival of friendly regimes, as in South Vietnam, or by stimulating expectations that when unfulfilled give rise to upheavals. Such dangers can be handled only by the most supple and intelligent leadership in the emerging countries, and by a considerable forbearance in the donor nations.

Experience has shown that foreign aid is not a useful way of bringing about political tranquillity in unstable lands. Rather, it is a means of providing an extra boost for those emerging nations which have the capacity and the desire to help themselves reach a higher stage of economic development. Once they reach that higher stage, such nations may turn out to be our friends or they may be our adversaries. Which they will be is something we cannot predict, and which foreign aid in itself cannot determine. Yet we cannot refuse to furnish assistance to the emerging nations without inspiring a climate of bitterness and resentment that will rebound against us and make our shortsighted selfishness seem like the greatest folly. As the richest and strongest of all the industrialized nations, as a power whose impact and whose influence is felt in every part of the globe, the United States has a special obligation to the poorer countries. To America and the other wealthy nations, foreign aid has become the new version of the "white man's burden"—not the burden of a superior civilization, as the nineteenth-century imperialists thought, but the burden of a superior technology whose benefits must be shared if they are to endure. This is the real meaning of foreign aid, and one we must learn if we are to find a way of living at peace in a revolutionary world.

The problems of development in the emerging nations are compounded by a catastrophic population growth that consumes new resources nearly as fast as they are produced, by the paucity of trained technicians and administrators, by the absence of a large middle class capable of providing stability and willing to invest its savings, by an inadequate transportation network that makes it difficult to expand markets and exploit natural resources, by an uncertain political climate that frightens foreign investors, and by economies that do not provide enough extra capital to plow into development. All these factors working together make it exceedingly difficult for many of the emerging nations to do much more than just keep their heads above water.

Except for a few countries which have the good fortune to be rich in the minerals the world needs—oil, copper, uranium—and which have attracted foreign investors willing to exploit these minerals, the backward nations cannot earn enough of the hard currency they need to develop and industrialize their economies. For some of these countries the problem can be met by selling more of their primary commodities and manufactured products in Western markets. But this in turn requires that the industrialized nations reduce further their tariff barriers and quotas on products from the underdeveloped countries. It also means commodity subsidies and stabilization agreements to insure them against wild fluctuations in the world prices of their primary products. In addition, the poorer nations need technical assistance and a certain amount of capital aid from the rich nations. This will permit them to save some of the hard currency they now spend on essential imports, and to invest those savings in economic development. These reforms—lower tariff and quota barriers, commodity agreements, and a foreign-aid pledge by the rich nations of 1 per cent of their gross national incomes—were urged by the developing countries at the 1964 and 1968 United Nations Confer-. ences on Trade and Development. Yet none of the industrialized countries are even approaching this goal, and in fact are mostly reducing their foreign-aid grants. In 1968 France led the list of donors with an aid figure of seven-tenths of 1 per cent of her gross national product. The United States trailed far behind with four-tenths of 1 per cent. An independent study by the Commission on International Development, headed by former Canadian Prime Minister Lester Pearson, in late 1969 recommended that the rich nations increase government aid (as distinct from private invest-ment) to seven-tenths of 1 per cent of GNP by 1975. For the United States this would mean an aid program of more than $8 billion. The Commission also urged that aid be international-ized by channeling 20 per cent through the World Bank and other such institutions by 1975 as compared with 10 per cent now.

Not only do the rich countries fail to provide enough aid for the developing countries—indeed, they have been cutting their aid budgets since 1968—but much of their aid money is used to pay the interest on their loans. This has become so severe that about half the aid from all donor countries, or nearly the total United States contribution, is used to carry the accumulated external debt of the poorer countries. From 1965 to 1967, according to the Pearson report, 73 per cent of new loans to Africa were used to pay old debts. In East Asia the figure was 52 per cent, in South Asia–Middle East 40 per cent, and in Latin America 87 per cent. By 1977, given the same amount of lending, these figures will jump to 121 per cent for Africa, and 134 per cent, 97 per cent, and 130 per cent respectively for the other areas. The poorer nations, in other words, will be paying out more for debt service than they will be receiving in aid.

Yet even if new lending is increased by as much as 8 per cent a year, only about one-third of the eighty backward nations will, within the present generation, be able to reach the "take-off" point where their own development becomes self-sustaining.

Aid can help the backward countries to bridge the gap between subsistence and growth. But so can trade, and if these countries could sell more of their exports at stable prices they would need less direct aid. The industrialized nations tend to trade mostly with one another and to erect tariff barriers against manufactured goods from the underdeveloped countries. The United States, for example, has low tariffs for raw materials, but these increase with the degree of processing. Cocoa beans from Ghana can enter with little or no duty, but processed cocoa has a high duty. This forces the poorer countries to concentrate on producing raw materials at the expense of industrialization.

To make matters worse, the demand for many of their primary products is falling, due to the greater use of synthetics. Man-made fibers, for example, now account for more than 60 per cent of world textile production. Further, prices for raw commodities have dropped an average of 7 per cent in the past decade, with natural rubber plummeting more than 50 per cent since 1960. The developing countries receive less for their agricultural and mineral exports, while being forced to pay increasingly higher prices for manufactured goods from the industrialized nations. Whereas in 1950 Colombia, for example, could import a jeep for the price of 17 sacs of coffee, by 1967 it took 57 sacs for the same jeep. As a result of such practices, the underdeveloped countries have actually seen their share of world trade shrink from 25 per cent in 1950 to 13.5 per cent in 1967.

The inability of the backward nations to gain a greater share of Western markets reinforces their economic dependence on the industrialized powers. This breeds resentment among elite groups in the new countries, who charge that the Western nations are deliberately trying to maintain the backward countries in a state of economic dependency. They back up these charges by figures which show that the mineral resources of the new nations remain largely under foreign ownership or are dependent upon foreign capital and foreign marketing organizations for their exploitation. The mineral wealth of Latin America—its petroleum, copper, and tin—is largely foreign-owned and controlled, with the profits from its sale being sent abroad. From 1960 to 1966 the United States received $2 billion more from the underdeveloped countries in the form of income than it sent abroad in investment capital. In effect the United States, together with other industrialized nations, is enriching itself at the expense of the underdeveloped countries. This is what an astute foreign observer means in stating that "American prosperity is, for the most part, based on the exploitation of the natural resources of the Third World and the repatriation to the United States of profits from the underdeveloped countries." [3] Although formally independent, many of the underdeveloped countries are so tied into the Western economy (to the former mother countries of Europe, in the case of Africa; to the United States, in the case of Latin America) that an independent economic policy is virtually impossible. For the new nations there is no alternative to the Western market—except for the communist countries of Europe, and this is an alternative which they find both economically and politically undesirable. The communist countries do not have the markets or the means to buy the products of the new nations, and so these formally independent new nations remain dependent on the West. It is this difference between the promise of political independence and the reality of Western economic control that the elites of the new nations call "neo-colonialism."

The backward countries have a legitimate complaint in their antipathy to neo-colonialism and their fears that foreign aid may be used to serve the narrow interests of the donor nation. But the détente has taken the sting out of the cold war, and the pleasures of "peaceful coexistence" are now becoming more appealing to both Russians and Americans than is the effort to win friends and influence people in the Third World through foreign aid. Thus the backward countries are now discovering that their political importance to the rich nations has decreased in inverse proportion to their own economic need. America and Russia do not need the poor countries for economic reasons, now that they and their industrialized allies produce most of their own food, trade mostly with one another, and use their advanced technology to develop synthetics which allow them to dispense with many of the raw materials the poor countries sell. They do not even need these nations for military purposes, now that guided missiles have taken the place of foreign air bases. For both Washington and Moscow the development of the new nations, whatever ideological meaning it may have, is not a political necessity so much as it is an economic chore, draining off funds they would prefer to use at home.

This is shown by the steady shrinkage of the United States foreign-aid budget in recent years. Since 1966 Presidential requests for economic and military aid have been cut about $1 billion a year. Appropriations for economic development dropped from $1.89 billion in fiscal 1968 to $1.38 billion in 1969, and about the same for 1970. The days of $2.5 billion aid programs are clearly gone for good. In fact, Congress is in such a mood of rebellion over aid, its uses, and all kinds of foreign involvements, that in its report on the 1970 aid bill the Senate Foreign Relations committee commented: "When all is considered, it is remarkable that the committee has recommended a foreign aid bill at all this year."

Aid is no longer a popular cause, even for liberals. But the need of the underdeveloped countries is as great as ever. Part of the reaction against aid is that it may lead us into unwanted military entanglements, such as Vietnam. Part is that the money can well be used at home for social welfare, the rebuilding of our cities, and the purification of our polluted environment. But part also rests on a misunderstanding of aid and a misallocation of its limited resources. We have spread our aid too thin, distributing it to some one hundred countries, and we are often more concerned with establishing our political "presence" than with making sure that our assistance can be effectively used. We have showered aid on some countries in excess of their capacity to absorb it—Indonesia is a classic example—and then complained because our money was wasted or fell into the hands of profiteers. We have "tied" our aid to purchases of American products and thereby provided a lucrative subsidy for a favored group of American firms at the taxpayers' expense. We have tried to use aid to make points against the Russians, to outflank Europeans in their former colonies, to buy the loyalty of local politicians, and even, in such places as South Vietnam, to create politically viable nations.

Foreign aid, as an instrument for waging the cold war, has been disappointing, and ultimately a failure. It has not bought us allies, won us friends, or created self-sufficient nations where there was no political consensus to support them. This, however, is not a reason for scrapping the aid program, for the need is no less even though the old justifications may no longer prevail. Rather, it is a reason to re-evaluate our whole attitude toward foreign aid and to reform the program so that it can be devoted to the real economic requirements of the emerging nations. In doing so, we may be able to spare ourselves a good deal of needless disappointment, as well as dangerous political involvement in countries where aid is used to shore up weak regimes that may later seek our military intervention on their behalf. Although we do not generally conceive of it as an imperial instrument, foreign aid has been used to reshape technologically backward societies along lines we consider to be desirable. When the strain upon the fragile framework of these societies becomes too great, we have felt compelled to step in with military assistance and even our own soldiers to prevent revolution and political upheaval. However innocent our intentions, this, too, is a form of imperialism, and we would do well to recognize it for what it is. Under the mantle of economic development we have intervened profoundly, and on occasion even tragically, in the politics of the nations we were ostensibly aiding. In places like Vietnam, foreign aid has been the prelude to military intervention.

The real justification for economic assistance to the poorer nations lies not in the tired vocabulary of the cold war, but in the need to raise two-thirds of mankind from stagnation so that a tolerable basis of coexistence can be achieved between the rich minority and the impoverished majority. This requires furnishing aid to nations in terms of their capacity to utilize it effectively, rather than in terms of the temporarily friendly policies they may follow. This cannot be done easily, and perhaps not at all, so long as aid is administered primarily on a nation-to-nation basis. Only by placing part of the economic assistance program in an international pool can the United States divorce foreign aid from narrow considerations of foreign policy and thus prevent the aid program from being used to justify future military interventions to prop up 'fragile client regimes. Putting aid on an international basis will also permit the United States and other industrialized nations to transfer capital funds to nations that may follow antagonistic policies. Such a course will not be easy to accept, particularly for those who have justified foreign aid as a means of buying friends. Yet it is integral to the whole problem of development, for we have to keep in mind that we ought to be aiding nations not for the political beliefs they espouse but for their ability to pursue economic development.

In determining the level of economic aid we will make available to the developing nations, we must be guided by a realistic assessment of what they can absorb, what other sources of assistance are available to them, and what efforts they are willing to make on their own behalf. By stressing that the United States can lend economic assistance only to those nations that are willing to help themselves, President Johnson has wisely sought to put the aid program on a more realistic basis. There are some nations which deserve far more aid than they receive; there are others which, in terms of their performance and their leadership, may not deserve any aid at all. The United States is not rich enough to provide for all the capital and technical needs of the poorer nations, nor should she try to do so. We have tried to encourage the Europeans to take on a greater share of the aid burden and we should continue to do so—although Britain may be doing all she can in the Commonwealth, and France is providing more than twice the amount of aid per capita that the United States does. In the parts of Africa where the influence, and the concern, of the former mother countries remains strong, it is to our interest to play as small a role as possible. The Europeans are more knowledgeable than we are in the problems of their former colonies, and it is to our advantage to allow them to furnish the bulk of technical and economic assistance. For the most part this has been our policy, although there remains a persistent attempt to retain an American "presence" in such countries —a presence that frequently backfires to our disadvantage.

In trying to use economic assistance as an instrument of the cold war, we have compromised the effectiveness of the aid program and oversold its political utility. Yet if we hope to achieve any kind of tolerable world order, foreign aid will be needed for decades, and perhaps for generations to come. As the world's richest nation, and as the dominant power in an alliance of the world's wealthiest nations, we have the ability to help the twenty or thirty nations that today are reaching the breakthrough point where their own growth may be self-sustaining, and we can also furnish the charitable assistance that will take the edge off the misery in which most of mankind lives. But we cannot create nations where there is no solid political consensus and sense of identity, nor should we try to build little Americas from unstable client states. Nation-building on a political level is not our business. We are not very good at it outside our own frontiers, and foreign aid is an ultimately dissatisfying element of imperialism. If we must have client states for our military security, then let us pay for them out of the military budget and not confuse our efforts with philanthropy or with economic progress. And if we are bent on forging an empire of ideologically acquiescent dependencies, let us at least be honest with ourselves about what we are doing.

In judging the future of foreign aid we should remember that it has three purposes: economic, political, and moral. The economic purpose is to supplement in key areas the efforts that the recipient poor countries are themselves making to stimulate their growth and modernize their societies. The political purpose is to reduce the threat of international violence in an anarchic world by lessening the need of peoples to resort to war to relieve their hunger and despair. Finally, the moral purpose of foreign aid is to narrow the chasm between a predominantly white minority and an impoverished colored majority—a chasm that cannot be deliberately maintained without undermining the moral values on which the West prides itself. That a man should be condemned to poverty, ignorance, and sickness for no other reason than that he happened to be born in Dacca rather than in Detroit is morally indefensible.

At best, if we are wise and lucky, foreign aid may help permit a relatively peaceful transition from a world of wealth for the few and misery for the many, to a world where the necessities of life and a reasonable hope for improvement are open to all. But we should be under no illusions as to what development entails. At best it is a cataclysmic process, uprooting old values, destroying ancient cultures, creating new conflicts, producing tormenting anxieties and unsatisfied wants. It is in the very nature of development to destroy the old social order and to build a different one resting on new classes, new values, new allegiances. The process will be long and tortuous, filled with bitter disappointments over the gaps that will inevitably occur between expectations and achievements. The poor will be less willing to accept their poverty with the old stoicism, the rich will become more desperate to hold on to their old privileges, and the rising generation of semi-educated politicians and intellectuals will be tempted to relieve popular frustration by demagogic propaganda and even by military adventures.

Are we willing to accept such disorder as the price of economic development? More important, can we accept the likelihood that in a number of countries the process of development will be led by governments hostile to capitalism—and that some of these countries may nationalize American-owned investments? Our economy could certainly stand it. United States assets in the Third World total only $16 billion in an economy whose gross national product is approaching $1,000 billion. But would our political and military leaders be willing to leave to the communists the arduous task of developing some of the more backward areas of the Third World? Our interventions to preserve the capitalist order in such places as Iran, Guatemala, Lebanon, Santo Domingo, and Vietnam would indicate that we prefer stagnation to development under anti-capitalist leadership. The record indicates, in Heilbroner's words, that "our present policy prefers the absence of development to the chance for communism—which is to say that we prefer hunger and want and the existing inadequate assaults against the causes of hunger and want to any regime that declares its hostility to capitalism." [4] Can these attitudes be changed before they lead to further interventions, to more Vietnams?

For the rich nations the problem is not how little foreign aid they can get away with, but how much can be usefully absorbed by the developing nations. This means distinguishing between regimes on the basis of their competence, not on whether they give lip service to anti-communism or proclaim their allegiance to free enterprise. The object of foreign aid is not to distribute money indiscriminately to anyone with his hand out. Our generosity, if not our resources, is too limited for that. Nor is it to win verbal allies for the obsessions of our foreign policy. Rather, it is to help alleviate human misery by aiding those who show a capacity to aid themselves, and by doing so to help create an international order where compassion will be joined to self-interest and where the poor may seek to join the rich rather than exterminate them. For those of us privileged to live in societies affluent beyond the imagination of most of mankind, foreign aid is not simply charity, but rather, as Oliver Wendell Holmes once said of taxes, our investment in civilization.

14. Prospero and Caliban

PROSPERO: *I pitied thee,*
        Took pains to make thee speak. . . .
        . . . I endow'd thy purposes
        With words that made them known. . . .

CALIBAN: *You taught me language; and my profit on't*
        Is, I know how to curse. The red plague rid you
        For learning me your language!
                                —SHAKESPEARE, *The Tempest* I, ii

🌿 🌿 🌿 CALIBAN'S curse seems to have taken on new meaning in the mid-twentieth century as the United States confronts the clamorous new nations of the Third World. With their extravagant vocabularies, insoluble problems, and dubious ambitions, many of them appear to be likely candidates for "the red plague" that so haunts American diplomacy. Among these nations the United States finds herself isolated and suspected of evil intentions, the richest nation on earth surrounded by a multitude of resentful beggars—Prospero in a world of Calibans.

Instead of being emulated as the model toward which less fortunate members of the family of nations should aspire, the United States is often an object of resentment and calumny. Her riches are seen not as a sign of superior virtue, but as a mark of superior skill in exploiting the poor and of good fortune in having inherited (or conquered) a continent of wondrous riches. Even her comparative youth is no point in her favor, since two centuries of national existence are an eternity to countries barely a decade or two old which have not yet even begun to enter their adolescence. Compared to Ghana or Pakistan, the American republic is virtually senile, a shameless example of what Sukarno used to call Oldefo in Indonesian Newspeak—an Old Established Force.

This attitude seems unjust and, even worse, unkind. After all, the United States not long ago was one of the new nations herself, and she has always, more or less, supported the principle of independence and self-determination for all. Indeed, a good deal of American popular folklore is wrapped up in the idea of resistance to the colonial powers of Europe. By the same token, American presidents such as Jefferson, Lincoln, Franklin Roosevelt, and recently Kennedy have become folk heroes to patriots in underdeveloped countries, who extol their principles and honor their memories, even though they seem to have little affection for the nation these men led.

The new nations find it hard to believe that at one time the United States was a dependent territory, producing primary products which were then shipped off to the mother country for processing and returned in the form of manufactured products at enormously inflated prices. Her economic life was largely under the control of foreign banks and businesses. She depended on loans from abroad (that is, foreign aid) to build her roads and railways, her ports and factories. The colonial settlers conquered an alien environment, virtually exterminated the original inhabitants, and finally achieved national unity only at the cost of a terrible civil war whose wounds are not yet healed. Until the beginning of the twentieth century the American republic was, in terms of the international balance of trade, primarily a furnisher of foodstuffs and raw materials, just as to this day she is one of the world's principal agricultural suppliers. Ex-colonial, long underdeveloped, non-European, the United States is in many ways like a fragment of the Third World that succeeded.

Having succeeded, however, she has discovered that her links of solidarity with the new nations are often more sentimental than real. As the leading industrial and financial power of the world, exercising virtually unchallenged hegemony over the western hemisphere and dominating, through her economic and military power, half of Europe and much of Asia and Africa as well, the

United States fits uncomfortably into the fraternity of former colonial nations. Indeed, to many in the Third World the United States is not so much ex-colonial as she is neo-colonial, exercising a power over their economies and making political demands upon them such as they no longer have to tolerate even from their old mother countries. Now that the European colonial empires have largely vanished or been reduced to a collection of curiosities such as Réunion, Aden, and Río Muni, the United States has taken the place vacated by the imperial powers of Europe.

To most Americans the idea that the United States could be an imperial power seems a contradiction in terms. We have long felt an ideological and emotional solidarity with the colonial nations as they sought to liberate themselves. After the Second World War we helped push the Dutch out of Indonesia, criticized French colonialism in Indochina and North Africa, and urged the British to leave India. But the cold war complicated our emotions, and the desire to contain communism led us to view our European allies in a rather different light. They were not so much virulent exploiters of unfortunate colonial peoples as demoralized old relatives who had to be nourished and protected. By the same token, the colonial nations seemed less like brave patriots struggling for freedom than like impetuous children who did not know the dangers facing them in the big world outside.

The dismantling of the European colonial empires, although aided and applauded by the United States, has increased, among the underdeveloped countries, the popularity of the Europeans and reduced that of the Americans. The new nations remain linked to Europe by strong cultural and economic ties that have not been seriously diminished by independence. Freedom has lent enchantment to the former colonial master and lessened the allure of the United States as the cheerleader of self-determination. Although the peoples of the Third World may look to the United States for expertise and technical know-how, they continue to look to their former mother countries for leadership and approval. And it is old ex-imperial Europe that has their affection, not young ex-colonial America.

Within the past decade there has been a remarkable reversal of roles between America and Europe. Whereas the United States once thundered against the arrogance of the Europeans who used their power to dominate their colonies and intervene militarily throughout the world, now it is the Europeans who have turned the same argument against the United States. For years the Europeans complained about the naïveté, the demagoguery, the over-simplification with which the United States viewed their colonial problems. Now the shoe is on the other foot, and Washington complains that the Europeans do not understand the burdens it has been forced to assume in Latin America, Asia, and Africa. "The European nations," Dean Acheson complained to a Senate committee, "are not interested in Vietnam. They don't understand it. It is a long way off. . . . These people are deeply concerned with their part of the world. We are the only power that has a sense of world responsibility." [1]

There is some irony, and much disappointment for us, in the attitude of the emerging nations toward the United States. We thought that America should be an ideal toward which they would naturally aspire. Our instinctive anti-colonialism, our sympathy for the underdog, our sense of mission, all contributed to the image of ourselves as honorary leader of the new nations, their moral inspiration as well as their economic benefactor. But there was more optimism than analysis in this belief, for it ignored the chasm of race, culture, wealth, and power which separates the poor nations from the United States, and the way in which we have taken over the role abandoned by their European masters. As a European economist has written:

In nearly all of Africa and a large part of Asia, the West—with all the admiration, all the envy, all the detestation that this term carries—has been more or less identified, until the middle of the twentieth century, with the various European colonial powers. But once the imperial privileges and the web of the metropolis were broken, the Third World discovered that behind Europe lay America. The diverse sentiments that the West inspired have been crystallized around her. After the demi-gods, they were confronted with the gods. [2]

This encounter with the gods could hardly have been reassuring to the new nations, for it made them the object of a rivalry they could not control. There were, to be sure, certain advantages to be gained from association with the super-powers: foreign aid to build up primitive economies, military assistance to create powerful armies, a certain prestige on the world stage. Yet they have not been willing to confide their fate to one, or two, or three super-powers, and have shown a remarkable agility in playing their suitors off against one another. New nations are nationalistic almost by definition. They do not want outsiders to interfere in their internal affairs, nor do they want to be lectured on their moral responsibility to uphold one "ism" or another. If they see the world divided between the powers of light and darkness, they are on the side of light, while the developed nations, communist or anti-communist, are among the forces of darkness. They have about as much interest in taking part in the Russo-American cold war as the young American republic had in joining the imperial struggles between Napoleonic France and the Holy Alliance.

The pioneers who swept across the Northwest Territories and Louisiana were building a nation of continental dimensions. There seemed to be no limits to her potential, and her builders thought it natural that this energetic nation should seek outlets beyond her own frontiers. The United States declared her alliance with all new states which, like her, had been born of insurrection, and she consigned to the historic ash-heap old imperial Europe with its archaic monarchies, its destructive civil wars, and its tedious class conflicts. Thumbing her nose at the Establishment, the young American republic was the communist China of the late eighteenth and early nineteenth centuries, raising the flag of sedition throughout the hemisphere, preaching the virtues of revolution in general, and issuing verbal broadsides against the imperial powers of the day. So enamored was she of revolutions that, had it not been for the restraining hand of George Washington, the United States might well have joined republican France in war against France's imperial enemies. It is not surprising that these gestures seemed insufferably impertinent to the conservative statesmen of Europe. "These United States of America," Prince Metternich wrote Czar Alexander indignantly,

> . . . in their indecent declarations they have cast blame and scorn on the institutions of Europe most worthy of respect, on the principles of their greatest sovereigns. . . . In permitting themselves these unprovoked attacks, in fostering revolutions wherever they show themselves, in regretting those which have failed, they lend new strength to the apostles of sedition, and reanimate the courage of every conspirator.[3]

This revolutionary strain that pulsed through the veins of the young United States now moves at a considerably slower pace. But it has been picked up by the new nations. Today, by a suitable irony of history, they are in the same relation to the United States that early nineteenth-century America bore to Metternich's Europe. They are impatient with all established authority that is not their own, sympathetic to all underdogs—except for neighbors with whom they may be feuding—and just as eager to instruct the great powers in principles of international morality as the great powers are to instruct them. They all pay homage to democracy, although it is often of the qualified variety: "people's democracy," "basic democracy," "guided democracy." Their attempts at working out democratic societies frequently bring patronizing smiles to the Western liberal, or indignation to the conservative. But it is well not to become overly emotional about their failures or overly pessimistic about their possibilities of improvement.

That all these nations pay allegiance to democracy should not, however, induce us to assume that their own definitions are an apt description of their political condition. Between the word and the deed there may be a considerable gap that even the best intentions may not be able to bridge. Democracy may be everybody's ideal; by stretching the definition far enough, it can even be made to include extremely unlikely candidates, yet with the world as it is today, it does not take a very highly developed sense of cynicism to wonder whether Western-style democracy may not be in for hard times in many, if not most, of the new nations. Everywhere it is hailed as having already arrived or, at worst, as being only just around the corner. Often it is praised in all sincerity, even by those whose conception of democracy would be—and frequently is—puzzling to most people in the Western world. But this verbal allegiance to democracy is the tribute vice renders to virtue, and we would do well not to take it literally. Those new and emerging nations which are gradually developing their own democratic institutions can be encouraged to keep up the good work, supported with foreign-aid grants, and feted as harbingers of the brighter tomorrow everyone desires. But it would be wise not to become overly preoccupied with the effort to bring Western democratic institutions to nations that have never experienced the economic and political changes—industrialization, the rise of a middle class, the waning of any aristocracy, the spread of education—that were the foundation of Western-style democracy.

These nations are going through a convulsion that will threaten not only their thin veneer of Western institutions but their very cohesion and perhaps even their national existence. As they face the problems of subduing tribalism, fighting off external enemies, creating national identities, initiating the long struggle for economic development, and even feeding their undernourished populations, they cannot put Western-style parliamentarianism at the top of their priority lists. Nor should they be expected to. The symbols of democracy—the choice between candidates, the secret ballot, the struggle of parties—mean little to people who have barely enough to keep alive and little hope of ever exercising political power within their lifetimes. While the masses would no doubt approve of democratic government, other things being equal, if it were offered to them, they cannot be expected to sacrifice more elementary needs to what is, in terms of their own experience, a political abstraction. Political democracy divorced from economic justice is less than half a loaf to those who are treated unjustly. And they are right, because the democracy which the privileged classes enjoy in economically backward states is often obtained at the expense of the underprivileged. "The masses in

the underdeveloped countries," the Brazilian economist Celso
Furtado has written,

> have not generally put the same high valuation on individual lib-
> erty that we do. Since they have not had access to the better things
> of life, they obviously cannot grasp the full meaning of the sup-
> posed dilemma between liberty and quick development. Also, if we
> were to assert that rapid economic development of socialist coun-
> tries was achieved only at the price of restricting civil liberties, we
> must then accept the corollary that the liberty enjoyed by the
> minority in our society is paid for by a delay in general economic
> development, hence is at the expense of the welfare of the great
> majority. . . . If the price of liberty for the few had to be the
> poverty of the many, we can be quite certain that the probability
> of preserving freedom would be practically nil.[4]

Democracy may be, as Churchill said, the worst form of government, except for all others. But it is not one toward which all nations must necessarily gravitate, or for which economic development offers any easy road. When democracy comes, if at all, it is
likely to be only after the development process has taken hold
and a middle class has been created with a stake in social mobility
and economic opportunity. In many of the new countries the
legitimacy of the government has not yet been established, and a
stable social order, which is the prerequisite of rational development, is still to be achieved. It has taken the West more than
seven centuries from the time of the Magna Carta to develop its
democratic institutions, and in some Western countries they are
not firmly established even yet.

The economic and political development of the backward
world is destined to be a long, agonizing, and often frustrating
process that will try the patience and the ideals of even the most
committed leaders. There are bound to be cases where the struggle will be given up before it is joined, and where the fusion of
democracy with economic development will seem almost unattainable. There will be a temptation in the West to despair over
these nations because the democratic ideals to which they pledge
allegiance may seem to be a cover for authoritarian methods. But
such despair is too easy, and it is also beside the point. The pri-

mary task of the new nations is to provide for the basic economic needs of their peoples. At some future date government by the people as well as government for the people may be possible. In the short run, at any rate, perhaps the best that we, or they, can reasonably hope for is that it not be government against the people.

Unfortunate though it may be, development in most of the backward countries can be carried out only by a certain degree of coercion. The more ambitious a country's development projects, the greater the degree of coercion likely to be employed. To prescribe more democracy for these nations before they have built up the superstructure which may (possibly) make democracy a reality, is to invite the failure of their economic ambitions without gaining any meaningful level of democracy. As George Lichtheim has explained:

> A relatively backward country which introduces the apparatus of parliamentary democracy *before* industrialization is complete may actually find that while the ruling elite of army officers, politicians, and intellectuals is on the side of forced-draft modernization, the peasant voters will have none of it. In a situation of this kind, the elite then faces the awkward choice of scrapping either democracy or modernization. In such case, if the ruling minority decides to press on with modernization against the will of the backward majority, it may find it necessary to seek a legitimation in "socialism." Its political doctrine will then be undemocratic and may come to bear some resemblance to either fascism or Stalinism—as the case may be—though in point of fact it simply serves to spread industrialization, quite possibly laying the foundation of a subsequent development along fairly ordinary capitalist lines.[5]

Thus, in dealing with the perplexing transition from economic feudalism to industrialization in the new countries, it is best not to be overly dependent on traditional definitions, not to place too great an emphasis on such loaded terms as "socialism" or "democracy." In a good many nations socialism is simply capitalism in different clothing—and pre-industrial capitalism at that. "Socialism" may simply be the label behind which a privileged oligarchy guarantees its profits and power, while paying a harmless obeisance to a fashionable ideology. To be a capitalist is to be historically obsolete and perhaps even an enemy of the people. To be a socialist, even if one is a landowner or a great industrialist, is to be in step with history. How natural, then, to be a socialist, particularly when everyone else is as well. Thus it is that the oligarchs of Latin America, like the communist dictators of Eastern Europe, solemnly display their socialist credentials.

Labels on nations, as on bottles, are often a poor guide to contents. There are societies proclaiming their pursuit of socialism and their devotion to democracy which are often incompetent at the former and indifferent to the latter. There are those, such as Indonesia during the heyday of Sukarno, that sacrifice development to grandstanding and pyramid-building: nations of sports palaces for people without shoes, air-conditioned hotels where millions have no roofs, Cadillacs for cities without paved streets. Which is simply to say that the absence of political democracy is not to be taken as an indication that rational economic development is being pursued. There seems to be no corollary between democracy and development. There are nations, such as India, which have made greater progress in parliamentarianism than in development; there are others, such as Egypt, which are furiously pursuing development, with an indifference to democracy as the West understands it; and there are those fortunate rarities, such as Tunisia, which have managed to pursue them both simultaneously. There is no formula that holds good for all the Third World because these are extraordinarily complex and diverse societies, as different from one another as Canada is from Japan, as Sweden is from Turkey. These nations are suffering from profound cultural, political, and economic shock. They are the victims of a world they did not make and cannot escape from. They are, perhaps, also its inheritors. As the Swiss historian Herbert Luethy has written:

All the "new nations" are at grips with the problem of forging a national identity, of inculcating common reflexes and a consciousness of mutual solidarity among divergent human groups penned inside more or less artificial and accidental frontiers. All their regimes employ, with varying degrees of success, the same familiar recipes long ago developed by European nationalist movements: education in the service of patriotism, the daily celebration of the cult of national leadership, national heroes, national symbols and national myths, and permanent mobilization against an indispensable common enemy. The exotic transposition of the myths and magic formulas of the deified race or nation sometimes prevents us from recognizing the old familiar face of *l'Europe des patries.*[6]

In holding up to the West the mirror of its own passions, they have made it exceedingly difficult for us to admire in ourselves that which we abhor in them. They are ourselves in exaggerated form, and at times the picture is not very inspiring.

For better or worse, the West, through the imperial powers of Europe, has imposed its image upon the entire world. That image, in all its horror and all its grandeur, is one both we and the underdeveloped countries must learn to live with, for we have no choice. This Westernization is what they want, and they attach the highest importance to it, even though we may question its values ourselves. This desire to be like Europeans, or at least to acquire the surface elements and the benefits of European civilization, is often contradictory, for it rests upon a conception of the West that often exists only in the mind of the beholder. What is new about the new nations is almost entirely European in origin. As a result of a colonial experience which they did not choose, but from which they received considerable material benefits, the nations of the Third World are imbued with the culture of ex-imperial Europe. Indeed, the Europeanization of the world is one of the most extraordinary phenomena of the twentieth century, one that is increasing in tempo even now that the colonial empires have almost entirely disintegrated. On the surface, the Third World capitals, with their obligatory skyscrapers, traffic lights, and sports palaces, often look like Europe writ small and somewhat gone awry. The shape of the new cities, the structure of the governments, the clothes people wear, the music they listen to, the films they see, the buses they ride on, the cars they drive, and in many cases even the languages they speak, come from the European mother countries—from the former hated rulers, who are now the benevolent friends. Whether they will it or not, the new nations have been imbued with a taste for Westernization which it is not within their power to reverse.

This is their hope, and it is also their tragedy, for it has placed them between two worlds, "one dead, the other yet unborn." They want the economic advantages the West has to offer, the skills, the medicines, the education, the machines, the mastery of environment that is the triumph of the Western man. They want all this, but they do not want to have to sacrifice their cultural heritage to obtain it. They want economic development—which is to say, Westernization—while at the same time they want to keep many of the customs on which they were raised. They want to be like the West, yet they want to assert those things that make them unique. But many of the things that do make them unique—bamboo huts, circumcision rites, women in veils, and part-time jobs between feasts and dances—are precisely what prevent them from becoming Westernized, that is, industrialized. If they retain their own customs (and these are often worthy and admirable customs which the West could do well to emulate), they can forget about orderly economic development and enjoy the benefits (not totally negligible) of an economically primitive society. If, however, they throw off their old customs and embrace the Western world—with its time-clocks, its ice-tray apartment houses, its smokestacks, and its psychiatrists—they are in danger of losing their identity.

Thus it is not surprising that, torn between conflicting motives of which they themselves are only partially aware, they simultaneously hate the West for taking away their identity and hate themselves for not being more Western—or, as they would say, more "modern." Economic aid, by speeding up the pace of development, intensifies these poisonous feelings of hatred and self-hatred. The plight of these nations is one which should elicit more sympathy than impatience, for it stems from national attitudes tragically divided between admiration and contempt, between emulation and rejection, between pride and self-abasement. These are people who blindly imitate the West, down to the jet airlines and the steel mills which have become the new objects of tribal worship, while they continue to proclaim their own superiority; people who reject their own culture, yet who cling to symbols such as tribal robes at the United Nations as a way of maintaining a cultural identity. Their pains are profound ones, for they are the birth pangs of the modern world.

We should not be surprised that the rulers of these new nations, when faced with tribal rivalries and other disruptive forces at home, should blame the West in general, and perhaps the United States in particular, for many of their problems. It is at least partly because they have been so courted by the great powers that they have been so vociferous. They have learned that a good deal of their political leverage depends on the volubility of their protests. Without a trained elite capable of stimulating development, with few developed resources and no possibility of gaining the capital they need for economic growth by their own efforts, the backward nations are forced to fall back on other methods to compensate for the short change history and nature have dealt them. They have to attack their own feudal structures by undemocratic methods, and they can wheedle aid out of the rich nations only by blackmail or threats of suicide. They must threaten to "go communist" or "join the imperialists," in hopes that Moscow or Washington will be alarmed and come rushing in with the money they need to keep their heads above water.

Possessed of the wealth, power, and influence toward which the backward countries aspire, we can afford to be sympathetic to their relatively modest ambitions and indulgent of their verbal excesses. There is, after all, something pathetic in the dilemma of Nasser, Castro, of the deposed Nkrumah, for their talents far exceed the meager material they have to work with. Egypt, Cuba, Ghana, however discordant a note they strike, cannot really hope to drown out the bellowing of elephants. If, by some historical accident, Nasser were the *Rais* of a united Arab world, if Nkrumah were the *Osagyefo* of all black Africa, if Castro were the *maximo líder* of Latin America, then we might have some serious cause for complaint. As it is, we can be thankful that these ambitious men are doomed to rule countries that can never offer them sufficient scope to implement their expansive dreams. How different the world might have been had Hitler been a Rumanian and Stalin a Turk. As it is, even the most vociferous demagogues of the Third World present a far greater headache to their own people than to the nations of the West they have been so curiously successful in taunting. Even they must be surprised that their high-pitched barks have sent the great powers scurrying for bribes.

But we live in a strange world where great nations devote major portions of their wealth to build nuclear arsenals for the specific purpose of never using them; where the super-powers feel more insecure than the pygmies; and where diplomatic influence rests more on showmanship and bravado than on military arsenals or economic strength. It is a world where communist Russia is more worried by the pretensions of communist China than by the challenge of capitalist America; where West Germany can have her nose tweaked by impoverished Egypt; and where the United States, the most powerful nation the world has ever known, feels threatened by seven million Cubans espousing a maverick brand of Marxism. It is a world of bluff, illusion, and imagination, in which power is more shadowy than real, where responsibility breeds caution, and where daring and a good sense of timing can reap astonishing rewards. It is a world where agility counts as much as brawn, and where a sense of measure can be even more important than a display of muscle.

This strange world of the post-cold-war era has been perplexing to all the nations of the West. Yet the Europeans, more experienced, perhaps, in the ways of the backward nations because of their past as colonial administrators, less idealistic by nature, have not put such high hopes in the Third World as Americans have, and consequently have not been so disappointed by it. Now that their empires are but a memory, the Europeans see their ex-colonies offering a means by which they can maintain world importance without the dangers and expense that are the tedious companions of empire. Where they once controlled directly through their colonial offices, they now control indirectly through their economic ministries, practicing a sophisticated neo-colonialism that is financially profitable without political dangers or costly military establishments. Thus the French run much of West Africa from Paris, the British invest enormous amounts of money and faith in the Commonwealth to assure that the sun never sets on their influence even though it has on their empire, the Belgians keep tight control of the economy of the Congo, and Dutch money slowly moves back into Indonesia. Even Franco Spain, with a blithe disregard for Marxist dogma, has kept its political, cultural, and economic links with Cuba in good order.

This revival of European interest in the Third World need not be considered a defiance of the United States. In fact, it could provide a great opportunity to spread the burden of developing the new states, to discard our mother-hen attitude toward their problems, and to ease the one-way dependence that is so humiliating for them and irritating for us. By preaching greater self-reliance for the new nations, and the need for Europe to reassume a sense of responsibility in areas to which it has been linked politically and sentimentally for decades, France may be doing the United States a good turn. We cannot assume the whole obligation of developing the backward nations. Nor should we try, for these nations can be induced to follow policies favorable to the West only by indirection and example rather than by commands and exhortations. If Europe can be persuaded to take on some of the chores of industrializing the backward nations, so much the better for us all. Then it may be able to do for the general interests of the West that which the United States cannot hope to do by herself. With a wealth of understanding and experience in the nations that were once their colonies, the Europeans can help provide the economic aid, technical assistance, and cultural leadership the new nations seek so desperately.

As we have seen, even with the help of the Europeans, and also the Russians, the effort to stimulate development with relative political stability is going to be an arduous task marked with disappointment and even with failure. There is a limit to what even the richest nations with the best of intentions can do for some two billion people living in poverty and despair, breeding themselves into asphyxiation, trying to squeeze a living out of sand and rocks, experimenting with various forms of tyranny, and all proclaiming that the future of the world revolves around them. The new nations have their own ideas as to what life is all about and how they should live it.

If we are going to interfere in the lives of other peoples—and foreign aid represents the most profound kind of interference—we owe it to ourselves to be realistic about what we can accomplish. We can send electric toothbrushes and giant tractors, but they are not likely to be of much use to people without electricity or without fields to plow. We can explain the virtues of the "free world" and the evils of the "international communist conspiracy," but we are unlikely to win any converts among people who have little interest in either. We can preach democracy and free enterprise, cloverleaf tollways and supermarkets, the Bill of Rights and the Tonkin Bay Resolution, but there will be few imitators among the recipients of our aid, and perhaps even few admirers. We may have a pre-packaged set of answers for them, but it will not do much good if they will have none of it. And perhaps much of it is not very good for them. Not everybody, after all, shares our admiration of the American Way, and even fewer are willing to follow it. A sense of proportion should also dictate a sense of restraint, and perhaps even a much-needed humility. Neither we nor the Russians nor the Europeans have any solutions for all the ills that wrack the underdeveloped nations, and we should be under no illusions about what we can achieve in an alien soil.

No matter how great our generosity and our discretion, the Third World is likely to be rocked by violence and subject to despotism for a long time to come. We cannot help this no matter what we do or how great our concern. All we know is that the violence and the despotism are likely to be even worse—perhaps so great as to engulf us—if we do not help the new nations in the painful task of development. Development is no cure-all. It is not even a prescription for social order. It is simply a way of stimulat-

ing the tolerable in order to stave off the disastrous. But it is unlikely to bring peace. As Heilbroner has warned:

> We must reckon with the likelihood that over the coming two or
> three decades as the pressures grow and the difficulties assert them-
> selves, the guidance of development will fall into the hands of
> dedicated revolutionary groups. . . . In most of the underdevel-
> oped nations the choice for the command post of development
> is apt to lie between a military dictatorship and a left-wing civilian
> dictatorship; . . . the necessity to hold down the level of con-
> sumption—to force savings—in order to free resources for the
> capital-building process will make for a rising level of frustration
> even under the sternest discipline. This frustration will almost
> surely have to be channeled into directions other than that of
> economic expectations. Hence a deliberately heightened national-
> ism, a carefully planned ideological fervor, even military adventures
> are a likely by-product of development.[7]

What appears over the horizon, therefore, is not a world of universal peace in which every nation cultivates its own garden of
economic development. More likely is a generation of revolution,
upheaval, and violence, a succession of pygmy wars that will
spread throughout the Third World and that may, if we are not
careful, afflict the industrialized nations as well. These conditions
are a reason for caution, but not a cause for despair, for development is an irreversible process. We cannot stop it; we can hope
only to channel it along lines that will permit the creation of a
tolerable world order.

There is a good deal we can do for the nations of the Third
World. We can give them lessons in agriculture and technology,
examples of democratic government and social equality, proof of
our goodwill and sympathy. There is also a good deal we can learn
from them, for we are neither so rich in knowledge nor so perfect
in conduct that we can afford to reject the learning of societies
far older than ours. But above all we shall have to recognize that
the Third World does not necessarily admire us, or want to be
very much like us. These new nations do not know what they do
want; often they thrash around in the swamp of their own foolish
rhetoric. But they are grasping for something different, some-

thing that will reflect their own historical experience, their own cultural identities, their own national aspirations.

Prospero can help Caliban, but he is doomed not to understand him. And when the magic scepter of an advanced technology is flung into the sea and Prospero returns to his kingdom from the island he has colonized, he may still be doomed to hear the curses of his former servant echoing in his ears.

15. The Pygmy Wars

When the war of the giants is over, the wars of the pygmies will begin. —WINSTON CHURCHILL

❦ ❦ ❦ SOMEWHERE along the banks of a muddy river in Central Africa a young postal clerk harangues his fellow workers to burn the mail sacks, steal the stamps, and take to the bush with the money orders. Deep in the Latin American rain forest a landless farmer hands out homemade machetes to the peasants for an assault on the local hacienda. On a coral reef somewhere along the Indian Ocean a band of teen-age soldiers in cotton shorts prepares an impromptu invasion of a neighboring island. In the icy peaks of the Himalayas a few rifle shots are exchanged as a border patrol swoops down to seize some frozen tundra and three dozen yaks. And in the windblown wastes of the Arabian desert sheiks on white ponies capture a mud-hut village and promptly proclaim it the capital of a rebel government.

What do these isolated acts have in common? They are all forms of rebellion against a government in power. What do the rebels want? To change or overthrow the regime that runs their (or a neighboring) country and install one more to their liking. Who are these people? Landless peasants, ambitious colonels, frustrated lawyers, restless students, embittered tribesmen, hungry slum-dwellers. Why do they do it? Because they are desperate, or because somebody has ordered them to, or because they think things will be better, or because they have been paid, or perhaps because they are bored. Will they succeed? Some will, some won't. Some will gain their ambitions, others will become disillusioned;

some will be made cabinet ministers, others will be shot as out-laws.

Who cares? We do, the Russians do, the Chinese do. Why? Be-cause these are the actors who carry out the skirmishes of the world revolution, a revolution that began with the collapse of the European colonial system in 1945 and has been gathering momentum ever since. As the anti-colonial tide swept from the Indian subcontinent to Southeast Asia, to the Middle East and then to Africa, scores of new nations were hacked from the old European empires and proudly took their place in the United Na-tions. Like our own war of independence—and often deriving inspiration from it—the wars of the colonial peoples wore down the European powers and drove them from their empires in Africa and Asia. Sometimes, as in the case of the French empire in black Africa, this was done without bloodshed. In other cases, such as Algeria, Indochina, and Cyprus, independence came only as a result of long and costly combat. Today the European em-pires are largely a memory, except for the Portuguese territories in southern Africa. Angola and Mozambique, the last major out-posts of European colonialism, may be the next scene of the long, and now virtually completed, drama of the colonized peoples for independence.

The passing of the European empires has not ushered in an age of peace. Rather, it has raised the curtain on another kind of war, one which has come in the wake of a dying colonialism. This kind of war can be seen in the conflicts between rival tribes which, freed from colonial restraints, are now able to give vent to ancient grievances. Such have been the disturbances that have rocked Burma, Iraq, Cyprus, and a good many states of Central Africa. These conflicts can be brutal, heartless, and exhausting. Usually they defy any easy solution because their roots lie so deep in the cultures and the traditions of those who fight them. Like the wars of religion and the wars of nationalism that were Eu-rope's stock-in-trade for three hundred years, these tribal wars are symptoms of a deep cleavage within the societies themselves.

Sometimes these are wars to unite tribes that may be on both sides of an international frontier (the Moslems of the Indian subcontinent, the Malays of East Asia, the Arabs of Palestine). At other times they are wars to secure the supremacy of one tribe over its rival within a country (such as the war between the pygmies and the Watusis in Burundi, or between the Ibos and the Hausas and Yorubas in Nigeria).

In addition to the anti-colonial wars and the tribal wars, there are the pygmy wars between some of the smaller nations. These wars are, for the most part, carried on sporadically, and often at a subdued level of violence. China's assaults on the Indian border posts in the Himalayas, the back-door war over Kashmir between India and Pakistan, the running feud between Israel and her Arab neighbors, Indonesia's "confrontation" of Malaysia, the proxy war between Egypt and Saudi Arabia over Yemen—these are all examples of limited war on a part-time basis. Such limited wars are possible because they are frequently carried out by guerrilla bands, so that nations can engage in combat without officially declaring war, and face-saving exits are possible when the operations are unsuccessful.

Finally, in a separate category, there have been conflicts designed to overturn the existing social order within a nation and to replace one ideology with another. Usually the communists have taken the offensive in such wars, as in the struggles in Greece and the Philippines in the 1940s, and in Malaya in the 1950s. Sometimes these conflicts over ideology have been allied with wars for independence, as in Indochina between 1946 and 1954. The communists like to label these struggles "wars of national liberation," on the assumption that the triumph of communism is equivalent to liberation. But there have been cases when anti-communist rebels have tried to topple a communist regime—such as the Hungarian revolt of 1956—and there may be cases in the future where the communist nations themselves could be victims of "wars of national liberation."

Thus war in the grand style, as it was known during the two great conflicts of this century, has been replaced by something rather different but perhaps even more disturbing, "another kind of war," as President Kennedy said in 1961 when he tried to grapple with an unfamiliar phenomenon, "new in its intensity, ancient in its origin—war by guerrillas, subversives, insurgents, assassins, war by ambush instead of by combat; by infiltration instead of aggression, seeking victory by eroding and exhausting the enemy instead of engaging him." These have been the new wars of the mid-twentieth century, the little wars of the forgotten peoples, the wars of rebellion, the wars of frustration, the wars of ambition, and, most troubling of all, the "wars of national liberation." These are the wars of the future already previewed by the conflicts of the present: the revolution in Cuba, the battle over Kashmir, the civil war in Vietnam, the uprising in Yemen, the rebellion in the Congo, the slaughter in Indonesia, and the mounting racial troubles in southern Africa.

These subdued and sporadic wars, fought by guerrillas with conventional weapons and for limited objectives, have something to offer everyone. For the great powers they provide a means of gaining political influence or shifting the balance in a strategic area without facing the perils of head-on confrontation. This is, to be sure, a delicate game, for there is always the danger that one of the atomic giants will overplay its hand and, instead of letting its clients carry on the fight, will become drawn into the war itself. Current examples hardly seem necessary. But as long as the super-powers keep a sense of proportion about their proxy wars, such conflicts can provide, to paraphrase Clausewitz, a way of carrying out warfare by other means. Thus they are not an anomaly in the atomic age, but rather its perfect expression.

It was by a guerrilla war that the Batista regime was overthrown in Cuba, that the Budapest rebels (temporarily) brought down the Soviet puppet regime in Hungary, and that the communist-led Vietcong nearly toppled the Saigon government before the United States intervened. In these cases, and others like them, guerrilla warfare became a natural outlet for discontent because all other channels of reform were closed. Usually guerrilla warfare has been successful only in regions where the rebels have popular support. For this reason it has been extremely difficult for outside powers to repress such rebellions, even for great powers like the United States. Indeed, guerrilla warfare is the only means by which small nations can hope to resist the overwhelming strength of the giants. In the jungles and deserts that are the foyers of guerrilla warfare, the super-powers are at a great disadvantage. The very things that make them great—their advanced technology, wealth, and sophisticated weapons—are of limited use against armed rebels. The more primitive a nation's economy, the less susceptible it will be to the sophisticated warfare conducted by the great powers. Unlike war between industrial giants, guerrilla warfare is a conflict directed not against cities, factories, and machines, but against men—and, more specifically, for the allegiance of men. Here the great powers are reduced to the level of their enemies, forced to carry on hand-to-hand combat in a foreign terrain they do not know and often over causes they do not understand.

What is particularly frustrating about guerrilla warfare is the extraordinary amount of disruption that a relatively small number of insurgents is able to inflict—and, conversely, how difficult it is for even great numbers of soldiers to repress a guerrilla uprising that has popular support. In Cyprus, for example, the British army outnumbered the Greek terrorists by more than a hundred to one; in Indochina and Algeria the French were vastly superior both in numbers and in equipment to native nationalists. Yet in both cases these powerful Western armies were unable to subdue the guerrillas and ultimately decided to withdraw rather than continue a seemingly perpetual struggle in which they had lost interest. Similarly, the ragged guerrilla band under Fidel Castro never numbered more than a few thousand, yet with virtually no outside assistance it was able to undermine the Batista regime, neutralize the army, and seize power in Cuba. Even the Irish rebels were a small band, ill equipped and no match for the British Army. Yet ultimately they won because they had the sympathy of the population.

The guerrilla wars of the twentieth century were initially struggles for independence. Now that this ambition has been achieved nearly everywhere, the focus has switched to political change. Sometimes these struggles are led by communists, as in Vietnam; sometimes by Marxist-inspired romantics who may eventually turn to communism, as in Cuba; and sometimes by those with only a vague commitment to ideology, as in Colombia. Communists have a vested interest in supporting—at least verbally—wars that are directed against constituted authority in non-communist nations. As Marxists, they see such wars as advancing the ultimate victory of communism. "There will be wars of liberation as long as imperialism exists, as long as colonialism exists," Khrushchev declared in 1961. "Such wars are not only justified, they are inevitable." But however great their verbal sympathy for such "inevitable" wars, the Russians have been careful not to tie themselves down in other people's revolutions. In the Congo, in Cuba, in Laos, they restrained their enthusiasm for wars of liberation which took them into deeper water than they cared to go. The current Russian attitude toward revolution was memorably expressed by Khrushchev when, rhetorically asking why the Soviet Union should help French workers seize power, he declared, "Who asked us to mix in their affairs? What do we know about them?"

Now that the Russians are busy practicing the pleasures of "peaceful coexistence," the Chinese are taking their place as cheerleaders of the world revolution. They argue that the future of the world revolution lies not in the working class of the industrial countries, as the nineteenth-century communist prophets believed, but rather among the peasant masses of the backward societies. With some justice they point out that the working class today in the industrialized societies is bourgeois, chauvinistic, and an integral part of the power structure. The Chinese have no need to resort to contorted ideology, they have only to cite the history of the past fifty years, to demonstrate that the focus of revolutionary movements has switched from the working class of the industrialized societies to the peasants of the economically backward nations.

Having challenged Russia for the leadership of the communist world, the Chinese now feel free to reject the old dogma that the industrial proletariat is the natural leader of the world revolution. It never had any relevance to the success of China's own revolution, and it has been an impediment to Peking's efforts to become the new Rome of world communism. As the peasant country par excellence, China has practical as well as ideological justification for switching the focus of the world revolution from the industrialized "cities" of the West to the "rural areas" of the Third World. Thus it becomes apparent that the real target of Lin Piao's doctrine is not the "imperialist" West but the "revisionist" East—not Washington so much as Moscow. China is attempting to disqualify Russia's Marxist credentials by linking her with the developed countries of the West and thereby naming her an enemy of the international peasantry.

Peking's prescription for revolution, on analysis, is little more than a plea for forbearance among the downtrodden and a glimpse of eternal paradise for those who are willing to work for their own redemption. It is a plan for do-it-yourself insurrections, based upon the military inability of China to operate beyond her own frontiers, and upon her obvious failure to shape the world according to her own wishes. Rather than a terrorizing blueprint for a Third World apocalypse directed from Peking, a Chinese version of *Mein Kampf*, as Secretary Rusk called it, the Lin Piao message represents a contorted effort by the Chinese to gain credit for upheavals over which they have no control. They are, in a sense, trying to hitch a ride on other people's revolutions by implying that every guerrilla uprising is really a war of "national liberation" master-minded in the Imperial City.

Obsessed with the nightmare of a world revolution directed from Peking, official Washington, alone of all the major capitals, seems to be taking the Chinese prescription seriously. Yet, judging from the record, it should be clear, as one scholar has pointed out, that

Peking is likely to apply the term "war of national liberation" to almost any revolution or rebellion anywhere in the Third World on the assumption that any violent disturbance can only propel the Chinese wave of the future and weaken the United States. It is one of the great triumphs of Peking's propaganda that Washington has come to agree with this view. If Washington had been in the same frame of mind with respect to "wars of national liberation" during the Algerian revolt, the United States would no doubt have thrown its full support behind the French policy of suppression.[1]

Although they have tried to buy their way into the affections of the new nations with unsolicited advice and a small foreign-aid program, the Chinese have not been noticeably successful in inspiring revolution, or even in supplanting the Russians and the Americans. The new nations are quite aware of China's game and have shown little susceptibility to Chinese efforts at subversion. The "second Bandung" conference at Algiers in 1965 collapsed when the Chinese tried to use it as an anti-Soviet forum, the inter-African conference at Nouakchott condemned China for meddling in African affairs, Peking's diplomats have been booted out of several African countries, the Indonesians brutally slaughtered their own communists, and communist North Korea has told the Chinese it will not accept their dictation. Even Fidel Castro has condemned Peking for interfering in Cuban affairs and flung the ultimate insult against the Chinese by comparing them with the "imperialists" on his doorstep.

Peking is learning that talk is cheap but that influence cannot be won by slogans gleaned from the wisdom of Comrade Mao. To the new nations China offers not much more than, literally, tea and sympathy, seasoned with a good deal of subversion. China is still too poor to furnish a market for their raw materials or supply the capital they need to industrialize their backward economies. China can be of some marginal use to the emerging nations because she shares some of their own economic problems. But where she has tried to enlist them as instruments of her own foreign policy, she has suffered the fate of America or Russia where they have tried to do the same. Indeed, her fate has been even worse, because she cannot outbid the richer nations in buying clients. The nations of the Third World have shown a firm determination not to be dragged into the Sino–Soviet quarrel any more than they are willing to be dragged into the cold war between communists and anti-communists.

It should now be apparent to all but the most confirmed ideologues that communism, like capitalism, is an economic tool, not an instrument for imposing political solidarity upon disparate nations. There is no more reason for nations to behave similarly because they profess an allegiance to communism than for them to behave alike because they call themselves Buddhists or Catholics. As a way of organizing primitive societies, as a messianic doctrine for the eventual salvation of the poor, as a "scientific" dogma in an age that worships technology, communism is bound to have a theoretical appeal to many of the elite in the aspiring nations. To imagine, however, that this appeal can be turned to the political advantage of Russia or China is to fly in the face of all the evidence to the contrary during the past two decades. Throughout the Third World communism has been an even greater failure in winning converts than has capitalism, and nowhere has it augmented the power of either Moscow or Peking. Communism is simply one of a wide variety of imported doctrines from the West, to be adopted where it is useful, discarded where it is troublesome, and distorted everywhere it fits uneasily.

Communism has tried, with little success, to profit from the legacy of colonialism, which left such scars upon the hearts and minds of the colonized peoples. Although Western colonialism helped raise the peoples of the new nations from a state of economic primitiveness, it taught them that they were inferior because their skins were dark or because they were technologically underdeveloped. The imperial nations of Europe moved into Africa and Asia not from a *mission civilisatrice*, although they later used that as a justification, but for profit and prestige. The colonial peoples—whatever they gained from their Western rulers in the form of medical care, education, and modern transport— were often cruelly exploited. The educated aspirants to leadership of their people felt this resentment most deeply. As Frantz Fanon, the West Indian Negro who became one of the guiding figures of the Algerian revolution, wrote: "The well-being and the progress of Europe were built on the sweat and the corpses of Negroes, Arabs, Indians, and Orientals. That we decide never to forget."

That communism should rarely have been able to profit from this bitterness toward the West is perhaps its greatest failure. Of all the nations which have come to independence since the end of the Second World War, only two have communist governments. North Korea became communist because that was the unwritten price of bringing Russia into the war against Japan; North Vietnam, because the communists led the anti-colonial war for independence. Our nightmares about communism's sweeping the Third World have been largely figments of our own imagination. All the nations we feared would "go communist"—Egypt, Syria, the Congo, Burma, Cambodia—have proved to be as suspicious of Moscow and Peking as they have been of Washington, London, and Paris.

There is, to be sure, always the possibility that communists may profit from the revolutionary situation that exists in most of the underdeveloped world. Indeed, it would be astonishing if they were not able to pick up occasional clients. The entire southern hemisphere is going through an upheaval of staggering dimensions. Throughout Africa, and in many parts of Asia, new countries have come to independence bearing few other signs of national identity than the arbitrary boundaries staked out for them by the departed European colonial powers. Africa alone is split up into more than fifty countries, many of them divided into feuding tribal regions, and nearly all of them at a primitive level of economic organization.

Some of these states cover areas larger than France or Italy, yet have populations barely as great as Lyon or Genoa. These countries have few developed resources and even less industry, and are at the mercy of fluctuating commodity markets controlled by the Western powers. Few of them have the trained cadre needed to implement their ambitious development schemes, nearly all of them are dependent on foreign-aid grants from Russia and the

West, and most of them are producing a discontented educated class for which there are no jobs. Some of these nations are not even capable of feeding themselves. Most are subject to a population explosion which is putting intolerable demands on their already limited economic resources and drawing large numbers of unemployed peasants into the cities, where they stimulate the crime and rootlessness that are common to most urban societies.

Many of the new nations, particularly those in Africa, were never meant to be nations at all but were simply plantations developed by the European colonial powers. That they now have adopted all the trappings of nationhood is the result of a historical accident. Some of them will almost certainly split up or be absorbed into larger units. The tribal animosities that have swept the Congo, Burundi, Nigeria, and the Sudan do not augur well for their continued existence as cohesive nation-states. Some of the poor states, such as Somalia, Chad, the Central African Republic, the Upper Volta, and Mali—or those sandwiched between powerful neighbors, such as Dahomey and Togo—may not be able to survive as independent countries. These weaker nations may well be subjected to an indigenous style of imperialism which bears the label of pan-African unity. But in some cases such imperialism may not necessarily be a bad thing, if erasing some of the arbitrary national boundaries in Africa can make possible a higher level of economic development and social stability. There is no reason why the nation-state in its present form, and the national chauvinism that goes with it, should be sacrosanct in Africa, or anywhere else.

Africa today is going through an upheaval that is a direct, and in many ways a necessary, consequence of its sudden passage from colonial status to independence. Until 1951 there were only four independent nations on the entire continent: Egypt, Ethiopia, Liberia, and South Africa. In the single year of 1960 seventeen new states were carved out of the French empire, and today nearly the entire continent of fifty nations—with the exception of the Portuguese territories, a few Spanish and French enclaves, and South-West Africa—is independent. Such a cataclysmic change

in the structure of a whole continent was bound to bring instability and violence, and the real miracle is that this violence has
been confined to relatively few areas, such as the Congo. Since
most of the new nations were unprepared for independence, it
was natural that they should be one-party states governed by char-
ismatic rulers who in most cases were the leaders of their independence movements. It was also natural that the authority of
these leaders would tarnish as the fruits of independence turned
out to be more meager than the people had been led to believe.
Public discontent led, in many cases, to increasingly repressive
measures by such leaders as Nkrumah in Ghana, and ultimately
to their overthrow, usually by their own armies. These military
coups, however, have not necessarily been repressive and in some
cases they have been attempts to stave off revolution. In such
countries as Algeria, Ghana, and the two Congos, the intervention of the army put a rein on the political adventurism of ambitious civilian leaders.

The army intervenes in Africa for the same reason that it intervenes in Latin America and in the unsettled states from Syria
to Indonesia: Western democratic procedures have not taken
hold, and civilian leaders have not been able to deal adequately
with the intractable new problems of nationhood. Throughout
most of Africa the nation-state came into existence before there
was any concept of a nation. Colonialism created a central government and rabidly nationalistic political groups. But it was not
able to submerge local and tribal loyalties into a single national
entity. This heritage is now being felt by the leaders of the new
states, who are trying to govern nations that do not yet have a
real sense of political cohesion. Their problems have been
exacerbated by the strains of economic development and by the
rising demands of their people for an improvement in the material
conditions of their lives. Authoritarianism and one-party states
have been a common, and often an unavoidable, way of dealing
with the pressures unleashed by independence.

Faced with the problems of rapid urbanization, expanding populations, inadequate economic development, deep-rooted tribal

animosities, feeble political superstructures, and achievements that fall far short of expectations, Africa is likely to be a foyer of revolution and upheaval for a generation and more to come. Neither democracy nor stability represents the norm in these new nations, for they are trying to forge a new identity from the ruins of a dead colonialism. In such circumstances, revolution is not an aberration, and even less is it a disease contracted from the outside. It is an integral part of the painful process of creating viable nations from colonial territories and political backwaters which have been stagnant for most of their modern history. Revolution, in such situations, is associated with modernization and the attempt to arouse a national consciousness. It is endemic in the development of the Third World, and has very little to do with the cold-war battles between communism and anti-communism.

Yet despite all the evidence to the contrary, official Washington still continues to behave as though most revolutions, even though they are not inspired by communism, will eventually fall into communist hands. This is why conservative, status-quo regimes look to us for support, and why the Pentagon is currently engaged in training young Americans, as well as officers from foreign armies, in the principles of anti-guerrilla warfare. The purpose of such warfare is to stamp out revolutions, and the reason for trying to stamp out revolutions is the assumption that they will fall under communist control. Thus, by a product of political subtraction that belies the evidence, we have convinced ourselves that revolution is virtually tantamount to communism and therefore a proper object of American suppression. Despite everything that has happened in Washington and the world during the past decade, our policy-makers still seem to agree with the analysis of President Eisenhower, who defended military and economic aid to Saudi Arabia on the grounds that its feudal king "at least professed anti-communism."

In this casually dropped phrase from the ex-President's memoirs lies the key to American foreign policy in the postwar period: anti-communism as an ideology. Although we might not admit it, we have been incapable of conceiving of any system other than communism that might replace the archaic economic and political structures in the Third World. From fear of change, rather than from approval of injustice, we are committed to the support of reactionary regimes that "at least profess anti-communism." We find ourselves in the situation of Metternich a century and a half ago: hostile to the extension of liberalism, yet unable to imagine a system to replace the collapsing monarchies of Europe, and thus driven to defend them by the use of force. It is, perhaps, not surprising that we should have become an un-revolutionary power. Our revolution, after all, is nearly two hundred years behind us, and in the interval we have grown rich and powerful beyond the dreams of the musket-wielding patriots of Concord and Lexington. We are not a young nation, but in fact the world's oldest constitutional democracy. It would indeed be remarkable if a rich, smug, and middle-aged nation with a very real economic interest in maintaining the status quo should brandish revolutionary slogans and urge the downtrodden peasants of the world to rise up against their masters. Yet there is a considerable difference between being an un-revolutionary power—like all the rich and self-satisfied nations of Western Europe—and being an anti-revolutionary power, dedicated to the suppression of revolutions.

If America, like Metternich's Austro-Hungarian Empire, has become an anti-revolutionary power, it is not from a desire to enforce her will upon other nations, but from an obsessive fear of communism, a fear which induces the belief that all revolutions are communist-inspired and directed against the United States. But these revolutions are not directed against us, and they are not manufactured to order by communists. They occur in politically backward nations because the status quo can be changed only by force. If reforms were possible through the ballot box in such countries, there would be no need for insurrection and no problem of "wars of liberation." We become targets of such revolts only insofar as we allow ourselves to become the prisoners of repressive local oligarchies or the defenders of exploiting American corporations. Yet in many countries this is precisely what has happened. "You can't be a nationalist without being anti-American," a young Philippine law student declared during anti-government riots in Manila in early 1970. That statement is a profound comment on American foreign policy.

"Wars of liberation" are merely one part of the disturbances that are now shaking the Third World and are likely to continue throughout this century. There will probably be wars for independence in the few remaining areas of foreign rule, such as Angola and Mozambique. There is quite likely to be a race war in southern Africa, unless there should be a radical change of policy in Rhodesia and South Africa. There will be a series of wars to overthrow reactionary regimes, or to replace despots, or to install military dictatorships, or to depose leaders who are unable to satisfy the new elites. There will be more *coups d'état* than it will be possible, or worth while, to count. In most of the Third World nations the army is becoming the final arbiter of power, either ruling directly in its own name or else through civilians who govern by its tolerance. Military coups are becoming standard practice throughout the Third World.

Aside from wars of national liberation and *coups d'état*, there will likely be a succession of civil wars in the new nations as the attempt to impose national unity comes into conflict with the powerful traditions of racial, religious, or nationality groups. Just as America herself had to experience a terrible civil war before the principle of national authority was finally accepted by all, so many of the new nations will have similar wars as the central governments try to impose their power on disparate and often hostile groups within the national boundaries. The war of the Kurdish tribesmen against the government of Iraq, of the Nagas and the Mizos against the government of India, of the feuding tribes in the Congo, of the Biafrans against the federal authorities in Nigeria, and the rebellion by the Negroes against the Arabs in the Sudan are simply a few current examples of what we can expect in the years ahead.

The turmoil of this revolutionary age is likely to continue for decades, perhaps for generations. This revolution, which has come from the breakdown of the European colonial world, the spread of a new technology, and the pressures of uncontrolled population growth, is that no power can hope to master. It is a revolution that has barely begun, and one in which communism is as incidental as is capitalism. This is a period of confusion and upheaval because it marks a transition from a world dominated by Europe to an anarchic world of nominally independent nation-states. Is it a revolution we can hope to control? And if so, what price are we likely to have to pay?

16. Isolation—or Intervention?

The plain truth is that the day is coming when no single nation, however powerful, can undertake by itself to keep the peace outside its own borders. —ROBERT S. McNAMARA

❧ ❧ ❧ THE debate over our world role is an urgent matter which America can no longer avoid. It is an argument between those who believe that American power and American responsibilities are limited, and those who believe that they are global; between those who see the defense of freedom as indivisible, and those who would limit our involvements to areas where our security is at stake and where we would not try to impose our ideals upon others. In the most elemental sense this is an argument about America's moral and intellectual responsibilities, and specifically about America's role in the world: whether she is, as John Kennedy said, "the watchman on the walls of world freedom," or whether, as John Quincy Adams advised, she should be the "well-wisher to the freedom and independence of all . . . [but] the champion and vindicator only of her own."

So far this argument has been carried on in a rather traditional vocabulary. Those who believe the nation to be overextended—militarily, intellectually, morally—are castigated as isolationists, or perhaps more charitably as neo-isolationists. Those who believe that America must intervene with her military power to prevent communist regimes from coming to power are labeled globalists. But the labeling, while convenient and perhaps unavoidable, does not do justice to either side. The so-called neo-isolationists do not want to turn the clock back to 1938 and retire to a Fortress America while the rest of the world goes up in flames. These neo-isolationists are, for the most part, convinced internationalists, supporters of foreign aid, NATO, and the Alliance for Progress. What they seek is not a denial of American responsibility but a retrenchment of American commitments to those areas which they consider vital to the national interest; more specifically, Western Europe and the western hemisphere. They believe that American military power should be used only to defend the vital strategic interests of the United States, and not to save non-communist governments in the Third World.

The globalists, on the other hand, feel that the United States has a moral as well as a national responsibility to prevent the spread of communism wherever the threat may arise. They reject the assumption of the neo-isolationists that one area of the world is more important than any other. Whereas President Kennedy declared that he was a Berliner, President Johnson more accurately reflected the globalist style by asserting that the United States is a Pacific power. The war in Vietnam is the proof of this conviction. Globalists believe that the United States is engaged in a struggle with communism that will, quite literally, determine the fate of the world. To retire from the struggle, or to refrain from using force to prevent an advance of communism, would, in this view, be ignominious. Not only would this represent a victory for a hostile ideology, but it would diminish America's stature on the world stage. Behind the appeals to a higher morality there lies a calculated consideration of national prestige. Globalists may be ideologues, but they are also confirmed believers in *Realpolitik*. The difficulty, however, occurs when the two come into conflict, when a commitment to ideology prevents a clear calculation of the national interest, or when a cynical use of power betrays basic moral principles.

This balancing of *Realpolitik* and political morality is a peculiar dilemma, but it is an American one, and it is shared equally by neo-isolationists and globalists. The former believe that calculations of national interest should determine whether or not the nation commits itself to military intervention in support of foreign governments. They would argue that only those nations whose security is crucial to our interests merit American military intervention in their support. However, because they are Americans and thus infused with a moral conception of foreign policy, they would make exceptions for certain non-strategic countries that are integral to the Western community, such as New Zealand, Israel, and Iceland. They would also argue that we should support only progressive, representative regimes that share our belief in political democracy. That such regimes are exceedingly scarce outside the Western world, even in countries that may be important to our national interest, is one of the dilemmas of the liberal neo-isolationists.

The globalists, for their part, speak movingly of the moral purpose of America as the defender of freedoms for those who are too weak to defend themselves. Yet they readily display a willingness to use American military power in such cruel ways as to make their moral imperatives appear as cynical self-justifications. "Sure of its moral purposes—surer of its own moral performance—America shall not be deterred from doing what must be done to preserve this last peace man shall ever have to win or lose," said Lyndon Johnson on June 6, 1965, as American planes strafed, bombed, and napalmed the villages of Vietnam. Behind the moral righteousness of the global interventionist lies the heavy rod of the Calvinist judge.

Thus morality and power blend in a strange combination that America's critics can look upon only as the most self-serving hypocrisy, but which all Americans will recognize as an expression of their own mixed, and often contradictory, feelings about the role of a nation engaged, in John F. Kennedy's words, "with a struggle we did not start in a world we did not make." There are no easy answers, no moral certainties, no sure rewards. There is only the reality of America's inextricable involvement in a recalcitrant world, and the gnawing fear that perhaps our great power is being dissipated uselessly, or, even worse, used in ways that diminish our worth to the world and to ourselves.

The United States is inescapably a world power, currently *the* world power, with all the responsibilities, the temptations, and the anguish that go with such overwhelming force. America did not choose to be a great power; she became a great power. She was born with great dreams and she had greatness thrust upon her. But once having achieved great power, once having had the responsibility of defending European civilization first from nazism, then from communism, the United States developed a sense of mission about the uses of her power. Just as she gradually picked up an empire in Europe and Asia to complement the one she had long enjoyed in Latin America, so she began to dream imperial dreams. She became absorbed not only in her own security and the defense of her closest allies from external aggression, but also in the effort to mold the world into an image conforming to her own conception of virtue.

This is, perhaps, a temptation common to many nations. But the extraordinary weight of America in the world balance transformed such an ambition from a dream into a program, albeit a rather dimly defined and only half-recognized one. American power, to a degree not fully conceived of even by the American people in whose name it is exercised, has been turned into an instrument for the pursuit of an American ideology. And that ideology is not merely the defense of the nation and its institutions, but something far more ambitious: the establishment of a world order on the American plan. It is this desire to translate American ideals into a universal political system that lies at the core of the current crisis in American diplomacy.

The vision of America as the enforcer of justice and the scourge of tyrants is a noble one. It goes back, in rhetoric at least, to the early days of the republic and corresponds to the image of the United States as a standard-bearer of freedom for peoples everywhere. It was not, however, until recently that this patriotic self-image was translated into a program of action and America was declared to have a responsibility to bring her concept of democratic self-government to peoples everywhere. Woodrow Wilson thought he would bring about universal justice through a League of Nations bound to principles of morality. Franklin Roosevelt, less idealistic but wiser in the ways of nations, sought to bring about the American Century by an accord of the great powers acting in cooperation through the Security Council of the United Nations. Lyndon Johnson, heading a government "sure of its moral purpose," would have had the United States achieve the world of justice and liberty that is every man's dream through the unilateral application of American military power. And Richard Nixon, even while sensing the public's rejection of such adventures as Cambodia, declares his belief that "this nation shall continue to be a source of world leadership, a source of freedom's strength, in creating a just world order that will bring an end to war."

Yet the freedom Americans are called upon to defend by the sword takes on an abstract ring when applied to societies outside the Western tradition. In the West "freedom" means the ability of men to choose, to change, and to reject the governments under which they live. To an Angolan rebel, however, it means independence from Portugal; to a Cuban revolutionary it means release from American economic control; to a Rumanian it means defiance of the Soviet Union; to white Rhodesians it means the right to dominate a black majority; to the Ibo tribesman of Nigeria it meant independence from the government in Lagos; and to the peasants of Brazil's northeast it means bread and a patch of land. These are not all freedoms which it is in America's power to grant, nor even necessarily freedoms which we would value.

The United States has intervened deeply in the affairs of countries where our national interests are often only remotely involved. She has done so in the name of freedom and in the struggle against communism. But we have not intervened in a good many countries where freedom is a mockery, such as Haiti, Paraguay, and Saudi Arabia; nor where it is confined to a privileged minority, such as in South Africa and Rhodesia; nor even where there was open communist aggression, such as in Tibet and Hungary. We did not intervene in these instances because the kind of freedoms that were being suppressed in the Caribbean and African dictatorships had nothing to do with our battle against communism. We did not intervene in Tibet because it was too remote and the issues were irrelevant; and we did not intervene in Hungary because we would probably have ignited a third world war. On closer inspection, therefore, it can be seen that our commitment to the defense of freedom and self-determination for all peoples is little more than a defense of the status quo that depends upon whether or not communists are involved. And if communists are involved, it depends on whether we think our intervention may have some chance of success. Where our theoretical compulsion to defend freedom everywhere has come into conflict with a threat to our own national survival—as in Hungary in 1956 and in the East Berlin riots of 1953—we have shown a prudent regard for survival.

What American postwar intervention boils down to in practice is not intervention against injustice or poverty for its own sake, but intervention against communism, where we can intervene without putting ourselves in direct conflict with Russia. It is not the virtues of freedom we are primarily worried about, but a threat to the status quo. Where injustice is combined with an absence of a communist problem, as in Haiti or Rhodesia, we have been indifferent to the call of our moral imperatives. Where a communist problem exists, as in Vietnam, we have found the defense of freedom to be an unshirkable obligation, even if performed on behalf of a regime which may be as indifferent to freedom as the communist one it opposes. When we decide when to honor our moral duty, the label the oppressor wears is exceedingly important.

This reluctance to become involved in the struggle against communism in instances where it is likely to trigger a sharp Russian counter-reaction is not necessarily to be criticized. Perhaps we might legitimately have intervened at Budapest, considering the moral issue at stake, and at least have tried to dissuade the Russians from invading Czechoslovakia, but in both cases we preferred stability. We have, on the other hand, certainly been right not to intervene in the unstable new countries of Africa, where Russia and China are unsuccessfully trying to outbid each other for African affections, and where any military intervention we might conceivably undertake could only rebound disastrously against us. Having had our fingers badly burned in the Congo, both we and the Russians have been reluctant to embroil ourselves in Africa's chronic troubles—and rightly so. Aside from economic and technical assistance mixed with heavy doses of forbearance, there is not much that we can do for the unstable, and still unmade, nations of Central Africa. Our guiding principles of anti-communism and self-determination have never meant very much in the context of tropical Africa, and our understandable unwillingness to act upon them in such places as South Africa and Rhodesia has revealed a deep, and often unconscious, hypocrisy in our foreign policy.

Our global mission against communism clearly is tinged with an elementary consideration of the possible, and fortunately so. Yet this has not liberated us from the rhetoric of a diplomacy that sees freedom and communism struggling for the soul of the world. But by now it should be obvious that this is not the real issue. The communists are not going to inherit the earth, and neither are we. They are not going to do it because communism no longer means more than a nodding allegiance to some rather antiquated economic theories of Karl Marx. The various communist parties have drifted so far apart, and have been so subordinated to the more potent ideology of nationalism, that in many cases it is no longer of any great significance whether or not a nation has a nominally communist form of government. Yugoslavia is communist; so are Albania and North Korea. What benefit does the Soviet Union get out of that? Or China, for that matter? Nicaragua is anti-communist; so are Taiwan and South Korea. What good does that do us? As far as the national interest is concerned, it makes little difference what kind of ideology a government professes, so long as it does not follow policies which are hostile or dangerous. We live perfectly well with a communist Yugoslavia, and could with a communist Cuba as well, if we could swallow our hurt pride. The Russians, by the same token, live at ease with an anti-communist Norway on one side of them and an anti-communist Iran on another.

What counts is not the label a regime may choose to attach to itself, but whether it poses a threat to us or to world peace. There are some communist countries such as Yugoslavia and, according even to Konrad Adenauer, the Soviet Union itself, that are a factor for stability and peace. There are some non-communist countries, such as the Congo and South Vietnam, that are a source of instability and danger. As far as the world's peace and our own national interests are concerned, the fact that a country is communist may be less important than how much rain it gets or how many pairs of shoes it produces. It is certainly less important than the policies it follows toward its neighbors, and how capable it is of meeting the demands of its own citizens for economic justice and social equality.

Small nations along the borders of Russia and China are not necessarily hostile to our interests because they are nominally communist. There are some communist governments that are more worthy of respect than some anti-communist governments. There are some anti-communist governments that are so unpopular with their own people that they cannot be saved. There are others which can be kept in power only by risks that are out of all proportion to the stakes involved. There are anti-communist governments that are not worth saving, regardless of how small the risks may be. And there are governments that, if the communists did take them over, would be more of a threat to the communist nations than to us. China is the classic example of a country which is a greater danger to Russia now that she is under communist control than she would have been under the control of Chiang Kai-shek.

Communism, in any case, is not taking over the world, and the reason has nothing to do with our military intervention. We intervened in Vietnam and thereby permitted the communists to seize the banner of Vietnamese nationalism against a new colonial power—that is, us. We did not intervene in Indonesia, a far more important country on any scale of power, when the communists threatened to seize control. If we had intervened militarily, it is likely that the Indonesian Communist Party would be running the government from Djakarta today, instead of having its leaders either dead or in prison. Indeed, as Singapore's anti-communist Prime Minister, Lee Kuan Yew, has said, after a bitter experience with the CIA, "If the Americans had been here, I'd have been in jail and tortured and died a commie."

The underdeveloped nations are unlikely to turn to the communists not because of the intervention of the CIA or the United States Air Force, but because they themselves have little sympathy for communism. Not a single nation which has come to independence since the Second World War has turned to communism, with the exception of Vietnam. The immunity of the new nations to communism has been remarkable. They have been, if anything, even more anti-communist than the old imperial nations of Europe. Even those which collect aid from the Soviet Union or from China do not show the slightest hesitation about jailing their own communists, outlawing the party, and expelling communist diplomats. Caught up in the ideology of nationalism, the new nations have rejected the pretensions of the communist giants along with the capitalist ones.

This does not mean that there will never be another communist government anywhere in the world. Perhaps one day there may be a communist Burma, or a communist Guatemala, or a communist Tanzania. What is important is not the label a regime chooses to pin on itself, but the policies it follows. Small communist nations in the southern hemisphere are no threat to the United States. Nor, as we should now have learned from experience, are they likely to remain the satellites of Russia or China for very long. The kind of government they choose to live under is their affair, not ours. We live perfectly comfortably with totalitarian governments of the Right; we even consider most of them allies and members of the "free world." We can learn to live with totalitarian governments of the Left as well, and let the Russians and the Chinese worry about the purity of their ideology.

If the notion that all communist governments everywhere are inherently evil and detrimental to our interests is the most pernicious myth of our foreign policy, then the second most pernicious myth is the belief that world peace depends on the maintenance of the status quo everywhere. In its basic form this myth declares that the current détente between ourselves and the Soviet Union rests upon a tacit agreement that changes in the boundary lines between the two systems—either by force or by unilateral action —are too dangerous to world peace to be tolerated. Greece and Hungary are given as examples where each side respected the existing demarcation lines: the Russians called off the Greek civil war, we refused to intervene at Budapest.

Yet this was reasonable only so long as there were in fact, as at the time of the Budapest riots, *two systems*: the communist world and ours. Any forcible change in the boundaries between the two systems could have been legitimately seen as a victory for one side or a defeat for the other. That was why President Truman intervened in Korea, and why the Russians stamped out the Budapest revolt. We could not allow South Korea to fall into their orbit, and they could not allow Hungary to fall into ours. If a loss for one side was not necessarily a victory for the other, reasonable men at least thought so at the time. There was, from the mid-1940s until the late 1950s, a bi-polar world.

But that is past history. The "communist world" does not exist any more, and neither does "ours." Therefore, to speak of boundaries and demarcation lines between the "free world" and the "communist world" is little more than cultural lag. Communist regimes may come to power in some countries and represent an actual net loss for the "international communist movement." The communist capture of China was hardly a "victory" for Russia, as Stalin had feared all along, any more than a communist Vietnam united under Ho Chi Minh would be likely to represent any kind of "victory" for China. The record has shown clearly that nationalism has triumphed over communism, even in those countries where the communists have come to power. In fact, it may well be that in certain instances (and Vietnam is probably one of them) national communism represents the best bulwark against Soviet or Chinese expansion. Cohesive, nationalistic states (whatever their political complexion) on the borders of great ones are a far more effective barrier to expansion, whether territorial or ideological, than are weak, divided ones.

Thus the idea that the détente between America and Russia rests upon a respect for "boundary lines" in the southern hemisphere is a delusion. The chaos of the underdeveloped world is a source of danger for both the super-powers, but not because a change of regime in some remote and backward country is going to upset the world balance. The only place the theory is still relevant is in those very few areas—notably Central Europe—where the vital interests of the great powers overlap. Neither side can change the boundary lines in Europe by force because neither America nor Russia could tolerate such a blow to her interests or her prestige. This is why the line down the center of Germany remains intact. It is also true that neither side can be allowed to upset the present military balance within the sphere of influence of the other. This was the point of the Cuban missile crisis. As we could not use Finland to set up a missile base, so the Soviets could not use Cuba for a strategic base against us. By establishing that principle, firmly but with suppleness, President Kennedy set the stage for the current détente. This détente rests on a mutual respect for the spheres of influence that are vital to the interests of the super-powers, not upon an agreement that present demarcation lines between communism and non-communism anywhere in the world shall never be changed.

To say, as many American policy-makers have been saying for the past few years, that the political status quo cannot be changed by force is to attempt to legislate stagnation into international politics. This has been tried many times in the past, but never successfully. There are always going to be people with grievances who will be forced to resort to arms to redress those grievances. That was the reason for Bunker Hill and the Bastille, for the Easter rising and the Moncada barracks. Where there are no free elections, no right of appeal, and no legal procedure for redressing grievances, then the status quo can be changed only by force. And in some countries the status quo is so intolerable to the people who live there that they will endure almost anything to change it. To dedicate American foreign policy to the perpetuation of the political status quo, except where it can be changed without violence, is to doom this nation to the role of a glorified prison warden. It would be to try to play Metternich's role on a world scale, with far greater power but with less justification and with little chance of success.

In seeking to ensure stability, we have been drawn into the suppression of progressive forces in cases where communists are, or may be, involved. Although it is not our intention to perpetuate the status quo, this has been the impact of our policy. As long as we are mesmerized by anti-communism and stability, it will be exceedingly difficult for us to accept the possibility that even violent changes in the political status quo in certain countries may not necessarily be hostile to our interests, or to prevent our foreign policy from being used to suppress popularly supported movements of political change. In assuming that we have an obligation to smother violent changes in the status quo by discontented groups within various countries, we are arrogating to ourselves the responsibility for being an international police power. We are doing so without anyone's consent and from no other motive than that we believe that our vision of a proper political order is valid for nations everywhere. This, whether we recognize it or not, is imperialism, and an imperial foreign policy cannot be maintained without considerable sacrifices at home and repression abroad. It can even lead to repression at home, as the Chicago "conspiracy" trial and the treatment of militants indicate.

Yet if military interventionism is an unsatisfactory policy, what is the alternative? A return to isolationism? Even though this may sometimes seem tempting to those disappointed by our inability to reform the world, it is hardly a real alternative. Whether we like the responsibility or not, the United States is the greatest power in the world. She cannot relinquish this power even by refusing to exercise it. America is fated to play a dominant world role during the remaining decades of this century, and perhaps for a good deal longer. So long as American power remains dominant in the world, it cannot be abdicated without inducing effects as great as those which arise from its exercise.

Were America to withdraw into a shell of isolationism, Soviet Russia would be the only great power left in the world. Although she seems to have turned her back on a policy of aggression, this has been in large part because of the counterbalance of the United States. If that balance were destroyed by a unilateral American abdication, Russian leaders would be tempted to embark upon a policy of diplomatic and military adventurism. The détente would be destroyed along with the power balance. Even if Russia were to resist temptations to open aggression, it would hardly be desirable to bestow the gift of world hegemony upon a nation that has shown such scant respect for democratic values within her own borders. A Pax Americana is dangerous and not even desirable. A Pax Sovietica would be a universal disaster.

Nor is it very likely. The United States has traveled too far from her old isolationism to take the road back. A whole generation of Americans has come to maturity since the cold war began, and another generation has moved into positions of responsibility after having spent its entire adult life in a period of American interventionism. The old isolationism is dead, and its most ardent practitioners have now become unilateral interventionists. America has not only turned her back on isolationism, she has forgotten it. Isolationism was never a viable object of American diplomacy. Today it is no longer even a conceivable one.

Instead of an isolationism that has become historically obsolete, a number of thoughtful observers favor a return to a spheres-of-influence policy. A formula of diplomacy long applied in Europe and pursued by the United States herself through the Monroe Doctrine, spheres-of-influence is based on the belief that great powers have certain proprietary rights in areas adjacent to their frontiers. These rights rest on the fact that areas which are contiguous to great powers are essential to their military security. Other powers recognize these rights and do not challenge their rivals on their home grounds unless they mean war. Just as the Lowlands have traditionally been in Britain's sphere of influence, and the Balkans within Russia's, so has the Caribbean been within ours.

This, of course, is precisely what Woodrow Wilson hoped to put an end to with the Fourteen Points and the League of Nations. Instead of proprietary rights for the great powers there was to be self-determination for all peoples, however weak and however strategically situated on other nations' borders. Wilson sincerely believed in these principles and died fighting for them. Yet such were his powers of self-deception that they did not prevent him from sending Marines to Veracruz, Haiti, and the Dominican Republic to quell disorders that threatened the tranquillity of "our own back yard." Wilson made an exception where the American sphere of influence was concerned, yet he nonetheless maintained that the system as applied elsewhere was inherently evil.

For all the scorn heaped upon the spheres-of-influence policy over the years, it remains a fairly accurate description of the way great powers behave, the United States included. We established our proprietary rights over the Caribbean, and indeed over the entire western hemisphere, in 1823 under President Monroe, and have shown no signs of relinquishing them. The Russians have their sphere of influence in Eastern Europe, which they have worked very hard to obtain and have no present intention of giving up. We may not like their hegemony over their neighbors any more than they like ours. But we both accept these spheres because we understand that they are areas which are considered vital to national security. Indeed, the only place where we do not recognize anybody else's sphere of influence is in Asia, where we believe that ours should extend to the borders of China, but that China herself should have no sphere of influence at all. This convenient state of affairs, of course, is made possible by the fact that China is so much weaker than we are. When China becomes a full-fledged nuclear power, we will most likely grant her in Southeast Asia what we grant Russia in Eastern Europe and demand for ourselves in the Caribbean.

Perhaps, then, spheres-of-influence is the logical alternative to globalism. Certainly no one has made a more persuasive case than

Walter Lippmann, when he wrote, in *support* of our invasion of the Dominican Republic:

> It is normal, not abnormal, for a great power to insist that within its sphere of influence no other great power shall exercise hostile military and political force. Since we emerged from isolation in the beginning of this century, American foreign policy has been bedeviled by the utopian fallacy that, because this is one world, special spheres of influence are an inherent evil and obsolete. . . . As a matter of fact, experience must soon verify the truth that spheres of influence are fundamental in the very nature of international society. Great powers will resist the invasion of their spheres of influence. . . . Recognition of spheres of influence is a true alternative to globalism. It is the alternative to communist gobalism which proclaims a universal revolution. It is the alternative to anti-communist globalism which promises to fight anti-communist wars everywhere. The acceptance of spheres of influence has been the dominant foundation of the détente in Europe between the Soviet Union and the West. Eventually it will provide the formula of coexistence between Red China and the United States.[1]

This is a compelling argument. As an antidote to unlimited intervention it has the merits of being logical, sane, and unprovocative. It would clearly spare us the agonies of such wars as the one in Vietnam, and it would relieve us of the terrible, self-inflicted burden of a moral responsibility for the fate of all mankind.

But for all its attractiveness, it also has certain drawbacks. If we accept that every great power has a sphere of influence, who is to decide how far the spheres extend? Does our sphere of influence end at the Caribbean, or does it extend all the way down to Tierra del Fuego? Does Russia's sphere end at the Oder–Neisse line, or at the Elbe, or perhaps along the Rhine? Even if we grant that great powers should have a sphere of influence, can they behave as they please within their corrals? Can the Russians stamp out with impunity revolutions such as the one in Hungary? Can we invade Santo Domingo whenever a regime we do not like threatens to come to power? A consistent spheres-of-influence policy would say yes, that, unfortunate as it may be, great powers must ensure that their small neighbors fall in line. This does not mean that the small powers must be abject slaves, but neither must they behave in a way that will embarrass or endanger their great neighbors. Finland cannot join NATO, Cuba cannot join the Warsaw Pact. Even assuming that small nations must not unduly irritate their big neighbors, how much liberty of maneuver are they allowed? As much as East Germany? As Rumania? As Santo Domingo? As Guatemala? Once the principle of spheres of influence is accepted, how can a line be drawn to delimit great-power domination?

Further, if we assume the morality of our sphere of influence in the Caribbean and Russia's in Eastern Europe, what do we do about China's sphere in Asia? As a great, or a potential great, power she merits a sphere of influence. But where does it stop, and how much control can she exercise within that sphere? To complicate matters, China does not stand alone in Asia. There are other potential great powers in the area: India, Japan, and Indonesia. Are they going to give China a free hand in the small nations on her periphery, or will they wrestle with her for the allegiance of these nations, some of which are on *their* peripheries as well and could be considered to fall within *their* sphere of influence?

Here we come upon the key dilemma of the spheres-of-influence doctrine: what happens when the spheres overlap? What happens when Indonesia and China struggle for a sphere of influence in Southeast Asia? When India and China struggle for influence over Burma and Nepal? When Japan and China struggle for influence over Korea? When Russia and China struggle for influence over Mongolia? Is this not the classic situation for the outbreak of war between powers who fear the sacrifice of their prestige if they seem to relinquish areas in their sphere of influence? To raise the question is to show that there are no easy solutions, even if we accept the spheres-of-influence theory as a working model. What it really offers is not a solution but a means of limiting great-power intervention in areas where only one great power has a vital interest.

A spheres-of-influence policy is no answer, for it puts the weak too much at the mercy of the strong, whether in Eastern Europe, in Southeast Asia, or in the Caribbean. But it is at least a beginning, for it forces us to recognize that some places are more important than others to the security of the great powers—that every spot on the globe is not equally vital to American interests, and that the political orientation of a country such as South Vietnam may be no more crucial to American security than the political orientation of Guatemala is to Chinese security. This is not to say that we should be morally indifferent to what happens in Vietnam, any more than the Chinese need be indifferent to what happens in Guatemala. Like all great powers, we are interested in crises wherever they occur. But all crises are not equally important to our security, and it is on the base of national security that an enlightened foreign policy must rest.

While national security should be the first guide of conduct for a nation's diplomacy, it cannot be the only guide, and particularly not for the United States, with her political idealism and her evangelical commitment to the betterment of mankind. An American foreign policy, if it is to have the support of the American people, must be something more than a policy of narrow self-interest.

A nation has interests that often transcend considerations of military security. Among those interests is the preservation of the community of nations to which the United States belongs by history, cultural affinity, and common values. America has a special responsibility to help those states with whom she is joined in this intimate community, even though they may lie outside her sphere of influence. But it is important to understand what the community of common values consists of and where its limits lie. It includes democratic nations that are earnestly seeking to preserve their own freedoms from outside aggression. It does not include feeble dictatorships which seek our support against their own population.

Throughout the entire postwar period the United States has embraced authoritarian and even fascist regimes because they were anti-communist and helped uphold the status quo. The dead-end of this policy was Vietnam, a war without end that tore American society to pieces. This kind of intervention, conducted in the name of anti-communism and perpetuated in order to retain a sphere of influence, has now been rejected by the vast majority of the American people. Vietnam has made many Americans aware of the terrible cost of their global empire and led to a pervasive mood of non-interventionism. But the lesson has yet to be fully learned in Washington, where the infatuation with intervention continues in Cambodia and in the CIA-led "secret war" in Laos, even though the language has been toned down.

In the delicate balancing of interests on which a new foreign policy must be built, discrimination is all: discrimination among competing interests, discrimination among competing nations, discrimination among competing claims. Some states are vital to our own security and therefore cannot be allowed to fall under the control of a hostile great power. Other states form a part of our own community of values and thus merit our involvement in their defense. But a good many states which seek American protection and which tell us that we have a responsibility to save them simply cannot be saved because they are too corrupt and discredited. Others may not be worth saving, because the difference between the oppression they are fighting and the oppression they practice at home may be marginal.

During the years ahead the real danger to world stability is likely to be not in Europe, which is prosperous, stable, and holds the key to its own unification, but in the states of the Third World, which are just rising to political consciousness and which are beset by tensions and divisions no outside power can master. These states will be chaotic, prone to violence and *coups d'état*, and tempted to aggression against their neighbors, no matter what we do. This violence is an inexorable part of the painful transition from a colonial world ruled from Europe to a world where there is no central source of authority and where a new balance has yet to be created.

There will be revolution in Latin America, upheaval throughout Asia and the Middle East, and violence in Africa, no matter what we or the communists do or refrain from doing. The most we can hope for is to try to restrain that violence and isolate it before it involves the great powers. This means refraining from cheap calls to "self-determination" and pious references to the "indivisibility of freedom," particularly when, in such places as Rhodesia and South Africa, we have no intention of acting upon them, and where our own record on the race question at home reduces much of our rhetoric to hypocrisy. It means standing back to allow the new nations to work out their own destiny as they see fit within their own frontiers, and showing restraint when violently nationalistic and anti-capitalistic regimes come to power. One hopeful sign of an evolution in American policy is shown by the Nixon administration's restraint toward the military government in Peru, which nationalized Standard Oil's holdings without being threatened by the Marines or even by a cut-off of American economic assistance. Peru, of course, had the good fortune not to be located in the Caribbean, where American military power could more easily be applied. Nonetheless, the precedent is a hopeful one.

When, if ever, is military intervention justified? Certainly not to protect American corporate investments or to defeat popular revolutions that threaten to be led by communists. Very few such revolutions represent a real threat to American security. There will, nonetheless, be instances when, if we have exhausted other possibilities, it may be necessary to intervene with American military power to defend a vital national interest. Intervention, like surgery, is not an evil in itself, but it must be applied sparingly and with consummate skill. Just as intervention cannot be a guiding principle in diplomacy, so non-intervention cannot be observed irrespective of time or place. All situations are not equally important. All do not justify American support, and even fewer justify American military intervention.

The crucial point is that a *unilateral* American military intervention is generally justified only if the security of the United States herself is involved. In cases of open aggression by one nation against another, or an eruption of hostilities that might endanger the peace of an entire area—such as war between Israel and the Arab states—it may be desirable for the great powers *jointly* to intervene, preferably under the auspices of the United Nations, to restore the peace. There is, however, no iron rule in such cases, for there are areas, such as Central Africa, where outside powers, even acting jointly, cannot hope to impose order and might be well advised not to try. Disturbances in such regions need concern us directly only where the region itself is of crucial importance to our interests, or where such disturbances may threaten world peace.

Finally, disturbances *within* a nation, however distasteful we may find them, must be the concern of that nation alone and cannot be the excuse for a military intervention designed to impose a form of government favored by the intervening power. If self-determination, which we continually proclaim as a guiding principle of international conduct, means anything, it means the right of nations to evolve their own forms of government. We would not tolerate interference in our own internal disturbances; by the same token, we cannot justify them abroad, except in the relatively rare cases where such disturbances represent a direct threat to our own security.

John F. Kennedy saw America playing the role of watchman on the walls of world freedom, protecting the weak from aggression and keeping the enemies of democracy at bay. Lyndon Johnson ordered the watchman to come off the walls and plunge into the melee below. But in becoming the defender of everybody's freedom, America has come perilously close to compromising her own. By defining freedom as the absence of communism, she has allowed herself to be drawn into fights on behalf of tyrannies not much better than the communism to which she is opposed. By failing to distinguish between struggles in which freedom is really at stake and those in which it is basically irrelevant, she has been used by those with little interest in her principles but a great desire to enlist her power. Instead of being the watchman on the walls of world freedom, America has too often been the dupe guarding the palace gate.

Rejecting isolationism, America has become entranced by global interventionism as a means of furthering her moral purpose. But to persist in this policy is to involve the United States in an unending series of quarrels, conflicts, and civil wars which will not make the world a better place but which may ultimately weaken the fabric of American democracy itself. There is no more urgent task for United States diplomacy than to find a path away from the benevolent imperialism of Pax Americana and toward a reconciliation with a world shattered into a plurality of nation-states.

17. The Plural World

The purpose of foreign policy is not to provide an outlet for our sentiments of hope or indignation; it is to shape real events in a real world. —JOHN F. KENNEDY

❧ ❧ ❧ WHAT is taking the place of a world divided between two rival poles is a world fragmented into scores of quasi-independent, quasi-neutralist political entities, some of them as large as India, others as tiny as Cyprus. These nations have inherited the world from the nuclear giants, and if they cannot hope to impose their will on all mankind, they can nonetheless prevent the super-powers from doing so themselves. The disintegration of the great power blocs and the rise to independence of the former colonial states have led to an atomization of the international order. Not only is there no longer a single source of authority, but there are no longer even several centers of authority, as there were until 1945. Now every nation is its own presbyter, so to speak, and Rome—both the Western and the Eastern variety—has been replaced by autocephalous national churches.

This neo-nationalism has been combined with a neo-neutralism that has effectively isolated the super-powers as sources of authority. Both the new states, which have evolved from the empires of Europe, and the European states themselves, which have emerged from under the shadow of the nuclear giants, have tried to insulate themselves from the foreign policies of the super-powers. Just as the French have cut loose from NATO and are casting out lines to Moscow and the Third World, so the Rumanians are seeking Western economic help and deprecating the utility of the

Warsaw Pact. This is not yet neutralism, because Europe is still the primary source of contention between Russia and America, and therefore freedom of maneuver is limited. But the movement is one of increasing detachment, as is shown by Western Europe's fear of becoming involved in war through American intervention in Asia. The Third World nations, for their part, have found it possible to avoid involvement in either power bloc while seeking aid from both.

In addition to nationalism, which has become the dominant ideology throughout most of the world—even in countries nominally communist—there is also a dispersion of power caused by the break-up of the nuclear monopoly held by America and Russia. France and China are already developing their own nuclear arsenals, and a number of other nations that have the necessary technological capacity—such as India, Japan, Israel, Sweden, Egypt, and West Germany—may eventually follow suit. Unable to agree on a system to halt the spread of nuclear weapons during a time when they enjoyed a world duopoly, America and Russia seem doomed to witness the proliferation of these weapons among a host of smaller powers. Had they been wiser and less obsessed with their ideological rivalry, they might have been able to devise a system to outlaw the production of such weapons. They certainly do not need them to augment their own power, for as continental nations possessed of enormous economic resources they can easily dominate any potential rivals with the conventional weapons of warfare. They do not need the Bomb to make them great. But once the Bomb was developed, incorporated into their military arsenals, and made into an international status symbol, it became an object of desirability for second-rank powers aspiring to the level of the great.

Unless the super-powers are able to agree on something more than simply a treaty of non-proliferation—unless they are able to provide realistic guarantees for the major non-nuclear powers and impose restrictions on their own independent arsenals—they cannot expect future great powers to forgo the temptation of nuclear independence. Nor, perhaps, should they be allowed to. A world dominated by one or two nuclear giants might well be less safe than a world in which a potential quest for global hegemony could be held in check by a combination of smaller nuclear powers—in which India and Japan could contain China; in which China and America might restrain Russia; or perhaps, given some totally unforeseen circumstances, in which Russia and a unified Europe might find it necessary to contain some future American government fallen into the hands of extremists. However remote this latter instance seems to us, it is not one which any responsible European statesman can dismiss as totally impossible. Diplomacy, after all, is the art of being prepared for the unthinkable.

Nuclear weapons have not, as many used to believe, made war impossible. Nor have they proved, as President Eisenhower once said, that "there is no alternative to peace." There is indeed an alternative to peace that does not involve a nuclear holocaust, and we have seen it going on for the past two decades in various limited wars around the earth's periphery. Non-nuclear war has become the substitute for the great war which the atom bomb has made impossible. War is not obsolete; it is simply conducted on a smaller scale. Since the development of the atom bomb there have been wars of conquest, such as Indonesia's absorption of Dutch New Guinea and India's of Goa; wars of occupation, such as Russia's action against Hungary and Czechoslovakia; border wars, such as those between India and China, India and Pakistan, Malaysia and Indonesia; wars of containment, such as Korea and Vietnam; and even wars by proxy, such as that between rival Congolese tribes sponsored by America and Russia. It is not war as such that is outlawed by the atom, but war conducted for the highest stakes with the supreme weapons. Outside Europe, where the vital interests of the super-powers do not overlap, limited war is not only possible but frequent, and increasingly likely in the future.

The spread of small wars under the cover of the unusable nuclear deterrent, combined with the virulent nationalism that has been transferred from Europe to the former colonies of the southern hemisphere, has led to a period of great danger for the super-powers, a danger of which they are only beginning to become aware. The decision between war and peace, which once lay exclusively in their hands, has now been dispersed to the scores of nations which are their allies and protectorates. A disturbance in any one of these client states could, if the super-powers allow themselves to intervene directly, draw them into a head-on conflict quite against their own will. The Middle East is obviously ripe for such an explosion.

Such a situation has been allowed to develop because both nations are not only great powers, with all the rivalries inherent in such status, but also ideological powers with global ambitions. Neither can, in terms of her own self-image, fail to express interest in quarrels in which the other is involved. To do so would be to ignore the ideologies they believe they are defending and thereby weaken the web of protectorates, clients, and allies they have accumulated over the past two decades. Their image of themselves as global powers rests to a large extent on their ability to retain ideological clients and allies. For this reason they have interpreted any forcible change in the status quo as a direct threat to their own interests.

Thus their nuclear balance is continually threatened by the mini-powers. The decision between war and peace in places like Vietnam and the Middle East lies in the hands of guerrilla bands, nationalist groups, and fanatical leaders who are not interested in the nuclear balance of the super-powers, or who seek to use it for their own ends. America and Russia have become involved in these quarrels because they have not been able to draw a line between their primary and their secondary interests. They have let themselves be sucked into the quarrels that are shaking the Third World because they are prisoners of the ideologies they believe they are defending.

A collision between the super-powers can be prevented, but it will require the willingness of both sides not to treat a change in the ideological status quo among the underdeveloped states of Africa and Asia as a threat to their vital interests. Only by putting these states into an ideological isolation can the balance between the great powers be preserved. This will not be easy. Astute leaders in the emerging countries will appeal for their help in the name of communism or anti-communism, and the great powers will be tempted to intervene because they will see the outcome of such insurrections as crucial to their role as global powers.

America and Russia cannot prevent "wars of national liberation" from occurring, any more than they can be sure who will ultimately benefit from them. But because of their common interest in halting the arms race and preventing a great-power confrontation, they must agree not to take advantage of any change in the status quo through military alliances or bases. This is the minimum on which any hope for cooperation rests, for otherwise it will be extremely difficult for either side to resist military intervention. There can be no possibility of eliminating guerrilla wars within the confines of a single country. The best the great powers can hope to achieve is to contain these wars so that they do not imperil the nuclear détente.

To do so, it will be necessary to divorce ideology from the vital questions of national interest. This will mean a retreat from interventionist policies that are essentially global to those based upon spheres of primary and secondary interest. In the vast areas of secondary interest throughout most of the southern hemisphere, the only workable rule of thumb must be that every nation should be allowed to have its own revolution without the intervention of outside forces. Sometimes such revolutions will bring to power regimes we do not like, at other times they will bring to power regimes we favor, but if we have learned anything over the past two decades it should be that no one can predict the course a national revolution will take.

A general policy of detachment from Third World insurrections will not be easy for many of us to accept, and it may be even more difficult for the Russians, with their messianic view of the communist faith, to accept. Even if we are able to follow a policy more closely based on national interest than on ideological compulsion, the Russians may not go along. Perhaps they will not be able to separate their ideology from their national interest, or refrain from intervening in the chronic disturbances of the southern hemisphere. This is a danger we must be prepared to cope with, although not by indiscriminate interventions of our own. But it is precisely because we want to persuade Moscow that such a policy of restraint in the unsettled areas of the Third World is to its interests as much as to ours, that we must re-evaluate our own diplomacy. This is not to say that world peace is going to be assured by a Russo-American condominium. Even if such a creation were desirable, it is no longer possible. But an accord between the super-powers in the Third World, just as they have reached an unwritten accord in Europe, is essential if the current détente is not to be destroyed by a new arms race and by Russian military interventions to match our own.

If such an accord is to have any meaning, there must be an agreement on the role the United Nations can be expected to play. When the international organization was established at the end of the Second World War, it was assumed that the power of decision would rest with the five great powers—America, Russia, Britain, France, and China. They were given permanent seats on the Security Council and the power to veto any proposals which threatened their national interests. They were expected to use their influence and their power to enforce agreements and dampen conflicts that threatened the peace. Under Roosevelt's plan, each of the great powers was to attend to its own area, while America, whose global interests overlapped them all, would ensure a favorable world balance through her power over Britain, France, and China. Composed in equal parts of idealism and self-interest, this was the design for the American Century—world peace through world law administered by the Security Council of the United Nations.

The American Century, as it turned out, lasted barely a few months, for it could not survive the collapse of great-power unity. Once the cold war broke out and the two great powers became bitter adversaries, there could be no hope of using the United Nations as an instrument of law enforcement. The veto ensured that the Security Council could not act contrary to the interests of any of the great powers, and the inability of the great powers to agree assured the paralysis of the Security Council. The United States, acting upon the fact that she controlled a majority of the votes in the General Assembly during the first fifteen years of the organization's existence, tried to break this impasse by circumventing the Security Council. Thus she was able to enlist the authority of the United Nations to justify the United States intervention in Korea. But the enormous expansion of the United Nations, particularly since 1960, caused by the break-up of the European colonial empires, has diminished American control over the General Assembly. This has led to an "agonizing reappraisal" of our attitude toward a forum in which a decisive two-thirds vote can now be made up of countries that possess only 10 per cent of the world's population and pay less than 5 per cent of the United Nations budget. Ironically, Washington has now taken a more benign look at the Security Council, which more accurately reflects the real power balance in the world, and in which the United States enjoys the right of veto.

The United Nations, therefore, is at a crucial juncture. While in many ways it is more necessary than ever before—especially to isolate small-scale conflicts and to provide a framework for economic development—its future prospects are dim. Perhaps the United Nations is not greatly important to the super-powers, for they certainly do not need it to augment their influence or protect their vital interests. But it does, for all its pettiness and inadequacies, provide a vitally needed forum in which the privileged minority is forced to account for its behavior to the impoverished majority, and it can also help the super-powers to avoid direct intervention in areas not really vital to their own security. The danger, of course, is that the United Nations can become a repressive force itself, tyrannizing the weak through majority votes in the General Assembly, and even denying the self-determination of cohesive ethnic minorities—as in Biafra—in the name of "stability" and the sacredness of the nation-state.

If it is to remain viable, the United Nations cannot lose the support of the super-powers, for without them it is nothing but a forum of the impoverished. Thus it must serve, or at least seem to serve, the interests of the great as well as of the small. The mini-powers would be well advised to take this into consideration in pushing "anti-colonial" resolutions through the General Assembly. The weakness of the United Nations rests on the very structure of the organization, which is based upon the legal fiction of equality for every member state, without, however, the means to enforce order. So long as such means are lacking, the system merely reinforces what amounts to international anarchy. The only feasible reform of the United Nations lies through a return to the original principles of the Charter, itself based upon the unavoidable truth that the major burden for peace-keeping rests upon agreement among the great powers. With their accord, minor disputes throughout the Third World can be isolated and neutralized. Without their accord, the United Nations cannot hope to be much more than an international debating society. The Security Council must regain some of the authority that has been taken over by the General Assembly, and various regional or functional organizations should be created so that the great powers may delegate peace-keeping tasks that it is inadvisable for them to administer directly. These steps would mean, ironically, a return to the principles envisaged by Franklin Roosevelt, who conceived of the United Nations as an instrument for the maintenance of peace through great-power unanimity. His analysis was essentially correct, even though he could not have predicted the countervailing power that would be exercised by scores of new nations. It is upon the creation of a balance between the demands of the great powers and the rights of the small powers that the future of the United Nations rests.

A re-evaluation of our role in the United Nations is merely part of a long-overdue reassessment of our role in the world. The mantle of empire now rides uneasily upon many American shoulders. The United States is not ancient Rome, although we maintain a global empire, and our standards are not those of Metternich, although we have been engaged in suppressing revolutions. America was not meant to maintain a shabby empire with Marines, napalm, and foreign-aid bribes, and the American people have become increasingly uneasy over the global interventions that have been carried out in their name.

Possessed of enormous power—which we have, for the most part, exercised with relative restraint—we have allowed ourselves to become intoxicated with it, to believe that it has given us a mandate to impose our own particular ideas of justice and virtue. Our great power has disturbed our sense of proportion and destroyed many of the old guide lines that once served as limitations. Power has proved to be a terrible dilemma to Americans, inspiring some with an exaggerated sense of mission, disturbing others with a guilty conscience, and perplexing many who seek to use it beneficially, yet who fear the infinite distortions to which any application of power is subject.

In grappling with the phenomenon of our enormous power, we have tended to lose sight of a crucial distinction that governs the use of power. That distinction rests not upon *whether* power should be used, but upon *when* and *how* power should be used— not whether power in itself is evil, but whether power indiscriminately applied may not be self-defeating as well as morally compromising. America is, in a sense, a prisoner of her own great power. She cannot ignore that power any more than she can repudiate it. But she can dissipate it on false or ignoble ends, and she can distort it into an instrument of repression that may betray her own values.

Power is an opportunity, but it is also a burden, for those who exercise it determine the fate of others. Something more than self-assurance of moral purpose is necessary to those who take on such a burden. It is not enough that power be applied for noble ends. History is a compilation of cases in which the most terrible crimes have been committed for the most noble reasons. It is not enough that the exercise of our power should bear the stamp of our virtuous motives. Those who suffer from the application of that power will not appreciate our motives, and we will have to live not with the purity of our motives but with the consequences our power has inflicted.

The lesson of imperial Britain is a lesson for contemporary

America. Like the United States today, Britain stood at the center of a great empire. For most of the nineteenth century she was the strongest power in the world, and the Pax Britannica was imposed for the purpose of managing her empire. It rested upon a balance of power in Europe and upon the acquiescence of the colonized peoples, who were subdued by the superior technology of the imperial nations. Britain was insufferably smug and hypocritical about her empire, engaging in inflated rhetoric about her moral purpose and the "anguish" that such heavy responsibilities inflicted upon the British conscience. Yet for all their cant about the onerous responsibilities of empire, the British did not allow their concern for stability in their distant outposts to involve them in costly wars. They had mercenaries to ensure order, or else they let the inhabitants fight among themselves and then concluded an agreement with the victor. They did not overly trouble themselves with the politics of their wards, they were not seduced by labels, and they did not allow their hypocrisy to interfere with a cold calculation of their national interest.

With great pain and despite considerable opposition from the hawks of the day, Britain brought her commitments into line with her resources and drew a clear distinction between conflicts that crucially affected her interests and those that did not. Whatever anguish the British may have felt over the power they possessed and the way in which it was applied, they were careful to reserve it for situations which they could hope to control and which were directly related to their national interest.

They were, in short, the opposite of the ancient Athenians, who wasted their substance in foreign wars, sent their fleet to its destruction in the tragic Sicilian campaign, and finally destroyed their own democracy by a policy of military adventurism. In ancient Athens the philosophers gave way to the demagogues, the virtues of the city-state were squandered in the effort to maintain an empire, and the interest of the community was lost in the search for new worlds to conquer. Athens was the opposite of Britain; one sought glory, the other searched for profits; one worried about its world mission, the other about protecting the interests of the nation. Thucydides described the glory and the tragedy of Athens, but it was Palmerston who provided the motto for Britain in declaring, "We have no eternal allies and we have no perpetual enemies. Our interests are eternal and perpetual, and those interests it is our duty to follow." It is the counsel of a man who did not confuse power diplomacy with a higher morality, and who knew the difference between the necessary involvement and the *beau geste*.

The hidden danger of power is that it conceals its own limitations. It is the breeding-ground of self-deception. The words of Edmund Burke to his English countrymen in 1790, when the explosions from revolutionary France seemed ready to shake all imperial Europe, are worth recalling:

> Among precautions against ambition it may not be amiss to take one precaution against our *own*. I must fairly say, I dread our *own* power and our *own* ambition. I dread our being too much dreaded. . . . We may say that we shall not abuse this astonishing and hitherto unheard-of power. But every nation will think we shall abuse it. It is impossible but that, sooner or later, this state of things must produce a combination against us which may end in our ruin.

Power, as Burke understood, is an instrument of inflicting evil as well as good, and therefore to be applied only with the greatest reluctance and discrimination when other measures of dissuasion have failed and where the vital interests of the nation are threatened. There are times when this may be so, as it was in Europe during and after the Second World War. In such cases we shall have no alternative but to intervene militarily in defense of our vital interests. But there will be other times, far more numerous, when we shall be tempted to intervene simply because we are powerful and think we can impose our will on others, using, of course, the most noble rhetoric of "democracy" and "self-determination."

If we can gain a sense of perspective about ourselves and what we conceive to be our mission, we may discover that the global quest that has so enchanted us for the past two decades, like the isolationism that came before it, is not a foreign policy but a search for the absolute. Globalism, like isolationism, has been a romantic retreat from the real world. Before the Second World War we thought we were too good for a corrupt world, and so we sought to preserve our moral purity through isolationism. When that failed twice, we then decided to purify the world by transforming it into our own image.

To turn away from the obsessive globalism that has dominated our foreign policy is not to turn our back on the world. On the contrary, a liberation from globalism will allow us to follow a freer role in world affairs, unhobbled by the obsolete dogmas of the cold war, the self-appointed responsibilities of a world policeman, and the crumbling alliances that inflate our national ego.

What we need are fewer historical compulsions, less Manifest Destiny, more skepticism about the ideals we are promulgating, and a greater realism about the causes in which we have become involved. Above all, we need to develop a sense of proportion about our place in the world, and particularly about ourselves as the pathfinders to the New Jerusalem. America has little to fear from the world, although perhaps a good deal to fear from herself —her obsession with an obsolete ideological struggle, her well-meaning desire to enforce her own conception of virtue upon others, her euphoria of power, and, perhaps most dangerous of all, the unmet, and often unacknowledged, inadequacies of her own society.

The experience of Vietnam has been a bitter lesson for America, destroying some of our most cherished beliefs about ourselves. It has caused many Americans to question not only the nature of our foreign policy, but of our society as well. It discredited the cold-war liberals and their policy of welfare imperialism, revealed the impact of what Eisenhower called the military-industrial complex on our national life, and radicalized a whole generation of young Americans. Vietnam was the most ambitious, and the most destructive, of our adventures in "nation-building," and in the wake of its failure, politicians are vowing "never again." But is this an exercise in rhetoric, or does it really mean there will be no more Vietnams?

18. No More Vietnams?

*The essential question is one which we should have to answer
if there were not a communist alive. Can we make freedom
and prosperity real in the present world? If we can,
communism is no threat. If not, with or without communism,
our own civilization would ultimately fail.*

—HENRY STIMSON

❧ ❧ ❧ YESTERDAY's heresy becomes today's cliché. What a few
years ago would have been labeled as isolationist, if not vaguely
traitorous, is now the new orthodoxy. "We cannot impose ideals
on others and still call ourselves men of peace," [1] President Nixon
declared, in outlining a new low posture for the United States and
a scaling down of foreign commitments. This is a far cry from John
Kennedy's summons to "pay any price, bear any burden, meet any
hardship, support any friend, oppose any foe to assure the survival
and the success of liberty" anywhere in the world. And it is welcome deflation from Lyndon Johnson's proclamation in the
Inaugural Address of January 1965 that "the American covenant
called on us to help show the way for the liberation of man."

After Vietnam, the Dominican Republic, and the Greek junta,
it is not so easy for an American President to speak with a straight
face of the nation's foreign policy being based on the "liberation
of man" or the "survival of liberty." The self-glorifying rhetoric
of the 1960s has given way to a more studied pragmatism based on
the old concepts of self-interest and balance of power. "Our in-

terests," President Nixon has told us, "must shape our commitments, rather than the other way around." Being a good politician, he recognizes that the nation is fed up with self-assumed obligations to set the world right and with undeclared wars conducted under the tattered banners of a discredited globalism.

No more Vietnams is what the public wants. Yet it is not enough to say that we made a mistake and won't do it again. Most people still believe that the war in Vietnam is some kind of aberration, an event totally without precedent in our national history, and one that will never happen again. But this is to ignore Korea, Lebanon, and Cuba. What is unique about Vietnam is not the fact of our intervention, but its scale. It has already cost some $100 billion, tied down three-quarters of a million men around Southeast Asia, and taken more casualties than the Korean War. Did we stumble into it by accident? Hardly. The war was a result of a succession of conscious political decisions made by three successive American presidents. Rather than a new departure in our way of looking at the world, it was quite consistent with the unexpressed principles of our foreign policy. Vietnam happened because it was time for it to happen, because we had the military power to make it happen.

Vietnam is precisely the kind of war the American military machine, as perfected in the mid-1960s, was designed to fight. When he came to power, John F. Kennedy inherited a military strategy based on "massive retaliation" with nuclear weapons. Clearly such a strategy was ineffective in dealing with the revolutionary disturbances shaking the Third World and imperiling American influence in such areas as the Caribbean and Southeast Asia. The ability to fight "limited war," Kennedy told Congress in a special defense message in March 1961, should be the "primary mission" of our overseas forces. An avid reader of the manuals of Mao and Che, Kennedy believed that guerrillas had to be met on their own terrain if forces of "national liberation" were to be defeated. Robert McNamara was brought in to reorganize the Pentagon and set up amphibious strike forces. In such cold-war intellectuals as Walt Rostow, Maxwell Taylor, Roger Hilsman, and

Richard Bissell, Kennedy found zealous advocates for the new counter-guerrilla warfare. Kennedy ordered the expansion of the Special Forces training center at Fort Bragg, and, over the Army's objections, reinstated the green beret as the symbol of the new counter-guerrilla elite force. In the fall of 1961 General Taylor, head of the Counter-Insurgency Committee, went to Vietnam with Walt Rostow and returned urging increased American intervention, including a military task force. In December Kennedy ordered the military build-up to begin.

The arms race took a dramatic jump during the next few years. Billions of dollars flowed into the Pentagon to increase American nuclear superiority and to provide weapons to fight insurrectionary movements in the Third World. The liberals around Kennedy believed they had a mission to bring about an American-style peace based upon political stability and economic development. They saw the underdeveloped nations achieving "take-off" points to economic growth through infusions of foreign aid and technical expertise. And they were convinced that world peace and American security demanded an ideological balance of power. They were ready to intervene wherever necessary to maintain that balance. American military power—both nuclear missiles and conventional forces— had been increased precisely for that purpose. After the Cuban missile crisis of October 1962, when they took the world to the brink of nuclear war and successfully faced down the Russians, they were ready to intervene wherever it seemed necessary.

Vietnam provided the opportunity in the guise of an obligation. Although American intervention in Vietnamese affairs extended back to the early 1950s, Eisenhower had clearly set the limits of American assistance to Saigon. The liberal interventionists, however, were eager to show that wars of national liberation would not pay. Vietnam was their showcase. When Diem failed to live up to their expectations, and when his brother showed signs of political independence verging on talks with the North Vietnamese, the right-wing generals were allowed to get rid of him. With the murder of Diem the legitimacy of the Saigon regime was undermined. This was followed shortly by Kennedy's assassination and the intensified American commitment to an anti-communist government in Saigon.

Under President Johnson, who eagerly embraced their theories of "nation-building" and communist containment, the liberals lost control of the war. Yet they dug in more deeply to vindicate themselves and the views they held. Vietnam was their war. "It took a visionary liberal administration," William Pfaff has written, "fully to translate the globalism of American rhetoric into a program of national action. Vietnam was deliberately made into a test of liberal international reform by the Kennedy and Johnson administrations—of liberal 'nation building,' carried on behind a shield of green beret counter-insurgent warfare—against the Asian communist 'model' of radical national transformation." [2]

By the time of Lyndon Johnson's electoral triumph, on a platform of peace and social reform, the Pentagon was ready for the full-scale military intervention that had been engineered in the White House. "McNamara's prodigious labors to strengthen and broaden the US military posture were about completed," according to Townsend Hoopes, a Pentagon official who turned against the war, ". . . US 'general purpose' forces were now organized to intervene swiftly and with modern equipment in conflicts of limited scope, well below the nuclear threshold." [3] In February 1965 Johnson began the bombing of North Vietnam, in June American troops were officially authorized to enter combat, and in July the President ordered an increase in American forces from 75,000 to 125,000. Within four years Kennedy's 16,000 "advisers" had swollen to an American expeditionary force of half a million men, and the Vietnamese civil war became an American war. As the economist Joseph Schumpeter wrote of ancient Egypt's military forces, "created by wars that required it, the machine now created the wars it required."

We intervened from a euphoria of power, generated in part by our success in the Cuban missile crisis and our military superiority over the Russians. The liberals wanted to prove that guerrilla wars were not the wave of the future, and were determined to keep South Vietnam as an anti-communist outpost in Southeast Asia. But they grossly underestimated the price. As the cost of intervention mounted, so the rhetoric rose to meet the occasion. What began as a military-aid program to a harassed neo-colonial outpost that had been abandoned by the French and picked up by Dulles was transformed into a full-scale war. The very scale of our intervention transformed the Vietnamese civil war into a test of American resolve. By our intervention we created the problem that was used to justify our involvement.

As the scale of war increased, so Washington sought various theories to explain why it was worth the cost. First it was to help our friends in the South deal with communist-led insurgents. Then it was to push back an "aggression" from the North, although Hanoi's troops did not enter the war until after the American intervention. We were there, it was said, to honor our treaty commitments, although the SEATO treaty provided only for consultation in case of attack, or to stop that amorphous but virulent force known simply as "Asian communism," or even to prevent the miraculously amphibious Chinese from invading southern California and speeding east along the interstate highway system. Vietnam, we were told, was a test case for wars of national liberation, and if the Vietcong were defeated, guerrillas from the Andes to the Sahara would turn in their rifles and slink home. In a moment of desperation, Lyndon Johnson even evoked the principle of envy, declaring that "they want what we've got," thereby suggesting that we are in Vietnam to defend electric carving knives and remote control TV from the greedy hands of the Vietcong. Later President Nixon, pursuing Johnson's policies while changing his tactics, again trotted out the balance-of-power theory, saying that to abandon the Saigon generals "would threaten our long-term hopes for peace in the world."

Nearly a year after assuming office with a promise to end the war, President Nixon presented a plan which called for the gradual withdrawal of American combat troops and their replacement by

South Vietnamese soldiers. The plan was tendered as a supplement to the peace talks in Paris between the United States and North Vietnam. Yet it was clearly meant as an alternative to negotiations, since no nation would reduce its military power in the field while conducting negotiations on its own withdrawal. The purpose of "Vietnamization," as Walter Lippmann pointed out, was "not to buy concessions from Hanoi with our military withdrawal, but to buy patience and endurance from the American people for an indefinitely long American occupation in South Vietnam." [4]

Vietnamization cleverly defused popular opposition to the war by withdrawing some of the troops while retaining the bases and the commitment to an anti-communist South Vietnam. Its drawback, as Hoopes observed, was that it committed the American people "to the endless support of a group of men in Saigon who represented nobody but themselves, preferred war to the risks of a political settlement, and could not remain in power more than a few months without our large-scale assistance." Yet what could the American people do about it? In the elections of 1964 and 1968 they twice voted for peace, first in rejecting Barry Goldwater and electing a man who said he would not send American boys to die in Vietnam, and then in repudiating the Humphrey–Johnson administration. Both times their wishes were ignored by presidents who circumvented Constitutional restrictions and pursued the war on their own authority for reasons they declared to be vital to the national interest.

If elections cannot change foreign policy, what is the validity of the political process? If Americans can be sent to die in battle as a result of decisions made by the executive branch, what is the meaning of the Constitutional obligation of Congress to declare acts of war? Traditional politics no longer provides a solution for political ills or implements the popular will. This has led to an increasing emphasis on direct action, on popular participation, on decentralization, and, when all else seems to fail, on violence. Unable to affect the decisions that control their lives—whether they be on the wars they die in, the polluted air they breathe, or the schools where their children fail to receive an education—the American people are driven to strike out against bureaucracy and many of the very principles of government that they have been trained to take for granted.

There has been a crisis of faith in the political process, just as there has been in the realm of science and technology. We have learned that technology destroys even as it creates, and that its gifts, such as DDT and the internal-combustion engine, are bought with our own lives. Our faith in man's future has been shaken as we realize that in the name of progress the very forces that make possible human life on the earth are being tampered with and perhaps inadvertently destroyed. In our political life, as in our personal lives, we are repelled by the cult of bigness, and are turning, more in desperation than in hope, to various forms of decentralization. Those who once believed that only big government could solve the problems of a complex society now put an equally abiding faith in the virtues of the local community.

Both radicals and reactionaries profess to find salvation in local control, the former in flight from the technology and the war machine that are oppressing their lives, the latter in an effort to hold on to the old ways. To both the Right and the Left, government itself has become a kind of enemy, and faith in political solutions has broken down. The whole society is pervaded by a deep and destructive sense of powerlessness. Among conservatives this feeling seeks its outlet against those who threaten the established order—hippies, drop-outs, militants. These are the people who chant that they love Mayor Daley and applaud police violence against young demonstrators. Among radicals this alienation and powerlessness results in desperate attempts to change unresponsive institutions. The universities, of course, are the obvious targets because there the ideals of community seem most betrayed by arbitrary and unresponsive administrators. This feeling was well expressed by the student newspaper at the Santa Barbara campus of the University of California, following rioting, mass arrests, and destruction: "If we have any community at all, it is a community based on common frustrations—born of powerlessness, alienation from one's pre-programmed life, and contempt for authoritarian institutions." It is a complaint that even conservatives could share, for it is a common American condition.

Vietnam intensified, although it did not create, this sense of powerlessness, of being unable to affect the decisions that can, literally, mean the difference between life and death. The war took perfectly decent young Americans, taught them to use napalm and machine guns, sent them across the world to a totally alien society with instructions to kill "communists," and justified this in the name of freedom. It is not surprising that some of our most sensitive young people, rather than fight a war they consider morally wrong, have preferred to go to jail or seek a saner life in another country. Nor is it even surprising that atrocities like those at Songmy have occurred, for the kind of war we are fighting in Vietnam is a brutalizing experience. It infects everything we do, and comes back to haunt us at home. We were all at Songmy, in one way or another.

There is a great revulsion in this country against the rhetorical globalism of the past two decades. A Harris poll taken early in 1970 showed six out of ten people saying Vietnam was a terrible mistake, with a full one-third volunteering that "we should mind our own business and stop policing the world." In these results the pollsters found "overtones of a new isolationism." No doubt Americans are tired of the violence that has been committed in the name of peace, of the two wars fought since 1950 for objectives that seem increasingly specious and hypocritical, of the unending interventions that are conducted in the tired vocabulary of anti-communism, of the sacrifice of their own social needs to an insatiable war machine that declares itself to be the repository of patriotism. No doubt they see no reason why more money should be spent on MIRVs and ABMs when America and Russia have already stockpiled nuclear weapons with the explosive power of fifteen tons of TNT for every man, woman, and child on earth.

But the people have always wanted peace, and they rarely get it—particularly when their leaders believe they have the power to obtain what they want by force of arms.

America is not aggressive by nature. As great powers go, it has been relatively restrained in its use of force. But it has undeniably used its power aggressively, not only in Vietnam, but in the Spanish-American war, and in seizing half of Mexico in the war of 1848. So long as that power is untempered, it will be used whenever military and political leaders think it should be used. So long as we have a military machine anywhere near its present size, it will always find work for itself to do. It will have bases to defend in one or another of the various unstable and revolution-prone countries of the Third World. It will issue solemn assurances, as Air Force generals did in Vietnam early in 1965, that a few well-placed bombs will take care of revolutionaries and communists. And there will be government officials, on loan from corporations and universities, who will tell us that American military intervention is necessary for something noble-sounding like stability or self-determination.

After Korea everyone said there would be no more Koreas. And there weren't. But there was Vietnam. Now it is a cliché to say there will be no more Vietnams. And there probably won't be—in Vietnam. But unless our military power to fight counter-revolutionary wars is reduced, and unless our attitudes change, there might very well be further American military interventions in Asia and the Caribbean. Even while President Nixon asserted that our allies should be able to defend themselves, he declared regarding Asia that "we shall provide a shield if a nuclear power threatens the freedom of a nation allied with us, or of a nation whose security we consider vital to our security and the security of the region as a whole." We are allied with forty-two nations and, judging from past behavior, consider virtually every non-communist country in the world as being vital to our security. Does that mean we are supposed to go to war whenever the President considers it "vital"? Who gave him the authority to provide nuclear shields for whatever Asian nations he desires? Even while saying there must be no more Vietnams, the administration conducted a covert war in Laos and invaded Cambodia without bothering to inform its government or the American Congress.

The legacy of globalism still weighs heavily on American foreign policy. Having intervened actively for thirty years, it has become almost a reflex action. Whenever there is talk of retrenching commitments, the global interventionists raise the specter of isolationism. They say that the experience of Vietnam may induce us to turn inward and ignore our responsibilities to the rest of the world. The danger is exaggerated. With the world's most powerful economy and mightiest military force, the United States could never again be isolationist. Regardless of how many Americans might desire it, the nation's economic and political interests make it impossible.

Yet it might not be a bad thing if we did ignore some of our self-assumed "responsibilities" for building democratic, capitalistic nations out of feudal societies. The results of isolationism could, in most cases, hardly be much worse than the results of our interventionism, which, except for Europe, have ranged from the stupid, as in Lebanon, Cuba, and the Dominican Republic, to the tragic, as in Vietnam. They have brought no credit on us, nor have they appreciably advanced the causes of freedom and self-determination we are ostensibly promoting. It long ago became obvious, even before Tet and Songmy, that the best thing we could have done for the Vietnamese was to have left them alone. "We had to destroy the village in order to save it," an American officer said as his troops moved into a lifeless wasteland of devastated homes and mutilated bodies. It could be the epitaph for our whole adventure in Vietnam.

By now it is a truism to say that we ought to set our own house in order before we declare ourselves responsible for the welfare of the entire world. It might even be said that we don't have any idea of what the welfare of other societies might be, and not very much understanding of how to improve our own. The emphasis is now on national priorities and on saving this country from drowning in its own pollution, or turning into a police state, or descending into the savagery of a race war. But powerful voices like President Nixon's still cling to the old rhetoric and warn us of the disasters that would occur "if America were to become a dropout in assuming the responsibility for defending peace and freedom in the world."

It is questionable that such disasters would occur, since outside of Western Europe (and in such countries as Greece and Portugal, not even there) the United States has not been occupied in defending peace and freedom. It has simply sought to maintain the status quo and prevent revolutionary groups, particularly those led or thought to be led by communists, from coming to power. The moral imperatives of our foreign policy, our interventions in support of self-serving oligarchies and military strongmen, have never fooled anyone but ourselves. America is not going to be a dropout in defending her own interests. No nation is, if it has the strength to do otherwise. But America would do well to cease the hypocrisy which seeks to justify its interventions in the name of a higher morality. Then it might be easier for our officials, not to mention the public they are supposed to be serving, to distinguish between interventions necessary to defend the United States and its most intimate allies, and those which spring from a euphoria of power.

No more Vietnams? It would be unwise to take any bets on it. The heady rhetoric of the 1960s has been deflated, but great power still provides an irresistible temptation. There will be a danger of more Vietnams until there is a world power balance that will make such unilateral interventions far more hazardous. Only then are we likely truly to have "our interests . . . shape our commitments, rather than the other way around." Undeniably we have learned something from Vietnam. But it may be simply that we should never again intervene in Vietnam.

If we are to avoid more Vietnams, we have to shake loose from our global fantasies and begin our perfection of the human race within our own frontiers. There is certainly a great deal to do within a society which a century after the liberation of the slaves still has not been able to grant the Negro full equality, a society which is plagued by violence in the streets and guilt in the heart, a society which has achieved unprecedented material riches and yet is sick from a debilitating alienation, and where the ideals of American democracy are mocked by the reality of radical prejudice, where individual decency is in constant conflict with social irresponsibility, where prosperity has assured neither justice nor tolerance, where private affluence dramatizes the shame of public squalor, where wealth has brought psychoanalysis, and where power has bred anxiety and fear.

Vietnam has not caused our troubles, but it has clearly intensified them and made Americans aware of their severity. It is not only the ideals of the nation that are being tested, but its very survival as a free society. Our power has not brought us security, any more than our wealth has brought us tranquillity. Nor have the noble ideals on which this nation was founded insured social justice for the millions of Americans who, because of race, or poverty, or misfortune, have been excluded from the system and the benefits it is supposed to provide. The dispossessed are now finding a voice, and their cause is being taken up by young idealists on campuses and elsewhere who, despite the hostility of their elders and mounting repression by the authorities, maintain a persistent belief that the promise of American life can be made real to all Americans.

For more than three decades this country has been absorbed in foreign affairs, foreign aid, and foreign wars. In the remaining years of this decade, and of this century, it might be better for America, and for the world, if we turn to the needs of our own divided, unhappy, insecure society. When he visited this country a century ago, Thomas Huxley wrote: "I cannot say that I am in the slightest degree impressed by your bigness, or your material resources, as such. Size is not grandeur, and territory does not make a nation. The great issue, about which hangs the terror overwhelming fate, is what are you going to do with all these things?"

What are we going to do with them? The task of diplomacy in

the years ahead is not to remake the world in the American image through wars of intervention and a self-deceiving imperialism. Rather, it is to help create, in cooperation with others, a tolerable international order from which the fear of instantaneous obliteration has been lifted. Having failed to bring the world democracy, we can at least try to make it safe for diversity. America's worth to the world will not be measured by the solutions she seeks to impose on others, but by the degree to which she achieves her own ideals at home. That will be a fitting challenge to our ideals and a test of whether "any nation so conceived, and so dedicated, can long endure."

Notes / Index

Notes

CHAPTER 1. A *Taste for Intervention*

The quotation at the head of the chapter by John F. Kennedy is from an address prepared for delivery at Dallas, November 22, 1963; that by General de Gaulle is from his *Mémoires de Guerre*, vol. 2, *L'Unité*. Paris: Librairie Plon, pp. 97-98. (Translated in 3 volumes as *War Memoirs of Charles de Gaulle*, New York: Simon and Schuster, 1958-1960.)

1. Dexter Perkins, *The United States and Latin America*. Baton Rouge: Louisiana State University Press, 1961, p. 19.
2. *Memorandum of the Subcommittee on National Security and International Operations of the Committee on Government Operations*, U.S. Senate, 89th Congress, 1st session, 1965, pp. 2-3.

CHAPTER 2. *The American Empire*

1. George Ball, "The Dangers of Nostalgia," *Department of State Bulletin*, April 12, 1965, pp. 535-36.
2. Arnold Toynbee, *America and the World Revolution*. London: Oxford University Press, 1962, pp. 29-30.
3. Kenneth Thompson, *Political Realism and the Crisis of World Politics: An American Approach to Foreign Policy*. Princeton: Princeton University Press, 1960, p. 124.
4. Dean Rusk, statement to the Senate Preparedness Subcommittee, *The Washington Post*, August 26, 1966.

CHAPTER 3. *After the Cold War*

1. George Kennan, "Polycentrism and Western Policy," *Foreign Affairs*, January 1964, p. 174.
2. N. Khrushchev, *The Times* (London), June 13, 1964.
3. John H. Kautsky, "Myth, Self-Fulfilling Prophecy, and Symbolic Reassurance," *The Journal of Conflict Resolution*, March 1965.

CHAPTER 4. *The Atlantic Mirage*

1. Henry Kissinger, "Coalition Diplomacy," *Foreign Affairs*, July 1964, p. 534.
2. Lester Pearson, address at Springfield, Illinois, June 11, 1966. *The Congressional Record*, June 14, 1966, p. 12501.
3. General Lauris Norstad, statement to the Senate Subcommittee on National Security and International Operations, May 6, 1966.
4. Walter Hallstein, quoted in David P. Calleo, *Europe's Future: The Grand Alternatives*. New York: Horizon Press, 1965, p. 78.
5. Harold Wilson, quoted in *The New York Times*, December 1, 1966.
6. Walter Lippmann, New York *World Journal Tribune*, December 15, 1966.

CHAPTER 5. *Nobody's Europe*

1. Charles de Gaulle, address at Strasbourg, November 22, 1964, *New York Herald Tribune* (European ed.), November 24, 1964.
2. Stanley Hoffmann, "Europe's Identity Crisis: Between the Past and America," *Daedalus*, Fall 1964, p. 1246.
3. Raymond Aron, "Old Nations, New Europe," *Daedalus*, Winter 1964, pp. 57-58.
4. Herman Kahn and William Pfaff, "Our Alternatives in Europe," *Foreign Affairs*, July 1966, p. 590.

5. J. H. Huizinga, "Which Way Europe?" *Foreign Affairs*, April 1965, p. 494.
6. Harold Macmillan, Hansard, 5th series, vol. 645, House of Commons, July 24-August 4, 1961, cols. 1490-91.
7. Harold Wilson, speech at Bristol, March 18, 1966, *The Sunday Times* (London), March 20, 1966.

CHAPTER 6. *One Europe, or Two?*

The quotation at the head of the chapter by President Johnson is from an address to the National Conference of Editorial Writers, New York, October 7, 1966.

1. Gustav Heinemann, Washington *Star*, March 11, 1969.
2. Willy Brandt, address to the Bundestag, January 14, 1970, *The German Tribune*, January 27, 1970.
3. Franz Josef Strauss, *The New York Times*, February 20, 1957, cited in R. J. Barnet and M. G. Raskin, *After Twenty Years*. New York: Random House, 1965, p. 47.
4. Charles de Gaulle, press conference, Paris, February 4, 1965.
5. Lyndon B. Johnson, op. cit., October 7, 1966.
6. Richard M. Nixon (see ref. in chap. 18).

CHAPTER 7. *Yellow Peril Revisited*

The quotation at the head of the chapter by Ambassador Joseph Grew is from Louis Halle, *Dream and Reality: Aspects of American Foreign Policy*. New York: Harper and Row, 1960, p. 171; that by Secretary McNamara is from hearings before the Senate Armed Services Committee, quoted in James Reston, *The New York Times*, March 3, 1966.

1. William Appleman Williams, *The Tragedy of American Diplomacy*, Delta, 1962, p. 38.
2. John K. Fairbank, *Hearings before the Senate Committee on Foreign Relations*, 89th Congress, March 1966, p. 103.
3. Dean Rusk, quoted in *The New Republic*, March 19, 1966.
4. Coral Bell, "Southeast Asia and the Powers," *The World Today*, Royal Institute of International Affairs, London, April 1965, p. 149.

5. John K. Fairbank, "The People's Middle Kingdom," *Foreign Affairs*, July 1966, p. 586.

CHAPTER 8. *Chinese Checkers*

1. Jean Lacouture, *Le Monde* (Paris), July 21, 1964.
2. Neil Sheehan, "Not a Dove, but No Longer a Hawk," *New York Times Magazine*, October 9, 1966.
3. George Ball, quoted in *The New Republic*, March 19, 1966.

CHAPTER 9. *New Balance in Asia*

The quotation at the head of the chapter by Walter Lippmann is from the *New York Herald Tribune* (European ed.), September 15, 1965.

1. George Kennan, "Japanese Security and American Policy," *Foreign Affairs*, October 1964, p. 22.
2. Konrad Adenauer, quoted in *The Observer* (London), September 19, 1965.
3. Harry Schwartz, *Tsars, Mandarins and Commissars*. Philadelphia: Lippincott, 1964, p. 239.
4. John K. Fairbank, "Reflections on 'The China Problem,'" *Diplomat*, September 1966, p. 39.
5. John Foster Dulles, *War or Peace*. New York: Macmillan, 1950, p. 190.

CHAPTER 10. *Pan-American Illusions*

1. Halle, op. cit., p. 157.
2. Alexis de Tocqueville, *De la Démocratie en Amérique*. Paris: Librairie de Médicis, 1951, vol. 2, p. 614.
3. "Ypsilon," "A Note on Inter-American Relations," in *Latin American Issues*, ed. Albert O. Hirschman. New York: Twentieth Century Fund, 1961, p. 55.

CHAPTER 11. *The Millionaire and the Beggars*

The quotation at the head of the chapter by Fidel Castro is from an interview with C. L. Sulzberger, *The New York Times*, November 7, 1964.

1. Robert J. Alexander, "Latin American Communism," in *Survey*, August 1962, p. 100.
2. John F. Kennedy, quoted in *Newsweek*, September 23, 1963, p. 70.
3. Barbara Ward, *The Rich Nations and the Poor Nations*. New York: Norton, 1962, p. 132.
4. Edmund Stillman and William Pfaff, *Power and Impotence*. New York: Random House, 1966, p. 149.
5. Theodore Draper, *Castroism: Theory and Practice*. New York: Praeger, 1965, p. 133.

CHAPTER 12. *Whose Hemisphere?*

The quotation at the head of the chapter by Lord Salisbury is from a reply to Secretary of State Richard Olney's note of July 20, 1895, regarding Britain's dispute with Venezuela over the boundary of British Guiana. The citation from President Johnson is with reference to the Dominican landings, *New York Herald Tribune* (European ed.), May 6, 1965.

1. Philip Geyelin, *Lyndon B. Johnson and the World*. New York: Praeger, 1966, p. 254.
2. Eduardo Frei, quoted by William P. Lineberry in "A Time to Act," *The New Leader*, October 10, 1966, p. 8.
3. S. E. Finer, "The Argentine Trouble," *Encounter*, September 1965, pp. 59-60.
4. Frank Tannenbaum, "Toward an Appreciation of Latin America," in *The United States and Latin America*. New York: The American Assembly, Columbia University, 1959, p. 57.
5. John Plank, "The Caribbean: Intervention, When and How?" *Foreign Affairs*, October 1965, pp. 47-48.

CHAPTER 13. *White Man's Burden*

1. Robert A. Heilbroner, *The Great Ascent*. New York: Harper and Row, 1963, pp. 87-88.

2. George Woods, "Poor Nations Need More Aid," *The Times* (London), September 16, 1965.

3. Claude Julien, *l'Empire American*, Grasset (Paris), 1968, p. 386.

4. Heilbroner, "Counter-revolutionary America," *Commentary*, April 1967.

CHAPTER 14. *Prospero and Caliban*

1. Dean Acheson, Senate Committee on Government Operations, 89th Congress, 2d session, April 27, 1966.

2. Pierre Moussa, *Les Etats-Unis et les Pays Prolétaires*. Paris: Editions du Seuil, 1965, pp. 56-57.

3. Metternich, quoted in Perkins, op. cit., pp. 46-47.

4. Celso Furtado, "Brazil—What Kind of Revolution?" *Foreign Affairs*, April 1963, p. 530.

5. George Lichtheim, *The New Europe*. New York: Praeger, 1963, p. 201.

6. Herbert Luethy, "Indonesia Confronted," *Encounter*, December 1965, p. 80.

7. Heilbroner, op. cit., pp. 157-59.

CHAPTER 15. *The Pygmy Wars*

1. Benjamin Schwartz, "Chinese Visions and American Policies," *Commentary*, April 1966, p. 55.

CHAPTER 16. *Isolation—or Intervention?*

The quotation at the head of the chapter by Secretary McNamara is from an address to the American Society of Newspaper Editors, Montreal, May 8, 1966.

1. Walter Lippmann, *New York Herald Tribune* (European ed.), May 5, 1965.

CHAPTER 17. *The Plural World*

The quotation at the head of the chapter by John F. Kennedy is from an address at Salt Lake City, September 26, 1963.

CHAPTER 18. *No More Vietnams?*

The quotation at the head of the chapter by Henry Stimson is from an article in *Foreign Affairs*, October 1947.

1. Richard Nixon, report to Congress, February 18, 1970, "United States Foreign Policy for the 1970s: A New Strategy for Peace." The other Nixon quotations in this chapter are from that report.
2. William Pfaff, "The Decline of Liberal Politics," *Commentary*, October 1969.
3. Townsend Hoopes, *The Limits of Intervention*. New York: McKay, 1969.
4. Walter Lippmann, *Newsweek*, December 1, 1969.

Index

Acheson, Dean, 53, 274

Adams, John Quincy, 3, 7, 305

Adenauer, Konrad, 53, 57, 102, 108, 116, 171, 312

Africa: Chinese communists in, 299-300; colonialism in, 293; democracy in, 305; foreign aid to, 267, 302, 306; independence movements in, 37-39; nationalism in, 306; tribal warfare in, 290-91, 299

Agency for International Development, 17

Albania, 40

Alexander I, Czar, 276

Alexander, Robert, 213

Algerian war, 293, 296

Alliance for Progress, 14, 122, 183, 191-92, 215-19, 231, 237, 247, 306; anti-Cuban policy of, 219-220; background of, 215-16; Castro on, 208; economic assistance by, 216, 218; failures of, 218, 250; Kennedy on, 216; opposition to, 218; program of, 216-17

American empire, 15-27; anti-communist ideology and, 16, 24-27; beginning of, 15-16, 21; Truman Doctrine and, 16, 21-23

American University, 116

Anti-communist ideology, 16, 24-27, 29-30, 157-63

Anti-Westernism, Chinese, 135-137

ANZUS treaty, 10

Appleman, William, 126

Arab-Israeli war (1967), 46

Arbenz, Jacobo, 202

Asia, 164-201; beginning of U.S. involvement in, 125-26; dominant military power in, 144; imperial-ism in 164-66; independence movements in, 37-39; nationalism in, 128-29, 163, 164; power balance in, 164-81; U.S. anti-communist attitudes and, 157-63; U.S. commitments in, 10-11

Austria, 33

Baghdad Pact, 149

Ball, George, 17

Bandung conference (1965), 299

Batista, Fulgencio, 182-83, 213, 214, 221; communism under, 238; economic colonialism under, 221-222; overthrow of, 295

Baylor University, 233

Bell, Coral, 135

Berlin crisis of 1961, 29

Berlin Wall, 9, 45-46, 104-105

Beyond the Mexique Bay (Huxley), 269

Bismarck, Otto von, 104

Bissell, Richard, 340

Bolívar, Simón, 182, 190

Bolivia, 219, 240; revolution of 1952 in, 212, 223

Boumedienne, Colonel Houari, 243

Brandt, Willy, 85, 106, 109

Brazil, 251, 317

Brogan, D. W., 24

Burke, Edmund, 15, 336

Castro, Fidel, 46, 85, 183, 213-31, 246, 283; admiration for, 243; on Alliance for Progress, 208; condemns Chinese interference, 296; on Cuban revolution, 220; foreign policy of, 214; guerrilla warfare of, 293; Washington tour of, 223